Vishwarup Darshan

The Restoration of Human Knowledge, Volume 2

Sandeep Chavan

Published by Gyrus Vision, 2025.

VISHWARUP DARSHAN

First edition. December 4, 2025.

ISBN: 979-8232419721

Written by Sandeep Chavan.

Table of Contents

To the seekers—those who look beyond appearances, question without fear,and dare to see the universe as a single, intelligent whole.May this vision deepen your clarity and expand your journey.

"The universe never hid its truth.It only waited for eyes that could see."

Disclaimer

This book is a work of independent interpretation and reflective inquiry. It does not claim to represent any religious institution, academic authority, or scientific establishment. The perspectives presented here draw upon ancient Indian texts, symbolic traditions, scientific concepts, and philosophical reasoning, but they are not intended to replace, contradict, or override established religious beliefs or scientific theories.

Readers are encouraged to approach the content with an open mind and to interpret the ideas in a manner consistent with their own understanding, experience, and discretion. All examples, models, metaphors, and analogies are illustrative in nature and should not be construed as literal descriptions of physical reality or doctrinal assertions.

This book is not a substitute for professional scientific, academic, psychological, or spiritual advice. Any resemblance to actual persons, events, or historical figures—outside of those referenced intentionally—is coincidental.

Statement of Originality

The interpretations, models, perspectives, and narrative structures presented in this book are original contributions by the author. While they draw from a wide spectrum of ancient knowledge systems and contemporary scientific insights, the synthesis, framing, explanations, and conceptual connections are uniquely developed for this work.

No part of this book has been copied or reproduced from any existing publication, research paper, or commentary. The content represents the author's independent thinking, experiential understanding, and personal approach to integrating science, philosophy, symbolism, and cosmology.

Author's Note

When I first began writing *Vishwarup Darshan*, it was an attempt to bring clarity to ideas that often remain buried under ritual, tradition, or symbolism. Over time, as my own understanding deepened, I realized that ancient cosmology, modern science, and lived human experience are not separate domains—they are different expressions of a single, intelligent architecture.

This updated edition reflects that evolution.

What you will read here is not a religious reinterpretation, nor an academic thesis, nor a celebration of mythology. It is a *decoding* **exercise**—a way of looking at ancient insights through a structural, consequence-driven, field-oriented lens. The purpose is simple: to show that the universe, in all its vastness and complexity, operates with coherence, intelligence, and order.

The ancients expressed this truth through symbols and stories because symbols survive when languages change, and stories travel where equations cannot. Today, science expresses the same truth through models, constants, and experiments. Neither approach is superior; both attempt to describe the same underlying reality.

This edition strengthens that bridge:

- by reorganizing the ideas more coherently,
- by refining metaphors with modern clarity,
- by removing distractions of ritual and belief,
- by revealing the intelligence embedded in every symbol and principle,
- by presenting a unified understanding of existence that is accessible to any reader.

I have written this book with the intention that you should never feel compelled to "believe" anything. Instead, I hope you feel encouraged to *see, question, interpret*, and *understand*.

If the ancient seers stood before us today, they would not ask us to accept their words; they would invite us to observe the universe with new eyes. This book is my attempt to carry forward that invitation in a modern language.

Thank you for opening these pages, for entering this exploration, and for giving this edition the chance to refine the vision it originally sought to offer.

May it expand your curiosity, strengthen your clarity, and deepen your relationship with the intelligence that shapes all existence.

— *Sandeep Chavan*

How to Read This Book

Vishwarup Darshan is not written as a traditional philosophical treatise or a scientific manual. It is structured as a journey—one that moves from ancient insights to modern understanding, from symbols to systems, from perception to reality. To get the most from it, approach the book with three simple principles:

1. Read Slowly, Let the Ideas Settle

This book deals with foundational concepts—time, intelligence, energy, cycles, symbolism, and the architecture of reality. These are not ideas to rush through.

Read one chapter at a time. Pause. Reflect. Allow the metaphors, models, and interpretations to settle in your mind.

This is not information; it is *orientation*.

2. Use Both Lenses: Ancient and Modern

The book consistently bridges two worlds:

- the symbolic depth of ancient Indian cosmology
- the analytical clarity of modern science

Do not choose one over the other. Allow both lenses to overlap.

When a symbol appears mythical, ask: *What principle is it encoding?*

When a scientific idea appears abstract, ask: *What deeper intelligence does it reveal?*

This dual-lens reading unlocks new clarity.

3. Treat the Chapters as Modules, Not Steps

You may read the book in order, but it is not mandatory. Each chapter is self-contained, designed as a *standalone insight* that fits into a larger framework.

If a particular theme calls you—time, evolution, intelligence, symbolism, cosmology—feel free to jump there. You will not lose context.

This is a book to revisit, not just read once.

4. Don't Search for Rituals or Beliefs—Look for Principles

This work does not advocate any ideology, religion, or practice.

It decodes *principles*, not prescriptions.

Its purpose is to help you see:

- the structure of reality
- the logic behind cosmic order
- the intelligence embedded in existence
- the meaning of ancient symbols
- the unity behind apparent diversity

Read with the intention to understand, not to adopt.

5. Engage With Curiosity, Not Agreement

You are not expected to agree with every interpretation. You are invited to explore.

Approach the ideas with curiosity, skepticism, reflection, and openness. The value of this book lies not in persuasion but in *perspective*—in offering a lens through which reality may appear more connected, coherent, and meaningful.

6. Revisit the Appendices—they Complete the Architecture

The appendices are not optional. They provide:

- cross-disciplinary mappings
- symbolic decoding
- scientific parallels
- structured models
- philosophical foundations

They anchor the book's central argument and bring the full picture into view.

Return to them as often as needed.

7. Make It Your Own Journey

This book is a map, not a destination. Use it to question, reflect, interpret, and build your own understanding of existence.

Whether you are a scientist, philosopher, seeker, student, or simply someone curious about the deeper logic of the universe, read with the awareness that your interpretation will evolve—as it should.

The universe is too large for one reading. Let each reading expand your vision.

Prologue

It began innocently, as many revelations do. A question asked casually, without intent, without preparation:

"Can a woman live her entire life without a man?"

It was a domestic question, shaped by daily life—but it carried a depth far beyond relationships. That night, as the conversation settled into silence, something shifted. The question refused to remain personal. It cracked open a doorway into duality, interdependence, and the fundamental architecture of existence.

Very quickly, I realized the question was not about man or woman at all. It was about balance.

Lakshmi and Narayana. Energy and Equilibrium. Flow and Stability.

Not as deities, but as principles.

Lakshmi revealed herself not as a symbol of wealth but as motion itself—energy in circulation, consciousness in action, the dynamic pulse that keeps the universe alive. Vishnu emerged not as a celestial figure but as the stabilizing intelligence that prevents motion from dissolving into chaos—a cosmic equilibrium that sustains everything from atoms to galaxies.

Suddenly, the ancient stories I had grown up hearing transformed. They were not stories. They were equations in disguise. They were models of the universe written in human language. Everything I had dismissed as mythology returned, not as belief, but as knowledge.

The Vedas were no longer scriptures. The Puranas were no longer legends. The Avatars were no longer mythological beings.

They became an integrated operating system of reality.

The Dashavatara mirrored biological evolution. The Yugas mirrored cosmic cycles. Vishnu, Lakshmi, and Shiva mirrored the three forces required for any system to exist—stability, motion, and renewal.

The deeper I went, the more impossible it became to ignore the intelligence encoded beneath. Modern science, with all its brilliance, seemed like a rediscovery of what the ancients had already mapped. The divide between God and Science began to dissolve. What remained was intelligence—pure, universal, omnipresent.

This book is not an interpretation. It is not an alternate reading. It is not a spiritual commentary.

It is rediscovery.

A restoration of the original design—the Vishwarup Darshan—the complete vision of reality that modern thinking has fractured into pieces.

You are not about to read mythology. You are not about to read science. You are about to see how both emerged from the same intelligence.

The question that began this journey was simple. The answer was everything.

Are you ready to see the universe without filters?

Chapter 1: The Need to Restore True Knowledge

Introduction

What if everything you knew about the universe was only half the truth? What if science—the sacred pursuit of rational minds—was merely a fragment of a far grander intelligence, not its ultimate authority? What if mythology—the dismissed poetry of ancient civilizations—was not just storytelling, but encoded knowledge that modern science is only now beginning to grasp?

And what if God was never meant to be sought, nor science to be worshipped?

The world you inhabit is shaped by two seemingly opposing forces: faith and reason. One tells you to believe without questioning. The other tells you to question without believing. Yet both have blinded you from seeing the complete picture.

Science gave you equations, but it cannot explain why intelligence exists. Religion gave you gods, but it never revealed where they truly reside. You were taught that the universe is random—yet every law of nature speaks of order.

If knowledge is meant to liberate, why does it divide? If truth is meant to be universal, why is it fragmented?

You have been handed reality in pieces, scattered like shattered glass. You see the reflections, but not the mirror itself.

Now imagine the mirror restored. Imagine seeing the universe as it truly is. You were never meant to choose between God and Science—for they were never separate to begin with.

The Grand Design Hidden in Plain Sight

The ancients did not struggle with this false divide. They did not separate physics from philosophy, nor mathematics from metaphysics. They did not draw boundaries between reason and reverence. They saw everything as one.

They wrote of Vishnu and Lakshmi—not as deities alone, but as twin forces of stability and motion, conservation and energy flow, the structured vacuum and the manifested universe.

They spoke of Brahma and Saraswati—not as separate beings, but as creation and wisdom, expansion and knowledge, the evolving cosmos and the intelligence that interprets it.

They revealed Shiva and Parvati—not as god and goddess, but as controlled destruction and nurturing transformation, the reset and renewal of cycles, the force that ensures stagnation never exists.

These were not myths. They were principles of existence, written in a language the world has forgotten how to read.

They knew time was relative. They understood energy was eternal. They saw intelligence not as a function of the brain, but as the governing principle of the cosmos itself.

And yet, you were told they were only stories. That the gods were symbols, or worse—fantasies. That their scriptures were religious, not scientific.

But what if they were neither? What if the Vedas were not religious texts, but the first scientific documentation of the universe? What if the Puranas were not mythology, but a coded framework of reality itself? What if everything modern science is discovering today had already been known—just in a language we no longer understand?

When Knowledge Became Faith and Science Became Blind

There was a time when knowledge was open and fluid. A time when intelligence was the guiding force of humanity. But somewhere along the way, it was lost.

It was broken into pieces. Knowledge became institutionalized. Wisdom became religion. Science became a closed system, rejecting everything that could not be measured.

The ancients never needed blind faith. They never divided knowledge into "scientific" and "spiritual." They simply understood.

But we became fragmented. We forgot. And now, it is time to restore what was lost.

The Vishwarup Darshan – The Grand Unification of Knowledge

This book is not about proving a belief system. It is not about validating one philosophy over another. It is about restoring truth itself.

You have been given fragments of reality. Now, we will connect them.

You will see how the Vedas and Puranas contain the first unified field theory. How Vishnu's Avatars align with human evolution. How Brahma and Saraswati represent the expanding universe and its intelligence. How Shiva and Parvati embody the cycles of destruction and rebirth. How Danavas and Rakshasas are not demons, but forces of disruption—entropy, instability, unchecked power.

Science is not the master of truth. It is only a subset of a much grander intelligence.

You will see how ancient knowledge and modern science are not rivals, but reflections of the same reality. You will understand why science without wisdom is dangerous, and wisdom without science is powerless.

You will see the Vishwarup Darshan—the Great Grand Theory of Everything—not as an idea, but as a reality that has always existed.

You were never meant to see in fragments. You were meant to see everything.

Turn the page. And witness what has been hidden in plain sight.

1.1 – The Illusion of Knowing

What does it mean to *know* something?

Is knowledge simply the collection of facts—the ability to measure, predict, and manipulate? Or is it something deeper, something beyond what can be tested in a laboratory or written into an equation?

For most people today, knowing means believing what is commonly accepted—what is taught in schools, published in journals, or written in sacred texts. But what if this knowledge is not the whole truth, only the fragments that survived the filters of time and perception?

You believe in science because it is measurable. You dismiss mythology because it is written as stories. You assume religion is faith and science is reason.

But what if that separation never existed? What if science is only our modern attempt to rediscover what was already known—fragmented, reduced, stripped of its wholeness? What if mythology was never meant to be "stories," but an encoded form of knowledge, preserving truths in a language beyond equations?

Reality is not limited to what you can measure—for even measurement itself depends on perception.

Time Dilation and the Ancient Understanding of Time

Take time, for example.

Modern physics tells us that time is not absolute. It stretches and contracts with gravity, speed, and energy fields. A second on Earth may be years elsewhere in the cosmos. This is time dilation—one of the fundamental aspects of Einstein's relativity.

A traveler near the speed of light experiences time more slowly than someone on Earth. An astronaut orbiting a black hole ages differently than one far from its pull. These are scientific facts—proven, measured, accepted.

But why does the idea feel familiar?

Because it was already described thousands of years ago in the Vedas and Puranas.

According to these texts, time is not universal—it flows differently across realms. A single day in Brahmaloka equals millions of years on Earth. A blink of Vishnu's eye marks the rise and fall of civilizations. The Bhagavata Purana, Vishnu Purana, and Mahabharata describe layered perceptions of time—mirroring relativity's time dilation.

The difference lies in language. Modern physics discovered time dilation through equations and experiments. The ancients preserved it through stories, symbols, and metaphors—the language of their era.

So the real question is: was their knowledge primitive, or simply written in a way we no longer understand? Did they lack mathematics, or did they choose to encode wisdom in forms that could survive millennia?

If modern physics had never been developed, would we have dismissed these texts as mere mythology forever? And if one fundamental truth—time dilation—was already encoded in the Puranas, how much more knowledge lies hidden within them?

The Mindset Trap – Science vs. Mythology

The problem is not what we know, but how we think.

We have been conditioned to see mythology as primitive and science as superior. But this assumption is arrogance—the arrogance of believing human civilization stands at its intellectual peak.

What if we are not at the peak? What if we are only rediscovering what was lost?

Imagine an advanced civilization disappearing tomorrow, leaving only symbols, sculptures, and stories. How would future generations interpret them? Would they recognize the truths encoded within? Or would they dismiss them as mythology—just as we have done with the ancients?

This is the illusion of knowing.

You think you understand the universe because science gives you equations and models. But models change. Equations are rewritten. Theories evolve. Truth does not change.

The ancients were not seeking equations. They were seeking truth.

Breaking the Illusion – Seeing Through the Right Lens

If you view the universe only through the fragmented lens of science, you will see equations, forces, and particles. If you view it only through blind faith, you will see rituals, gods, and deities.

But if you step beyond both—if you break the illusion of separation—you will see Vishwarup Darshan: the true, interconnected, intelligent design of everything.

This book is not about arguing for science or religion. It is not about proving one over the other. It is about restoring the original knowledge—the knowledge that was never meant to be fragmented, but has always existed as one unified whole.

The illusion of knowing has kept you blind. Now, it is time to see.

1.2 – Why Science is Not the Final Truth

Science has given us extraordinary advancements. It has split atoms, carried us to the moon, and decoded the human genome. It has predicted storms, manipulated matter, and built machines that extend human capability beyond imagination.

Yet for all its triumphs, science remains incomplete. It tells us how the universe behaves, but not why it exists at all. It measures energy, but cannot define intelligence. It explains motion, but not the purpose behind it.

Science is powerful, but it is not the master of truth. It is a tool—one that allows us to observe, measure, and manipulate. But observation is not understanding. Measurement is not wisdom. The real question is: can science ever explain the nature of intelligence itself?

The Fragmented Nature of Science

Science does not study the universe as a whole. It breaks reality into pieces, each with its own laws and boundaries. Physics studies forces and motion. Chemistry studies atoms and reactions. Biology studies life and evolution. Psychology studies thought and behavior.

Each branch acts as if it exists independently—as if physics does not shape chemistry, as if the mind is not an extension of biology, as if intelligence is an accident of evolution.

But the universe does not function in fragments. It operates as one seamless system. A tree does not exist apart from the soil. The body does not function apart from the mind. The planets do not move apart from the fabric of space-time.

Truth is not a collection of models. Truth is whole. Truth is intelligence itself. And science, for all its complexity, is still only a tool trying to measure what intelligence already knows.

The Greatest Minds Looked Beyond Equations

If science were the final truth, why did the greatest minds look beyond it?

Newton, after discovering motion and gravity, turned to philosophy, alchemy, and ancient texts, convinced that mathematics alone could not reveal the deeper order of reality.

Tesla spoke of energy, frequency, and vibration, insisting that intelligence existed beyond matter, and that science was only scratching the surface.

Einstein, who rewrote physics with relativity, admitted: "The most incomprehensible thing about the universe is that it is comprehensible." He sensed intelligence behind the mathematical beauty of the cosmos.

Heisenberg, pioneer of quantum mechanics, said: "The first gulp from the glass of natural sciences will turn you into an atheist, but at the bottom of the glass, God is waiting for you."

None of them rejected science. None rejected logic. They simply realized there was something greater than equations—something beyond what science could measure.

Science is Not the Master—It is a Mirror

The mistake of modern thinking is confusing measurement with meaning. Science does not create intelligence. It only measures its effects.

It can record electrical signals in the brain, but not explain where thoughts come from. It can map DNA, but not explain why life exists. It can define gravity, but not explain why its laws exist at all.

The Vedas understood this long before physics. They spoke of intelligence not as a human trait, but as the governing force of the universe itself. This intelligence is not supernatural. It is not outside the cosmos. It is the cosmos.

Science can tell us how things work. But it cannot tell us why they exist. That is the difference between a tool and the truth.

Tracing the Outlines of Intelligence

Science is a mirror. It reflects only what we are capable of perceiving.

To an ant, the world is soil and leaves. To a fish, reality is water. To a human, science is an attempt to explain what is already there—but only as much as our limited minds can grasp.

When science measures the universe, it is tracing the outlines of intelligence without ever fully seeing it.

Imagine an ancient sculptor working on a hidden statue. With each discovery, science chips away at the stone, revealing fragments of the form beneath. But it does not know what the final shape will be. It does not even know if it is carving a statue at all.

The ancients did not chip at the surface. They saw the full structure. They did not divide knowledge into physics, chemistry, and biology. They saw Vishwarup Darshan—the complete design of reality, without division, without gaps.

Science is still carving. Intelligence is the hand that sculpted it in the first place.

The Universe is One Intelligent System

There is no "science" separate from reality. No "spirituality" apart from existence. Everything is one.

The force that binds galaxies is the same that binds atoms. The intelligence that guides a bird to build its nest is the same that guides humans to build civilizations. The rhythm that creates seasons is the same rhythm that creates breath in your lungs.

The mistake we made was breaking knowledge into pieces. But truth does not exist in pieces. Truth is seamless.

And it is time to see the universe as it truly is.

1.3 – What if mythology wasn't just stories?

For centuries, mythology has been dismissed as mere storytelling—imaginative tales woven by people trying to explain what they did not understand. We were told ancient scriptures were religious texts, that the gods within them were symbolic figures meant to inspire devotion, and that such stories had no place in the world of logic and rational thought. But what if that assumption is entirely wrong? What if mythology was never meant to be taken as stories at all, but as a coded framework of knowledge—preserving truths far more advanced than we realize?

The greatest civilizations did not separate science from spirituality, nor divide philosophy from physics. To them, reality was one seamless system. They didn't write in dry equations or academic papers; they encoded their understanding into narratives—because narratives carry wisdom across generations, across cultures, and across time. Read these ancient texts with the right lens—not as religious doctrine, but as an encoded knowledge system—and a deeper reality begins to appear, one modern science is still reaching toward.

The Vedas and Puranas as structured intelligence

The Vedas and Puranas are not collections of myths or religious commandments. They are early attempts to document the fundamental nature of existence. The Vedas focus on cosmic laws, energy, and intelligence—describing the architecture of reality. The Puranas encode truths about evolution, destruction, balance, and transformation—through allegory and symbol. Because they were transmitted orally and symbolically, later generations mistook them for fantasy. What was structured knowledge became ritual; scientific insight became dogma; a complete understanding became fragmented stories of gods and demons. Decode them correctly, and a revelation emerges: they were speaking of intelligence, energy, and cosmic forces—constructive and destructive—written in the language of their era.

Vishnu's Dashavatara as a narrative of evolution

If you were to describe life's ascent, you would begin in water, move to land, then emerge into intelligence, society, and cosmic awareness. Vishnu's ten Avatars mirror this arc with uncanny precision:

- **Matsya (Fish):** Life begins in the oceans—first emergence in water.
- **Kurma (Turtle):** Transition from water to land—amphibious adaptability.
- **Varaha (Boar):** Dominance of land creatures—mammalian resilience.
- **Narasimha (Half-man, half-lion):** Hybrid thresholds—early primate bridges between animal and human.
- **Vamana (Dwarf):** Small yet catalytic—first hominids shaping tools and pattern recognition.
- **Parashurama (Warrior):** Human force as destroyer-controller—early civilizations, warfare, deforestation, raw agency.
- **Rama (The Ideal Human):** Order, ethics, and law—civilization stabilizing through moral frameworks.
- **Krishna (The Strategist):** Mastery of intellect and dharma—philosophical and strategic sophistication.
- **Buddha (The Enlightened):** Awakening to inner intelligence—self-awareness and compassionate wisdom.
- **Kalki (The Final):** Reset through correction—humanity's inflection toward destruction or transcendence.

This is not coincidence. It is a structured representation of evolutionary progress. Modern science needed centuries to articulate evolution; the ancients encoded it in a timeless narrative accessible to a farmer and a philosopher, a child and a sage. What was dismissed as myth becomes a scientific blueprint in story form. If they knew this, what else did they know?

Danavas and Rakshasas as entropy and imbalance

The Puranas describe battles between Devas and Asuras, Vishnu and Rakshasas, light and darkness. The missing explanation is that Devas represent constructive cosmic intelligence—the sustaining forces of evolution and order. Danavas and Rakshasas represent destructive vectors—entropy, imbalance, unchecked power, systemic destabilization. They were never literal demons. They are embodiments of imbalance so it can be seen, understood, and corrected. Vishnu's Avatars intervene not to "kill demons," but to restore equilibrium whenever destruction outpaces balance. Modern physics echoes this: creation and entropy must remain in tension; when imbalance reaches a threshold, a reset occurs and a new phase begins. The universe is a living cycle of order and chaos. The ancients captured this in stories because they knew: humans remember stories; they forget equations.

Restoring the lens of understanding

Mythology was never meant to be taken literally, nor dismissed as fantasy. It was meant to be decoded. It contains cosmology without telescopes, evolution without DNA sequencing, psychology without neuroscience, physics without formal equations. Seeing it through the right lens is not about proving mythology right or science wrong. It is about seeing the complete picture as it was originally intended: unified, intelligible, alive. We were never meant to choose between science and mythology—they were never separate. Once you understand this, the next question becomes unavoidable: what else have we misunderstood?

Turn the page, and step deeper into the truth.

1.4 – The Great Mistake: When Knowledge Became Faith

There was a time when knowledge was not something to be believed—it was something to be understood.

There was no division between seeker and scientist, philosopher and mathematician, spiritual and empirical. Knowledge flowed freely, adapting and evolving as human consciousness expanded.

But something changed. Somewhere along the journey of civilization, knowledge ceased to be a path of discovery and became a system of control. What was once open and fluid became institutionalized. What was once explored became restricted. What was once wisdom became doctrine.

The greatest mistake of human history was this: we turned knowledge into belief, discovery into dogma, truth into systems of faith and authority. And in doing so, we lost the essence of intelligence itself.

From Universal Understanding to Divided Systems

The ancients did not see knowledge in fragments. Physics was not separate from metaphysics, medicine was not apart from consciousness, astronomy was not divorced from spirituality. To them, everything was interconnected.

But as civilizations grew, power structures formed. With power came control. Knowledge that was once universal became reserved for the privileged few. Ideas that were fluid became fixed into rigid texts. What was once shared openly became owned and guarded by institutions.

This shift was gradual, unfolding over centuries, until one day humanity forgot that knowledge was once free. People were told to believe instead of seek, to accept instead of experience, to follow institutions—religious or scientific—rather than explore truth themselves.

Religion claimed ownership of wisdom. Science claimed ownership of reason. And in this divide, we forgot something fundamental: truth does not belong to any institution. Truth does not require faith or validation. Truth simply is.

Ayurveda, Yog, and Astronomy – From Daily Life to Forgotten Science

Consider the ancient sciences of Ayurveda, Yog, and Astronomy. Once, they were not "alternative" practices or mystical curiosities. They were ways of life—practical, precise, deeply connected to reality.

Ayurveda was a complete understanding of how body, mind, and nature interact. Yog was a method to align human consciousness with universal intelligence. Astronomy was the study of cosmic cycles, time, and the energetic influence of celestial bodies.

Today, these systems are dismissed as unscientific because they do not fit laboratory validation, commercialized into superficial trends, or re-explored in fragments—where modern research "discovers" meditation, fasting, or plant medicine as if they were new.

But science is not validating them—it is catching up. The mistake was never in these ancient sciences. The mistake was forgetting that they were based on direct experience, not blind belief. Knowledge was tested by reality itself. If something worked, it was kept. If it failed, it was discarded. Proof was lived, not demanded.

When Science Became Another Faith

We often criticize religion for demanding blind faith. But what of science?

Do you truly understand quantum mechanics, or do you simply believe what scientists tell you? Do you personally verify medical research, or do you trust institutions without question? Do you conduct your own experiments, or do you accept published findings as truth?

Most people do not understand science. They believe in it. And when belief replaces understanding, science becomes another form of faith.

Religious faith believes in what cannot be proven. Scientific faith believes in what has been "proven"—until a new discovery overturns it. Neither approach leads to truth. Because truth does not belong to belief or validation. Truth belongs only to intelligence.

Restoring Knowledge as Truth, Not Belief

The world today is full of arguments. Religious followers claim their texts hold ultimate truth. Scientists claim their methods are the only path to knowledge. Both are mistaken.

Truth is neither religious nor scientific. It does not belong to temples or laboratories. It does not need priests or peer reviews. Truth is self-existent.

It can be found in the Vedas and in quantum physics. It can be seen in Yog and in neuroscience. It can be experienced in meditation and in discovery. But to see it, you must let go of belief. Knowledge was never meant to be followed. It was meant to be understood, experienced, and evolved.

When you see this—when you truly understand—you will no longer need to choose between science and spirituality. You will see they were always one.

Breaking the Great Divide

This is where the journey shifts. This is where you step beyond faith and beyond institutions. The question is no longer science versus religion. The question is:

What is knowledge when free from both? What does intelligence look like when unrestricted? If we break the illusion of separation, what do we see?

The answer is Vishwarup Darshan—the ultimate, unified knowledge of everything. And once you see it, there is no going back.

Turn the page. And let intelligence reveal itself.

1.5 – Breaking the False Divide: The Unity of God & Science

For centuries, humanity has been caught in an endless debate—God versus Science. One side insists, *"Believe in God, even without proof."* The other demands, *"Believe only in what can be measured."* One calls for faith without reason. The other calls for reason without wisdom.

And yet, both are incomplete.

God and Science were never meant to be opposites. Truth was never meant to be divided.

What if God is not a being to be sought, but the intelligence that exists within all things? What if science is not a belief system, but merely a method—one of many—to understand and manipulate reality? What if the real problem lies not in God or Science, but in how we have misunderstood both?

This is where the false divide breaks. This is where we step beyond illusion.

The Illusion of Separation

There was a time when science and spirituality were one. The ancients did not see God as an external ruler, but as the supreme intelligence governing all things. They did not see science as separate from the divine—it was simply a way to study the patterns of creation.

But over time, this unified truth was split into extremes. Religion claimed that truth required no proof—only belief. Science claimed that truth must be proven, or it was meaningless. One closed its eyes to reason. The other closed its eyes to wisdom. And in doing so, humanity became blind to the full nature of reality.

Why did we ever separate them? Because one side feared the power of reason, and the other feared the power of intelligence beyond measurement. The result was a world where faith became blind, and science became soulless.

But the truth was never divided. Only our perception was.

God Is Not a Being—God Is Intelligence

Ask a religious follower, *"Where is God?"* and they will point to the heavens. Ask a scientist, *"Where is intelligence?"* and they will point to the brain. Both are mistaken.

Intelligence is not limited to human thought. God is not a distant being. God is the intelligence woven into the fabric of reality itself.

When a plant turns toward the sun, that is intelligence. When planets orbit in perfect balance, that is intelligence. When the human body heals itself, that is intelligence. When quantum particles defy classical physics, that too is intelligence.

Everything in existence operates with intelligence—not random chaos, not blind luck, but precise, self-organizing, universal intelligence.

This is what the ancients called *Brahman*—the Supreme Intelligence, the Source. This is what modern thinkers sense but struggle to define, because they try to reduce God to a being, or intelligence to neurons in a brain. But intelligence is not limited to brains. It is not limited to human understanding. It is the universe itself.

This is why seeking God outside is meaningless. God is not something to be found—it is something to be realized. Not in temples, not in scriptures, but in the very intelligence that moves the cosmos.

Science Is Not a Belief System—It Is a Tool

Science is powerful, but it is not the master of truth. It is a tool—a method to measure, predict, and manipulate the world. It studies patterns, discovers laws, and applies knowledge.

But science is limited. It can measure the chemistry of thought, but not explain where thoughts come from. It can map the universe, but not explain why it exists. It can study consciousness, but not define what consciousness truly is.

Science measures only what it can detect. And the most powerful forces in existence are beyond measurement.

Love cannot be reduced to brain chemicals. Intuition cannot be reduced to neural activity. Consciousness cannot be reduced to brainwaves. These are experiences, not equations.

Science, for all its power, is limited to observation. But truth exists with or without measurement. The wind existed before air pressure was measured. Gravity existed before equations described it. The mind existed before neuroscience studied it. Intelligence exists whether we can measure it or not.

So the real question is: is science searching for truth, or only for what it can measure? If science refuses to look beyond measurement, it is not a pursuit of truth—it is only a pursuit of data.

Restoring the Unity

God is not a ruler in the sky. Science is not the ultimate path to truth. They are not opposites. They are two sides of the same intelligence.

God is the intelligence behind the universe. Science is the method of understanding and applying that intelligence. One is wisdom. The other is application. One is the unchanging source. The other is the evolving discovery of that source.

The problem was never in God or Science. The problem was in how we misunderstood both. We turned God into blind faith. We turned Science into blind measurement. But knowledge was never meant to be blind. It was meant to be seen completely.

And when you see beyond the illusion, you realize: you do not need to believe in God. You do not need to reject science. You only need to understand that both were always pointing to the same truth.

Once you see this truth, you will never again ask, *"Is it science or God?"* Because you will finally understand—it is both.

And that is Vishwarup Darshan—the complete vision of reality.

1.6 – The Truth Hidden in Plain Sight

We live in an era of information overload, yet knowledge has never been more fragmented. We wield powerful tools, advanced technologies, and scientific breakthroughs, but the fundamental questions remain unanswered—questions the ancients had already explored.

How was the universe created? What is time? What is consciousness? Is there an ultimate intelligence guiding everything?

We think we are progressing, but in truth, we are only rediscovering what was already known. The answers exist, but we have been conditioned to look in the wrong places.

If you believe the Vedas are merely religious texts, you are mistaken. They are the first scientific documentation of reality itself. If you believe the Puranas are only myths, you are mistaken. They are the earliest recorded framework of cosmic evolution. If you believe ancient civilizations lacked scientific knowledge, you are mistaken. They understood the universe, time, intelligence, and cosmic cycles with a clarity we are only beginning to glimpse.

The evidence is everywhere—if you know how to see it.

The Vedas: Scientific Documentation of Reality

The Vedas are not books of prayer, nor cultural scriptures. They are the oldest, most comprehensive documentation of universal laws.

The *Rigveda* describes the nature of reality, time, space, and energy. The *Yajurveda* lays out cosmic cycles, movement, and balance. The *Samaveda* encodes vibrational frequencies of creation—sound as the foundation of reality. The *Atharvaveda* details health, medicine, and human physiology in alignment with the cosmos.

These are not texts of blind faith. They are structured like scientific treatises—precise, mathematical, observational. Yet modern scholars, bound by fragmented frameworks, dismissed them as "religious." Science demands evidence. But what if the evidence is encoded within these texts, written in a language modern minds fail to decipher?

The Puranas: Framework of Cosmic Evolution

The Puranas were never meant to be taken as simple stories. They are the first recorded framework of cosmic evolution.

The concept of *Yugas* aligns with astronomical cycles. The descriptions of creation mirror modern cosmology—the universe expanding and contracting in cycles. The *Dashavatara* maps the evolutionary journey from aquatic life to higher intelligence. Even Brahma's lifespan—trillions of years—echoes modern physics' understanding of cosmic time.

Is this coincidence? Or is it evidence of a lost knowledge system we have failed to recognize? What if these texts were never intended as religion, but as advanced recordings of universal dynamics? What if our misinterpretation of them is the greatest intellectual failure of our time?

Ancient Civilizations Knew More Than We Think

We assume ancient civilizations were primitive, bound by superstition. Yet the deeper we look, the more undeniable their sophistication becomes.

Temples and pyramids aligned with astronomical precision far beyond what should have been possible. Vedic structures integrated geometry, resonance, and architecture seamlessly. The *Sushruta Samhita* recorded advanced medical and surgical techniques centuries before modern medicine confirmed them. The Upanishads spoke of *Bindu*—creation from a single point—eerily similar to the Big Bang.

Were these guesses? Or is it time to admit that too many "coincidences" point to a lost science?

Why Modern Science Cannot See the Truth

The tragedy of modern thought is its refusal to accept what does not fit its framework. If it cannot be measured, it is ignored. If it is written in symbols, it is dismissed as myth. If it predates modern theories, it is assumed accidental.

But truth does not depend on validation. The wind existed before meteorology. Gravity existed before Newton. DNA existed before Watson and Crick. Reality does not wait for science to catch up.

The Vedas, the Puranas, and ancient civilizations do not need modern approval. They were always true. We simply forgot how to read them.

The Next Step: Seeing with the Right Lens

The truth has been hidden in plain sight—not because it was secret, but because we were taught not to see it. We were conditioned to believe ancient wisdom was outdated, that science was the only path, that reality was only what could be measured.

But now, we stand at a turning point. We are beginning to realize we have been looking through a broken lens. The ancients were not mistaken. They did not need validation. They already knew.

And now, it is time to see what they saw. This is where past and future converge. This is where truth is restored.

This is Vishwarup Darshan—the complete vision of reality.

Turn the page. Step into the knowledge that was never lost—only forgotten.

1.7 – The Need for Vishwarup Darshan: The Grand Theory of Everything

You have been given only fragments of truth. Each fragment, on its own, seems logical, convincing—even complete. Science gave you one part. Spirituality gave you another. Philosophy added more. Religion created its own version.

But no one gave you the whole picture.

You were told to choose between God and Science. You were told to pick a side—reason or faith. You were told that knowledge must be categorized, divided, separated.

And that was the greatest deception of all.

Because truth has no sides. Intelligence does not exist in fragments. Reality is not divided—it is one seamless, interconnected whole.

For centuries, we have studied reality in pieces. Now, it is time to see it completely.

Restoring the Whole Picture

This book is not here to prove a belief system. It is not here to defend or attack religion. It is not here to validate science, nor to reject it.

It exists for one reason only—to restore the complete vision of truth.

We will decode the myths, showing how ancient knowledge was never just "stories" but encoded wisdom. We will dissolve contradictions, showing how religion and science are not rivals but reflections of the same intelligence. We will bridge the gap between ancient texts and modern discoveries, showing how forgotten knowledge aligns with today's most advanced theories.

By the end, you will no longer see the universe as scattered knowledge. You will see it as Vishwarup Darshan—the complete and unified truth.

This is not a theory. This is not a philosophical argument. This is not a new belief system. This is intelligence itself. And once you see it, there is no going back.

The Last Illusion

Most people approach knowledge with preconceived ideas, trying to fit new information into the framework of what they already know. That is why truth remains hidden.

A scientist rejects what cannot be measured. A religious follower rejects what contradicts faith. A philosopher debates endlessly but never experiences truth directly.

But real truth does not need acceptance. It does not need faith. It does not need debate.

The sun does not need belief to rise. Gravity does not need approval to function. Consciousness does not need validation to exist.

So the real question is not whether you believe in Vishwarup Darshan. The real question is whether you are ready to see it.

Because once you do, you will realize: you never needed faith, you never needed proof—you only needed the right perspective.

The Grand Theory of Everything

What lies ahead is not just another book. It is not a theory, a hypothesis, or a new interpretation. It is a restoration of what was always known but forgotten.

You will see how the universe operates—not just through physics, but through intelligence itself. You will understand how ancient knowledge aligns with modern discoveries, revealing a hidden order beneath everything. You will witness how every aspect of reality—energy, consciousness, time, evolution—follows a single, unbreakable law. You will finally see the Vishwarup—the whole, the complete, the undeniable.

This is not just about reading. It is about awakening.

Because when you truly see Vishwarup Darshan, something shifts forever. You will no longer look at the universe in fragments. You will no longer ask whether God and Science are separate. You will no longer be bound by illusions that have controlled human thought for millennia.

You will see the entire system as it truly is.

This is the last question you will ever need to ask. This is the final answer you have been searching for.

Turn the page. And witness Vishwarup Darshan—the Grand Theory of Everything.

Interlude: A Pause Between Fragments

You have journeyed through the first chapter—an unveiling of fragments, illusions, and forgotten truths. Perhaps your mind feels full, perhaps your heart feels stirred. That is the nature of rediscovery: it is not only information, but a shift in perception.

So let us pause.

Close your eyes for a moment and imagine the universe not as equations or scriptures, but as a vast, breathing presence. Imagine knowledge not as something to be owned, but as something to be felt. Imagine truth not as a debate, but as a quiet recognition.

The ancients did not rush. They did not consume knowledge as data. They lived it, slowly, rhythmically, as part of their daily existence. In this pause, you are invited to do the same.

Reflect on what you have read. Notice how the divide between God and Science begins to dissolve when seen through the lens of intelligence. Notice how myths transform into codes, how fragments merge into wholeness. Notice how truth feels less like something to prove, and more like something to remember.

This interlude is not about answers. It is about stillness. It is about allowing the ideas to settle into your own rhythm, your own awareness.

Because Vishwarup Darshan is not just a theory—it is a way of seeing. And to see clearly, sometimes you must first be still.

Take this moment. Breathe. Let the weight of centuries fall away. Let the fragments begin to align.

When you are ready, turn the page. The journey continues—but now, you carry the resonance of wholeness within you.

Chapter 2: The Ancient Universal System

The Original Grand Theory

For centuries, modern science has searched for a unified theory—a single framework that could explain everything, from the motion of galaxies to the subatomic dance of particles. The pursuit has led to astonishing discoveries: Einstein's relativity, quantum mechanics, the standard model of particle physics, and the ongoing quest for a Theory of Everything—one equation to unite gravity, electromagnetism, and the fundamental forces of nature.

Yet, despite all progress, an unsettling realization remains: science is fragmented. Each discovery opens deeper questions rather than final answers. Relativity and quantum mechanics, two of the most successful theories, remain incompatible at their core. The search continues for the missing piece—something that could weave contradictions into one seamless understanding.

But what if this unified knowledge was never truly lost? What if our ancestors had already documented the Grand Theory of Everything—not in equations, but in a language we have misinterpreted for centuries?

Fragmentation vs. Wholeness

Modern science is reductionist. It breaks reality into pieces, studying each in isolation. Physics examines forces and motion. Chemistry studies matter and reactions. Biology explains life. Neuroscience maps the brain. Each field progresses independently, yet none answers the most fundamental question: *What is intelligence, and why does the universe function as it does?*

The ancients, however, never divided knowledge. For them, everything was part of one interconnected system. Physics was not separate from philosophy. Biology was not apart from cosmic law. The universe was not either mathematical or divine—it was both, seamlessly woven into one intelligent framework.

They spoke of Vishnu and Lakshmi—not as mythological figures, but as cosmic forces of equilibrium and energy. They described Shiva—not as a deity of destruction, but as the principle of transformation, ensuring the universe never stagnates. The Vedas did not separate the material from the spiritual—they revealed an all-encompassing intelligence governing everything from human consciousness to planetary motion.

For them, knowledge was not just intellectual pursuit. It was revelation.

Why Do We Assume Ancient Wisdom Was Primitive?

The modern world has been conditioned to believe ancient civilizations were scientifically ignorant, bound by myth and superstition. This assumption is rooted in arrogance—the belief that progress is linear, that earlier societies were inferior, and that we, as modern humans, stand at the peak of evolution.

But what if progress is not linear? What if knowledge has been discovered, lost, and rediscovered across history?

Consider this: ancient Indian texts described the relative nature of time—where time passes differently in different realms—long before Einstein introduced time dilation. The Dashavatara, Vishnu's ten incarnations, align with biological evolution, suggesting an understanding of life's progressive development. The Yugas, cosmic time cycles, map onto astronomical and climate rhythms, echoing astrophysics' view of planetary and galactic evolution. Temples and structures were built with resonance, vibration, and cosmic alignment that modern engineers are only beginning to explore.

Are these coincidences? Or evidence of a lost system of knowledge—encoded in symbols, stories, and philosophy rather than laboratory data?

The Possibility of the Original Grand Theory

If knowledge is universal, and if intelligence is the fundamental fabric of reality, then humanity has encountered the same truths repeatedly—only to lose and rediscover them in different forms.

Modern science explains the universe mathematically. Ancient wisdom explained it through intelligence and balance. But what if both were describing the same reality—just from different perspectives?

This book does not propose a new theory. It does not seek to create belief or argument. It seeks to reconstruct what was already known—what was encoded in scriptures, myths, and the lost teachings of ancient civilizations.

It is time to look beyond the illusion of separation. It is time to rediscover Vishwarup Darshan—the Complete Universal Vision.

2.1 – The Cosmos as a Unified Intelligence

Modern science often describes the universe as a mechanical system—a vast expanse of particles, forces, and fields, all interacting according to strict mathematical laws. It is seen as intricate but soulless, governed by cause and effect yet devoid of deeper intelligence or purpose.

The ancients saw differently. To them, the cosmos was not a machine but a living, conscious system. It was governed not by random interactions, but by an underlying intelligence that structured and sustained everything. This intelligence was not confined to the human brain; it existed at all levels of reality, from the smallest particle to the grandest celestial body.

The Vedas did not ask, *"What are the laws of physics?"* They asked, *"What is the intelligence that makes these laws possible?"* The Upanishads did not seek to explain how the universe works mechanically. They sought to understand why it works at all. Their answer was Vishwarup—the Universal Form of intelligence.

Vishwarup – The Universe as a Single, Intelligent Entity

The *Bhagavad Gita* describes Vishwarup Darshan—the moment when Arjuna, through divine vision, sees Krishna in his universal form. What he witnesses is not a human deity, but a grand, all-encompassing cosmic intelligence. Within this vision, he sees galaxies without end, time converging into a single moment, creation and destruction unfolding simultaneously, and the forces of nature intertwined in perfect harmony.

This was not mystical fantasy. It was realization: the universe itself is intelligence, a self-regulating, interconnected whole. Vishwarup is not religion, nor blind faith. It is insight into reality—a truth modern physics is only beginning to glimpse.

Intelligence Beyond the Human Mind

Science limits intelligence to the human brain, treating it as an evolutionary accident. But if intelligence were only human, how would nature itself exhibit profound order, adaptation, and balance?

A single cell repairs itself, replicates, and adapts. A tree grows toward sunlight, sustains ecosystems, and renews life. A beehive functions as a coordinated superorganism, though no bee holds the master plan. Galaxies rotate in elegant patterns, bound by invisible laws. Subatomic particles shift between wave and particle, as though aware of being observed.

These are not accidents. They reveal intelligence as fundamental, preceding complexity, preceding life, preceding measurable reality. The sages called it Brahman—the Supreme Intelligence, the source of all existence. Not a deity with emotions, but the self-organizing principle of the cosmos.

Beyond Scientific Models – Asking Why, Not Just How

Science has given extraordinary insights into how the universe works. It describes expansion, energy, and forces. But it struggles with the deeper questions:

Why does the universe follow precise mathematical laws? Why does energy transform into matter in exact ratios for life? Why do quantum particles behave as if aware of observation? Why does time bend with gravity and motion?

These are not technical puzzles. They are questions of intelligence. The ancients answered them not with equations, but with symbols and allegories—Vishnu as balance, Lakshmi as flowing energy, Shiva as transformation, Brahma as creative intelligence. These were not figures of devotion, but expressions of cosmic principles.

The Universe as a Living System

If intelligence is woven into existence, then we are not separate from the universe—we are expressions of it. Our thoughts are not just neural signals. Our consciousness is not an accident. We are the universe becoming aware of itself.

The ancients did not worship the universe as external. They recognized themselves as part of the same intelligence that governs stars, atoms, and time. Vishwarup Darshan is not a vision of God outside us. It is the realization that all existence is one unified, intelligent system.

Science tells us how the universe behaves. Vishwarup Darshan tells us why. One without the other is incomplete. To truly understand reality, we must restore the lost connection between knowledge and intelligence.

Everyday Analogies of Cosmic Intelligence

This universal intelligence is not abstract—it is mirrored in systems we encounter daily.

The internet, a vast network of information, reflects cosmic intelligence. Millions of independent systems interact seamlessly, much like galaxies and natural laws. AI algorithms learn and adapt, echoing nature's inherent intelligence. Yet unlike the internet, the universe's intelligence was never created—it simply is.

The human body is a microcosm of universal intelligence. Trillions of cells function without conscious command. The heart beats, lungs breathe, and the immune system protects—all self-regulating, just as the cosmos sustains balance.

Ecosystems reveal the same truth. Forests regenerate, trees communicate through roots, Earth regulates climate and cycles, predator and prey sustain equilibrium. Intelligence is not limited to thought—it is the governing principle of existence.

Bringing It All Together

The internet connects and organizes. The body sustains itself. Ecosystems balance and renew. Each mirrors the intelligence of the cosmos.

The ancients did not separate science, philosophy, and spirituality. They knew reality is one seamless, intelligent whole. Vishwarup Darshan is not abstraction—it is the fundamental nature of existence, hidden in plain sight, waiting to be seen.

And now, it is time to see it again.

2.2 – The Missing Element in Modern Science – Intelligence as the Governing Principle

Modern science has given humanity astonishing power. We can map DNA, observe distant galaxies, and split atoms. Yet for all its achievements, science remains incomplete—for it can describe how things work, but not why they exist at all.

Science is a tool of observation and measurement. It can quantify energy, motion, and forces, but it struggles with purpose. It studies what is already there, but it cannot answer the deeper questions: Why does the universe exist? Why do natural laws follow mathematical precision instead of randomness? Why does matter organize itself into patterns—from atoms to galaxies? Why does life evolve toward higher intelligence?

Science remains silent because it does not recognize intelligence as a fundamental principle. It assumes intelligence emerges from complexity, rather than being the very fabric of reality itself.

The ancients saw differently. They understood that intelligence is not an emergent property—it is the first principle that governs all existence. Before energy. Before matter. Before time. There was intelligence.

Science Explains the Mechanics, But Not the Purpose

Science today is divided into specialized fields. Physics explains motion and forces. Chemistry explains atoms and reactions. Biology explains life and evolution. Neuroscience explains the brain and perception. Each provides extraordinary insights into how the world operates. Yet none can answer why intelligence exists in the first place.

The Big Bang Theory describes how the universe expanded from a singularity. But it does not explain what caused the singularity, why the laws of physics emerged with perfect consistency, or why energy behaves in predictable patterns instead of chaos. Physics can describe gravity, but not why mass attracts mass. Chemistry can explain molecular bonds, but not why atoms have inherent order. Biology can explain DNA replication, but not why life seeks survival and complexity.

Knowledge without intelligence is incomplete. The ancients already knew this.

The Ancients Saw Intelligence as the First Principle

The Vedic system did not see blind forces acting without direction. It described a supreme intelligence woven into existence—an intelligence preceding matter and energy, universal and infinite.

They called it **Brahman**—the supreme consciousness pervading all. They described **Rit**—cosmic order ensuring balance, much like fundamental laws of physics. They saw **Dharma**—not as morality, but as the natural intelligence guiding harmony.

This was not faith-based knowledge. It was observational, experiential, logical. They understood that energy follows patterns dictated by intelligence, matter organizes with purpose, and life evolves toward higher awareness. Intelligence was not a byproduct of the universe—it was its foundation.

Supreme Intelligence – The Source of All Phenomena

If intelligence is not limited to the brain, and if the universe functions with mathematical precision, then intelligence must be intrinsic to reality itself.

It ensures galaxies rotate in harmony instead of chaos. It allows DNA to encode life with perfect efficiency. It governs the emergence of consciousness, enabling adaptation and awareness.

This intelligence is not random, nor supernatural. It is the first principle—the organizing force behind all things. Just as gravity organizes planetary motion, electromagnetism binds atoms, and quantum entanglement reveals hidden connectivity, there exists a higher intelligence that governs all forces, matter, and consciousness.

Modern physics calls it the search for a unified field theory. Ancient wisdom called it **Vishwarup Darshan**—the vision of universal intelligence. One seeks it through equations. The other already saw it as undeniable reality.

Bridging the Gap Between Science and Intelligence

Science is beginning to acknowledge signs of intelligence. Quantum mechanics suggests particles behave as though aware of observation. Chaos theory reveals hidden order within disorder. Fractal geometry shows nature replicates itself through mathematical structures. Neuroscience cannot define consciousness beyond brain activity.

These discoveries point toward the same truth the ancients understood: intelligence precedes complexity, the universe is finely tuned to sustain order, and life is not accidental but an expression of intelligence itself.

Science and ancient wisdom are not in conflict. They are approaching the same truth from different angles. What remains is for humanity to break free from the illusion of separation and recognize: science is a tool for understanding intelligence, and intelligence is the reason science exists. Together, they form the complete picture of reality.

Analogy: The Blueprint and the Architect

Imagine a skyscraper under construction. Engineers design every detail—load distribution, structural integrity, systems woven into balance. When construction begins, every beam and pillar follows the blueprint.

Ask why the building is structured so perfectly, and a worker might answer: "Because of the laws of physics—gravity, material strength, load distribution." Technically correct, but incomplete. The skyscraper did not emerge by chance—it was designed before a single brick was laid.

Science studies the materials—the atoms, forces, motion. But the blueprint—the intelligence behind the design—is what science does not fully account for. Just as a skyscraper requires an architect, the universe requires underlying intelligence to give rise to precise laws, self-regulating ecosystems, and conscious beings who can question existence itself.

Without intelligence, the skyscraper collapses before it takes form. Without Supreme Intelligence, the universe dissolves into chaos instead of sustaining life.

The ancients saw the universe not as a building, but as an intelligent creation following a blueprint of order, balance, and evolution. This blueprint was Dharma, Rit, Supreme Intelligence—the unifying force behind existence.

And just as a skyscraper requires an architect, the universe itself reflects an intelligence that precedes it.

This is the missing element in modern science. This is what the ancients already understood. This is Vishwarup Darshan—the realization of Supreme Intelligence that governs all things.

2.3 – The Vedic Model of the Universe: The First Grand Unified System

Modern science continues its search for a Grand Unified Theory—a single framework to explain all fundamental forces, from gravity to quantum mechanics. Yet thousands of years ago, the Vedas had already described a unified system of reality, one that did not separate the physical, the energetic, and the conscious, but saw them as different expressions of the same truth.

Unlike modern texts, which rely on equations and measurements, the Vedas did not quantify reality mathematically. They structured knowledge as an interconnected whole, using concepts, principles, and experiential wisdom to explain existence. Far from being scriptures of worship, they stand as some of the earliest scientific and philosophical treatises—presenting a system where energy, intelligence, and balance form the very fabric of the universe.

The Three Core Layers of Existence

At the heart of the Vedic model lies a profound structure of reality, expressed through three foundational layers:

Sat – The Foundation of Reality Sat is ultimate truth, eternal and unchanging beyond time and space. It is pure existence, beyond form and perception, the infinite intelligence underlying all matter and energy. In modern terms, it resembles the quantum field—the unseen fabric from which particles arise. As the Upanishads declare: *"Satyam eva jayate"*—truth alone prevails.

Rit – Cosmic Order Rit is the rhythm of reality, the laws that govern existence. It ensures balance and predictability, guiding planetary motion, the flow of energy, and the evolution of life. In physics, Rit parallels gravity, thermodynamics, electromagnetism, and quantum mechanics. The Rigveda states: *"Ritam cha satyam cha"*—cosmic order and truth are one. Reality is not chaos, but structured harmony.

Dharma – The Principle of Balance Dharma sustains harmony. Often misunderstood as religious duty, it is the universal principle of equilibrium, applying to atoms, galaxies, and human consciousness alike. In physics, Dharma resembles the tendency of systems toward equilibrium—entropy balancing disorder, homeostasis sustaining life. As Krishna declares in the *Bhagavad Gita*: *"Whenever Dharma declines, and chaos rises, I manifest to restore balance."* Dharma is not imposed—it is intrinsic to the universe itself.

Interconnectedness in the Vedic Model

Unlike modern science, which separates energy, matter, time, and intelligence, the Vedas saw them as inseparable.

Energy (*Shakti*) is the driving force of creation, always in motion (*Gati*), evolving and transforming. Time (*Kala*) is cyclical, marked by expansion and contraction, mirrored in Yugas and echoed in cosmology's Big Bang and Big Crunch. Intelligence (*Buddhi*) is not a product of biology—it is the guiding principle of evolution itself, embedded in reality, visible even in quantum phenomena where particles behave as though aware.

Everything is connected. Nothing exists in isolation. The Vedas understood this long before modern science began rediscovering it.

The First Grand Unified Theory

Physicists today acknowledge what the ancients already knew: the universe operates through precise laws, not randomness. Energy and motion are constant, but structured. Time is relative, governed by cycles. Intelligence is embedded in existence, not confined to human thought.

The Vedas did not separate science from spirituality, nor philosophy from physics. They saw everything as one continuous field of intelligence, motion, and balance—a model of reality as relevant today as it was millennia ago.

This is not mythology. This is not doctrine. This is Vishwarup Darshan—the recognition of the universe as an intelligent, unified whole.

Analogy: The Universe as a Symphony Orchestra

Imagine an orchestra performing a grand symphony. Each instrument has its own sound, rhythm, and purpose. Yet none play in isolation. Each follows a score, guided by a conductor, ensuring harmony. If one section falters, the performance collapses.

Now imagine someone who has never heard music entering the hall. They see violinists moving bows, pianists striking keys, a conductor waving hands—but without hearing the music, it all seems random.

This is how modern science often studies the universe—observing notes without recognizing the symphony. Physics measures forces and particles. Chemistry studies harmonies of atoms. Biology examines the musicians—life itself. But the music—the intelligence guiding the performance—remains unseen.

In the Vedic model, this intelligence is structured as Sat, Rit, and Dharma. Sat is the existence of the music itself. Rit is the law of harmony ensuring rhythm. Dharma is the balance that keeps everything aligned.

Without intelligence, the orchestra is noise. Without Sat, Rit, and Dharma, the universe is chaos. The ancients understood: the universe is not random—it is a symphony, orchestrated by intelligence, balance, and rhythm.

What science sees as separate fields are simply sections of the same orchestra, all playing their role in the grand cosmic symphony that is Vishwarup Darshan—the complete vision of universal intelligence.

2.4 – Vishnu as the Stabilizing Force – The Concept of Cosmic Equilibrium

In modern physics, equilibrium is a fundamental principle. It governs gravitational balance that keeps planets in orbit, the conservation of energy in thermodynamics, and the self-regulating mechanisms of ecosystems. Everywhere, the universe seeks stability.

The ancients understood this universal tendency and encoded it in the concept of Vishnu. Vishnu is not merely a deity—he is the force of preservation and balance, the principle that prevents collapse into chaos. Unlike Shiva, who embodies transformation, or Brahma, who symbolizes creation, Vishnu represents the sustaining intelligence that maintains order in an ever-changing reality.

This is not religion. It is a profound recognition of cosmic equilibrium, a truth that aligns seamlessly with physics, biology, and systems theory.

Vishnu's Avatars as Evolutionary Milestones

The Dashavatara—the ten incarnations of Vishnu—are often seen as myth. Yet when examined through the lens of evolution and cosmic balance, they reveal a deeper truth. Each avatar emerges at a critical phase of evolution, serving as a reset mechanism to restore equilibrium when disorder rises.

Matsya, the fish, marks life's emergence in water. Kurma, the turtle, signals the transition to land. Varaha, the boar, reflects the dominance of mammals. Narasimha, half-man and half-lion, embodies the hybrid threshold toward humanity. Vamana, the dwarf, represents primitive human development. Parashurama, the warrior, mirrors the rise of conflict and civilization. Rama, the ideal human, establishes order. Krishna, the strategist, masters intellect and dharma. Buddha, the enlightened one, awakens inner intelligence. Kalki, the future avatar, heralds the destruction of imbalance and the beginning of a new cycle.

This sequence mirrors biological and societal progression. Just as evolution unfolds in stages, Vishnu's avatars represent adaptive corrections that prevent collapse. Every time chaos rises, equilibrium returns. This is not mythology—it is the recognition of self-regulating systems.

The Structured Vacuum – Vishnu's Principle of Balance

Modern physics now recognizes that "empty space" is not empty at all, but a structured vacuum—a field of organized energy, filled with fluctuations that give rise to particles and forces. The ancients saw this equilibrium as Vishnu himself.

Just as the vacuum sustains galaxies in motion, Vishnu sustains cosmic stability. Just as quantum fields regulate energy interactions, Vishnu is the foundation of order. Just as energy transforms but never vanishes, Vishnu preserves existence by maintaining balance.

This vision aligns with Shesha Naag, the cosmic serpent upon which Vishnu rests—a symbol of infinite cycles of creation, preservation, and dissolution. Vishnu does not impose order. He is the order itself, ensuring stability amid constant change.

The Laws of Equilibrium – Nature's Self-Regulation

Nature never tolerates extremes for long. Systems self-correct when pushed too far. Planets remain in orbit through gravitational balance. Ecosystems regenerate through food chains. The human body fights disease through homeostasis. The universe expands at a fine-tuned rate, balanced between dark energy and gravity.

Vishnu represents this tendency. His presence does not prevent change—it ensures change unfolds without collapse. In modern terms, Vishnu is feedback loops, thermodynamic balance, and cosmic inflation. He is the silent force ensuring Shiva's destruction does not lead to chaos, Brahma's creation does not lead to unchecked expansion, and all things return to rightful cycles.

Bringing It All Together

The ancients did not divide energy, stability, and transformation. They saw motion requiring stability, creation requiring structure, destruction requiring renewal. Vishnu embodies this universal law—the intelligence that keeps everything aligned.

Without Vishnu, Shiva's destruction would collapse the system. Without Vishnu, Brahma's creation would expand into disorder. Without Vishnu, the cosmos would be unsustainable. His role is central—not as a ruler, but as the stabilizing principle of existence itself.

The universe is not random. It is finely tuned, continuously adjusting, adapting, and restoring itself—exactly as Vishnu has always been described. This is Vishwarup Darshan: seeing Vishnu not as myth, but as the living intelligence of balance.

Analogy: Vishnu as the Gyroscope of the Universe

Imagine a gyroscope—a spinning device that stabilizes airplanes, spacecraft, and bicycles. Despite external forces, it remains steady, continuously adjusting to prevent collapse.

Now imagine the universe. Just as a gyroscope stabilizes motion, Vishnu stabilizes creation and destruction. Just as a gyroscope self-corrects when tilted, Vishnu ensures equilibrium amid constant change. Just as an airplane would crash without stabilizers, the cosmos would collapse without Vishnu's balancing force.

A gyroscope does not resist motion—it allows movement while keeping it sustainable. Brahma's creation is thrust, Shiva's transformation is turbulence, and Vishnu is the gyroscopic intelligence that ensures forward motion without collapse.

This is why Vishnu rests on Shesha Naag—the serpent of infinite cycles. Without Vishnu, the cosmic gyroscope fails, energy collapses or explodes, and evolution loses meaning. Stability is not passive—it is active, intelligent, and embedded in existence itself.

This is Vishwarup Darshan—understanding Vishnu as the stabilizing force of the cosmos.

2.5 – Lakshmi as the Force of Motion – Energy in Constant Flow

In modern physics, energy is never static. It is always in motion, constantly transforming from one state to another. The law of conservation of energy declares that energy can neither be created nor destroyed, only transferred or converted.

The ancients understood this long before equations gave it form. They described this eternal motion through Lakshmi—not merely as a goddess of wealth, but as the fundamental force that drives creation, sustains life, and ensures the universe remains dynamic.

Lakshmi is the counterbalance to Vishnu. Vishnu holds the universe together, preventing collapse into chaos. Lakshmi ensures that energy never stagnates, that creation continues, and that life evolves. Together they embody the duality of the cosmos: stability and motion, structure and transformation. Without stability, motion becomes erratic. Without motion, stability decays into lifeless stillness. Lakshmi is Shakti itself—the active principle that keeps existence alive.

Lakshmi as the Eternal Flow of Energy

From the cosmic to the microscopic, everything is driven by movement. Electrons orbit nuclei, sustaining matter. Planets revolve around stars, maintaining celestial balance. Rivers carve landscapes, wind distributes heat, blood circulates through the body. Everywhere, energy flows.

Lakshmi represents this ceaseless motion. She is depicted with golden coins flowing from her hands—not as symbols of material wealth, but as representations of energy in circulation. Wealth, like energy, must move to sustain balance.

This understanding resonates even with economics: money has value only when it circulates, resources benefit societies only when used, and stagnant economies collapse just as stagnant energy decays. Lakshmi ensures that energy flows, transforms, and creates.

The Conservation of Energy – Ancient Insight

Physics teaches that energy cannot be created or destroyed, only changed in form. Vedic thought expressed the same principle: Shakti is eternal. Creation is not new energy but rearrangement. Destruction is not annihilation but transition—matter dissolving back into energy.

This is why Lakshmi is inseparable from Vishnu. Vishnu maintains structure; Lakshmi ensures it remains dynamic. Without conservation, the universe would collapse into nothingness. Without flow, existence would freeze into stillness. Every light, sound, movement, and thought is Lakshmi manifest.

Why Motion and Change Are Essential

In nature, stagnation leads to decay. A river that stops flowing becomes lifeless. A planet that ceases rotation cannot sustain life. A society that resists change collapses under rigidity. A mind that refuses to evolve becomes stagnant.

Lakshmi is not static wealth but dynamic abundance. The Vedas teach that nothing remains fixed forever—motion is the law of nature. Seasons change, cells die and renew, civilizations rise and fall, stars burn out and seed new worlds. Lakshmi ensures that energy never ceases, that progress never halts, that life never becomes stale.

This is why Vishnu always requires Lakshmi by his side. Without energy in motion, balance is meaningless.

Lakshmi as the Dynamic Force of Reality

Lakshmi is not a goddess to be worshipped for gold. She is the principle of movement, transformation, and energy flow. She is the current that drives evolution, the force that sustains life, the energy that fuels transformation.

Her presence ensures the universe remains alive, never frozen, never stagnant. Vishnu provides stability; Lakshmi provides motion. Together they form the duality of existence—order and flow, structure and transformation. Vishwarup Darshan is incomplete without Lakshmi, the universal force of energy in motion.

Diwali – The Celebration of Energy Flow

Diwali, the Festival of Lights, is often seen as welcoming Lakshmi into homes for prosperity. But its deeper essence is not material—it is the celebration of energy flow, renewal, and transformation.

Every year, Diwali resets energy cycles. Homes are cleaned, debts settled, records renewed, lights lit. Cleaning removes stagnation, lamps activate energy, gifts circulate joy, gatherings renew enthusiasm. Diwali is not about attracting wealth—it is about creating conditions where energy flows freely.

This principle extends into Vastushastra, the ancient science of architecture. Spaces are designed to channel energy efficiently—open light, flowing water, uncluttered paths. Prosperity arises not from static structures but from vibrant circulation.

Lakshmi as Renewal and Enthusiasm

The prosperity celebrated during Diwali is not financial alone—it is new energy, new enthusiasm, renewal. Businesses begin, homes fill with light, old things are discarded, new things brought in. Rangolis at entrances are not decoration but energy patterns activating flow.

Lakshmi is not an idol in a temple. She is motion, enthusiasm, progress. Diwali is not just ritual—it is a reminder that prosperity is circulation, not hoarding. Without flow, there is no prosperity. Without enthusiasm, no growth. Without renewal, life stagnates.

Bringing It All Together

Lakshmi is not gold. She is circulation. She is not stored wealth. She is enthusiasm that creates opportunity. She is not an idol. She is the principle of continuous movement, progress, and transformation.

When people pray to Lakshmi, they align themselves with the natural flow of energy that sustains prosperity in all forms. Vishwarup Darshan sees Lakshmi as essential—she is the energy that keeps existence moving forward, ensuring that neither individuals, societies, nor the universe itself ever stop evolving.

2.6 – Shiva as the Necessary Reset – The Force That Prevents Stagnation

In every system—physical, biological, or cosmic—stagnation leads to decay. If nothing changes, if energy does not flow, if evolution halts, the system begins to collapse.

This is where Shiva enters—not as a god of destruction in the traditional sense, but as the principle of transformation and renewal. Shiva is not against creation, nor stability, nor motion. Instead, he ensures that creation does not become rigid, stability does not turn into stagnation, and motion does not dissolve into disorder.

He is not merely a destroyer, but the force of transformation—dissolving what is outdated so that new possibilities can emerge. This principle is embedded in physics, biology, and cosmic evolution.

Shiva and Entropy – Transformation as Renewal

In thermodynamics, entropy measures disorder and transformation. If a system is too rigid, it collapses. If energy does not dissipate and reorganize, instability follows. If life does not evolve, extinction arrives.

Shiva embodies this universal law. Stars must explode in supernovae for new elements to form planets and life. Cells must die through apoptosis for the body to regenerate. Forests must burn to clear old growth and allow biodiversity to thrive.

These are not acts of destruction for their own sake—they are cycles of renewal. Shiva is this principle of dynamic balance, expressed in his cosmic dance, the Tandava: creation, preservation, and transformation in continuous rhythm.

Cosmic Cycles – The Vedic Vision

Ancient Indian knowledge did not see time as linear. It recognized cycles:

- *Srishti* (Creation) – Brahma brings new structures into existence.
- *Sthiti* (Preservation) – Vishnu maintains and stabilizes them.
- *Laya* (Dissolution) – Shiva transforms, making way for renewal.

Modern cosmology mirrors this: the Big Bang expands the universe, heat death drains its efficiency, and collapse or rebirth resets the cycle. The ancients described this as the pulsation of the cosmos, where destruction is never final but a phase of renewal.

This is why Shiva is Mahakaal—the Master of Time—governing cycles so existence never becomes static.

Shiva's Role in Preventing Stagnation

Without Shiva's force, stars would never explode, and life's elements would never form. Old cells would never die, leading to disease. Civilizations would never change, leading to oppression and decay. Ecosystems would collapse under imbalance.

Shiva ensures dynamism. His presence is seen in volcanoes that destroy land yet create fertile soil, in evolution where species must adapt or perish, in psychology where growth requires shedding old limitations.

His energy is not reckless destruction but intelligent transformation—removing what no longer serves so progress can continue. This is why he is called Shiva, the Auspicious One: his presence prevents life from being trapped in outdated patterns.

Shiva as the Cosmic Reset Mechanism

Shiva is not a god to be feared, nor a force that seeks elimination. He ensures that creation does not become rigid, equilibrium does not stagnate, and energy continues to flow meaningfully.

This is why Brahma, Vishnu, and Shiva must coexist. Brahma initiates, Vishnu sustains, Shiva renews. Together they form the eternal cycle where nothing is truly destroyed—only transformed.

The ancients understood that life, the universe, and thought itself must evolve—or else become irrelevant. Shiva is the reminder that without transformation, there is no progress.

This is Vishwarup Darshan—the realization that transformation is not destruction, but the essential rhythm of existence.

Analogy: Shiva as the Forest Fire That Revitalizes Life

Imagine a forest growing undisturbed for decades. Dead leaves and branches accumulate, blocking sunlight, depleting soil, suffocating new growth. Then a natural fire occurs. It burns away the old, releases nutrients, opens space for biodiversity, and awakens seeds that germinate only after fire.

At first glance, the fire seems destructive. In truth, it is renewal. Without it, the forest chokes itself. With it, life thrives.

This is Shiva's role. If energy is not recycled, ecosystems collapse. If societies resist change, they stagnate. If Shiva's force did not exist, the universe itself would become static and unsustainable.

This is why Shiva is associated with fire—destroying, purifying, and making space for beginnings. This is why he is depicted in meditation—because transformation is guided by wisdom. This is why his cosmic dance symbolizes cycles of renewal—showing that change is continuous, not chaotic.

The forest does not fear fire, because it knows renewal is life. Similarly, Shiva is not destruction for its own sake, but the necessary force that ensures old systems dissolve, new possibilities emerge, and existence remains in harmony.

This is Vishwarup Darshan—the recognition that endings are beginnings, and transformation is the heartbeat of the cosmos.

2.7 – The Puranic Model of Evolution – A Scientific Blueprint in Disguise

For centuries, the Puranas have been dismissed as mythology—collections of divine stories meant for devotion. Yet a deeper examination reveals something profound: the Puranas contain a structured model of evolution, one that mirrors modern scientific discoveries. The Dashavatara (Ten Avatars of Vishnu) align with stages of biological evolution. The Yugas (Cosmic Time Cycles) parallel astronomical and geological cycles. The cyclical nature of cosmic expansion and contraction resembles modern cosmology's Big Bang and Big Crunch.

The ancients did not view evolution as random. They saw it as guided progression, where consciousness and intelligence evolve over time, shaping reality itself. This challenges the modern assumption that scientific advancement is recent, suggesting instead that the Puranic model was an early blueprint of cosmic and biological evolution.

The Dashavatara – Evolution Encoded in Mythology

One of the most striking parallels between Puranic knowledge and modern science is the Dashavatara—the ten incarnations of Vishnu. Each avatar appears at a critical moment of imbalance, restoring order while also representing a stage in the evolution of life.

Matsya, the fish, represents the first life forms in water—the emergence of aquatic life. Kurma, the turtle, marks the transition between water and land—the rise of amphibians. Varaha, the boar, symbolizes the domination of land life—the emergence of mammals. Narasimha, half-man and half-lion, reflects the hybrid transition from animal to human—the stage of early primates. Vamana, the dwarf, represents the first human-like figure—primitive hominins such as Homo erectus. Parashurama, the warrior with an axe, embodies the rise of civilization and conflict—hunter-gatherer societies and warfare. Rama, the ideal human, signifies the establishment of societal order—early kingdoms and structured civilization. Krishna, the divine strategist, represents mastery of intellect and dharma—philosophical and ethical evolution. Buddha, the enlightened one, marks the realization of inner intelligence—the age of wisdom and spiritual awakening. Finally, Kalki, the future avatar, represents the destruction of imbalance and the reset of the cycle—the future of humanity, whether through destruction or transcendence.

The transition from aquatic to terrestrial life mirrors evolutionary theory. The rise of intelligence and ethical consciousness aligns with human civilization's intellectual progress. The final avatar suggests that evolution is not only physical but also intellectual and spiritual. This is not coincidence. What modern biology describes as random evolution, the Puranas describe as purposeful progression toward higher intelligence and balance.

Yugas – Cosmic Time Cycles and Astronomical Alignments

The concept of Yugas in the Puranas parallels astronomical cycles that modern science is only now beginning to understand. The four Yugas describe the progressive decline of dharma and the rise of entropy over time, much like thermodynamics where systems tend toward disorder.

Satya Yuga is the Golden Age—harmony, truth, and long lifespans, corresponding to a stable cosmic period with minimal entropy. Treta Yuga is the Silver Age—a gradual decline of dharma, marking the beginning of planetary and biological shifts. Dwapara Yuga is the Bronze Age—materialism rises, lifespans shorten, and planetary and societal changes increase. Kali Yuga is the Dark Age—chaos, ignorance, and ethical decline, paralleling high entropy and accelerating environmental and social crises.

These Yugas resemble astronomical cycles such as the Precession of the Equinoxes, a 25,920-year cycle. They also align with geological epochs where Earth underwent dramatic climate and evolutionary shifts. Kali Yuga, marked by rapid technological advancement but increasing ethical and environmental challenges, closely resembles our current trajectory.

If this model is correct, time is not linear but cyclical. Civilizations and life forms evolve, peak, and reset through transformation. This correlates with modern theories of mass extinctions, climate cycles, and cosmic evolution, proving that the Puranic understanding of time was deeply scientific.

The Expanding and Contracting Universe – Big Bang and Big Crunch

Modern cosmology describes the Big Bang as the universe exploding from a singularity into expansion. Yet many physicists propose that the universe may not expand forever—it could contract back into a singularity, leading to a new cycle.

The Puranas already described this process. Brahma's Day and Night depict the universe expanding during the day and contracting at night in endless cycles. Srishti (Creation) and Pralaya (Dissolution) describe the universe being born, expanding, stabilizing, and dissolving back into potential energy. Vishnu's Cosmic Breath symbolizes rhythmic pulsation—the universe expands as he exhales and contracts as he inhales.

This aligns with the oscillating universe theory, quantum physics suggesting fluctuating states, and discoveries that space-time itself is dynamic. The Puranas were not describing myths, but early explanations of cosmic cycles that science is only now exploring.

Bringing It All Together – The Puranas as a Scientific Framework

The Puranic model is not mythology—it is a structured knowledge system. It encodes evolution in the Dashavatara sequence. It describes time as cyclical, aligning with astronomical and geological cycles. It explains cosmic expansion and contraction as creation and dissolution. It sees evolution not as random, but as guided intelligence.

Modern science is slowly rediscovering what the ancients already knew. What we call evolution, entropy, and cosmic expansion—they called Vishnu's Avatars, Yugas, and Pralaya. This is Vishwarup Darshan—the realization that ancient wisdom and modern science are two perspectives of the same universal intelligence.

Analogy: Evolution as the Software Updates of the Universe

Imagine a smartphone operating system that evolves through updates. The first version is basic, functional but limited. Over time, updates enhance performance, fix bugs, and introduce new features.

Matsya is Version 1.0—the first working form, like aquatic life. Kurma is Version 2.0—expanding capabilities, moving between water and land. Varaha is Version 3.0—fully functional on land, like mammals. Narasimha is Version 4.0—a hybrid transition, testing new capabilities. Vamana is Version 5.0—a compact, efficient form, like early hominins. Parashurama is Version 6.0—advanced features but primitive aggression. Rama is Version 7.0—a stable, structured system, civilization emerges. Krishna is Version 8.0—intelligence and strategy take precedence. Buddha is Version 9.0—inner optimization and wisdom. Kalki is Version 10.0—the final upgrade, preparing for the next cycle.

The Yugas act like software lifecycles—entropy builds up, requiring resets. The Big Bang and Big Crunch resemble hardware reboots—systems reset for fresh beginnings. The Puranic model suggests the universe operates on self-correcting updates, much like AI adapting over time.

Evolution is not random—it is structured progression, like software upgrades. If an app stops updating, it becomes obsolete. If species stop evolving, they go extinct. Just as smartphones need updates, the universe, life, and intelligence need continuous evolution to sustain balance and progress.

This is Vishwarup Darshan—the realization that cosmic evolution is not blind, but intelligently structured, much like technological advancement.

2.8 – The Universe as an Interconnected Web – Everything is One System

In the modern world, knowledge is fragmented. Physics, biology, chemistry, psychology, and philosophy are treated as separate fields, each operating in isolation. But the ancients did not divide knowledge this way. To them, the universe was not a collection of separate objects, forces, and events—it was a single, interconnected whole.

They understood that everything emerges from one intelligence, which they called Brahman. Everything remains connected at all levels of reality—physical, energetic, and conscious. What science is only now rediscovering, they already knew: separation is an illusion, and the universe is fundamentally a web of relationships. This is Vishwarup Darshan—the complete vision of reality, where everything is recognized as part of one unified system.

Brahman – The Singular Intelligence Behind All Existence

In Vedic philosophy, Brahman is not a deity or supernatural force. It is the underlying reality from which everything emerges—the source of matter, energy, space, and time. Brahman is not limited by form; it is the intelligence that governs the cosmos. It is both immanent, existing within everything, and transcendent, beyond everything.

Modern physics is arriving at a similar understanding. Quantum fields permeate all space, showing that even "empty" space is structured and connected. Energy and matter are interchangeable, as Einstein revealed, proving that all existence is simply different expressions of the same fundamental reality. Consciousness studies now suggest that intelligence may not be confined to the brain, but could be an inherent property of the universe itself.

This aligns with the Vedic vision: everything is connected because everything originates from one source. Nothing exists independently—every action, thought, and event ripples through the entire system. Vishwarup Darshan is the realization of this unity, breaking the illusion of separation. The more science advances, the more it confirms what the ancients already knew: the universe is not a machine, but an intelligent, interconnected system.

Quantum Entanglement – Science Confirms the Interconnected Universe

One of the most groundbreaking discoveries in modern physics is quantum entanglement. When two particles become entangled, they remain connected regardless of distance. A change in one particle instantly affects the other, even across millions of light-years.

This challenges the classical view of separateness and confirms what the ancients believed: everything in existence remains fundamentally connected. Space and time do not divide reality as much as we assumed. Consciousness, energy, and matter are not independent—they are part of one continuous field.

In the Vedic framework, this is why Brahman is described as omnipresent and all-pervading. Reality is not built from disconnected parts, but from one inseparable whole. What modern physics calls entanglement, the ancients understood as the unbreakable connection between all things. The universe is woven together beyond the limitations of time and space. This is Vishwarup Darshan—the awareness of how everything is interlinked at all levels of existence.

The Web of Reality – How Everything Affects Everything Else

If everything is connected, then nothing exists in isolation. Every action, thought, and event creates ripples that affect the entire system.

We see this in ecosystems, where the extinction of one species disrupts the entire food chain. We see it in climate systems, where a change in one region alters weather patterns globally. We see it in economics, where a financial crisis in one country reverberates across the world. We see it in human consciousness, where ideas and emotions spread, shaping societies and histories.

The ancients never saw individuals, societies, or nature as separate from the cosmos. They understood that every living being is part of a larger system, every thought and action has unseen effects, and the distinctions of "I" and "you," "this" and "that" are illusions. In Vishwarup Darshan, Krishna shows Arjuna that all things—past, present, and future—are part of the same intelligence. There is no true separation, only the perception of separation.

This realization breaks the illusion and allows one to see reality as it truly is.

Bringing It All Together – The Universe as One Unified System

Modern science and ancient wisdom now converge on the same truth: the universe is not built from separate pieces, but is one interconnected system. Quantum physics, energy fields, and consciousness studies point to a unified reality. Vedic philosophy has always recognized this, calling it Brahman—the singular intelligence behind everything.

Vishwarup Darshan is the complete awareness of this unity, beyond all illusions of division. The idea that "I am separate from the universe" is an illusion. The idea that "humanity is separate from nature" is an illusion. The idea that "science and spirituality are separate" is an illusion.

There is only one system, one intelligence, one reality. It is all one interconnected whole.

This is Vishwarup Darshan—the grand vision of seeing everything as one.

2.9 – Where Science and Ancient Knowledge Meet – Reconstructing the Lost Grand Theory

For centuries, science and ancient knowledge were seen as opposites—one rooted in measurable facts, the other in wisdom passed down through texts and traditions. Yet as scientific discoveries advance, we are beginning to realize that many of the truths modern physics now uncovers were already known to ancient Indian cosmology, expressed in a different language.

Science is rediscovering concepts that the ancients had already described. The parallels between quantum physics, cosmic evolution, and Vedic cosmology are too precise to dismiss. The holistic nature of ancient wisdom, which integrates science, philosophy, and consciousness, remains more relevant today than ever. This is Vishwarup Darshan—the realization that the universe operates as an interconnected, intelligent system, where science and ancient knowledge are two perspectives of the same truth.

How Science is Rediscovering What Was Already Known

Modern breakthroughs align with ancient cosmology in ways that suggest the Vedas, Upanishads, and Puranas were not primitive speculations, but encoded knowledge of the cosmos.

Quantum mechanics reveals wave-particle duality, showing that particles exist as both waves and matter until observed. The Vedas described this as *Maya*—the illusion that reality is not fixed, and perception shapes experience.

Cosmology suggests the universe undergoes cycles of expansion and contraction, the Big Bang followed by a possible Big Crunch. Vedic cosmology spoke of Brahma's Day and Night, endless cycles of creation and dissolution.

Quantum entanglement proves particles remain connected across vast distances. The Upanishads described Brahman as indivisible and all-pervading, where everything is connected at a fundamental level.

Einstein's relativity shows that time is not absolute, but shifts with gravity and velocity. Hindu cosmology described multiple layers of time—Yugas,

Kalpas, and Brahma's lifespan—where time flows differently in different realms.

Biology teaches that life evolved from water to land, then to advanced species. The Dashavatara of Vishnu follows the same path—from Matsya the fish, to Narasimha the half-human, to fully developed beings like Krishna and Buddha.

These parallels suggest that ancient wisdom and modern science are converging toward the same understanding—only through different methods. Science breaks reality into equations. The Vedas explain reality through interconnected principles. But the truth behind both is the same.

Parallels Between Modern Physics and Ancient Cosmology

What modern science calls the quantum field, ancient wisdom called Brahman—the all-pervading source from which reality emerges. The Big Bang is Srishti, creation as expansion of cosmic energy. Entropy is Adharma, imbalance leading to destruction. The multiverse is Lokas, multiple planes of existence. Wave-particle duality is Maya, perception shaping reality. Dark matter and dark energy are Prana and Shakti, invisible forces influencing all things.

This proves that ancient wisdom was not primitive storytelling, but a deep understanding of reality encoded in symbolic language.

Why the Vedic Approach is Still Relevant

In an era of fragmented knowledge, the Vedic approach offers a holistic perspective. It unifies science and philosophy, integrating physics, chemistry, and biology into one reality. It accounts for consciousness, describing it as the foundation of existence rather than a byproduct of the brain. It provides ethical and ecological wisdom, with Dharma aligning with modern environmental concerns. It bridges material and spiritual knowledge, integrating technology with inner awareness and universal intelligence.

As science evolves, it becomes clear that ancient knowledge provides the missing piece—the recognition of intelligence behind all systems.

How Vishwarup Darshan Restores Holistic Knowledge

Vishwarup Darshan is not just about seeing the universe as vast and interconnected—it is about restoring the lost unity of knowledge. Science is not separate from philosophy. Consciousness is not separate from physical reality. The universe is not mechanical—it is intelligent.

By reconstructing this lost Grand Theory, Vishwarup Darshan teaches us that the Puranas, Vedas, and Upanishads were advanced knowledge systems. Science and ancient wisdom are two sides of the same truth. True knowledge is holistic—it does not separate physics from consciousness, nor mathematics from philosophy.

What science discovers through research, the ancients knew through direct realization. This is Vishwarup Darshan—the vision where all knowledge converges into one complete understanding of the cosmos.

Bringing It All Together – The Science of Vishwarup Darshan

The universe is not fragmented—everything is interconnected. Ancient wisdom and modern physics align in fundamental ways. Vishwarup Darshan restores the original knowledge lost in separation. What we call science, spirituality, physics, and metaphysics are not separate disciplines—they are all expressions of the same truth.

Vishwarup Darshan is not new—it is the rediscovery of what was always known. This is the future of knowledge—where science, ancient wisdom, and human consciousness evolve together.

Analogy: Vishwarup Darshan as the Internet of Knowledge

Imagine the internet—a vast network where information flows seamlessly, linking diverse fields, industries, and people. At first glance, someone unfamiliar might assume physics websites are separate from biology, history databases unrelated to quantum computing, music and economics isolated. But in reality, everything is interconnected.

Vishwarup Darshan is the same. Modern science treats disciplines as separate. Ancient wisdom integrated them into one seamless understanding. Vishwarup Darshan reveals that no field of knowledge can be understood in isolation.

Just as the internet connects diverse information, allowing physicists to collaborate with neuroscientists or historians with AI engineers, Vishwarup Darshan connects science, philosophy, and consciousness, showing that the universe functions as one intelligent system.

Imagine someone who only reads one website and believes that is the entire internet. That is what happens when we study only physics, only spirituality, or only biology. When you finally realize the entire web of knowledge, you see Vishwarup Darshan—the unified vision where all disciplines merge into one.

This is why ancient knowledge must be revisited—not as religion, but as lost science. This is why modern science must expand—not just measuring forces, but recognizing intelligence. The future of knowledge is holistic, where all fields are connected, just as the internet seamlessly links data worldwide.

The internet of knowledge already exists within the universe itself. We only need the right lens to see it.

This is Vishwarup Darshan—the grand realization that everything is one.

2.10 - Conclusion: Seeing the Universe as It Was Always Meant to Be

For centuries, humanity has sought to understand the universe by walking two separate paths—one through science, the other through spirituality. Science has given us measurement, equations, and technology, yet it struggles to explain why intelligence exists at all. Spirituality has given us wisdom, interconnectedness, and purpose, yet it often lacks the logical structure needed for universal acceptance.

Each, on its own, is incomplete. Science without intelligence is an empty framework—it explains how, but not why. Spirituality without logic is blind—it inspires belief, but cannot provide precision. But what if they were never meant to be separate? What if the ancients had already unified knowledge into a seamless system—one that integrated science, intelligence, and cosmic order?

This is Vishwarup Darshan—the realization that everything is part of one complete truth.

The Lost Grand Theory of Everything

Science has spent centuries breaking reality into fragments, attempting to reverse-engineer the cosmos piece by piece. Yet the more we analyze, the more we encounter paradoxes, uncertainties, and missing links. Ancient knowledge never suffered from this problem—because it never separated reality into disconnected fields.

The Vedas, Upanishads, and Puranas already described cosmic expansion and contraction, what we now call the Big Bang and Big Crunch. They spoke of Brahman, the interconnected nature of reality, which modern physics now explores through quantum entanglement and unified field theory. They encoded the evolution of species in the Dashavatara, mirroring biological evolution and natural selection. They described multiple dimensions of time in Yugas and Kalpas, anticipating relativity and time dilation. They spoke of Vishnu's stability as the structured vacuum, now studied as quantum fields and zero-point energy. They revealed Shiva's role as necessary destruction for renewal, which science now recognizes as entropy and thermodynamic cycles.

This was never religion—it was the lost Grand Theory of Everything. The next step is not to pit science against ancient wisdom, but to integrate them into a single, holistic understanding of reality. Vishwarup Darshan is that realization—the vision that restores what was lost.

The Next Step: Restoring the Complete Vision of Reality

Modern science is reaching a turning point. We are beginning to see that reality is not random—it is structured by intelligence. Consciousness is not separate from physics—it is fundamental to existence. The universe is not mechanical—it is a self-regulating, evolving, interconnected system.

What the ancients knew intuitively, we are now proving mathematically. This means we are not discovering new truths—we are remembering what was already known. The next step is to stop looking at reality in fragments and begin to see Vishwarup Darshan—the complete, unified vision of existence.

This is not the end of knowledge—it is the beginning of a new era. An era where science embraces intelligence as a core principle. An era where spirituality is reconstructed through reason and evidence. An era where humanity learns to see the universe not in pieces, but as one interconnected whole.

This is Vishwarup Darshan—the true Grand Theory of Everything, hidden in plain sight all along. And now, it is time to see the universe as it was always meant to be.

Interlude: Resting in the Vision

You have walked through fragments of knowledge, seen them dissolve, and felt them reassemble into wholeness. Perhaps your mind is full, perhaps your heart is stirred. This is the nature of rediscovery—it is not only information, but a shift in perception.

So let us pause.

Imagine the universe not as equations or scriptures, but as a vast, breathing presence. Imagine knowledge not as something to be owned, but as something to be felt. Imagine truth not as a debate, but as a quiet recognition.

The ancients did not rush. They did not consume knowledge as data. They lived it slowly, rhythmically, as part of their daily existence. In this pause, you are invited to do the same.

Reflect on what you have read. Notice how the divide between science and spirituality begins to dissolve when seen through the lens of intelligence. Notice how myths transform into codes, how fragments merge into wholeness. Notice how truth feels less like something to prove, and more like something to remember.

This interlude is not about answers. It is about stillness. It is about allowing the ideas to settle into your own rhythm, your own awareness.

Because Vishwarup Darshan is not just a theory—it is a way of seeing. And to see clearly, sometimes you must first be still.

Take this moment. Breathe. Let the weight of centuries fall away. Let the fragments begin to align.

When you are ready, turn the page. The journey continues—but now, you carry the resonance of wholeness within you.

Chapter 3: The Vedic Encoding

How the Vedas Encoded Science Without Equations

In the previous chapter, we saw how modern science is gradually rediscovering principles that ancient Indian knowledge had already established—structured cosmology, evolutionary biology, quantum mechanics, and the interconnected nature of reality. This raises a profound question: if the ancients possessed such insights, why did they not express them in mathematical equations and formulas, as modern science does?

At first glance, the absence of numbers and explicit physical models in the Vedas and Upanishads might seem like a limitation. Yet when examined closely, it becomes clear that this was no omission, but a deliberate encoding strategy. The ancients did not see knowledge as something confined to calculations. Instead, they used symbols, metaphors, allegories, and experiential practices to capture the essence of reality.

This method of encoding allowed for multi-layered interpretation—a transmission of wisdom that was both timeless and accessible. To the common person, Vedic stories offered moral and ethical guidance. To the philosopher, they revealed metaphysical truths. To the scientist, they hinted at universal principles that could be observed, tested, and understood.

Unlike modern science, which prioritizes quantification and rigid formulas, the Vedic approach prioritized direct experience, observation, and mental models. This transition—from experiential wisdom to mathematical abstraction—was one of the greatest shifts in human thought. Equations allow for precision and repeatability, but they often strip away the qualitative essence of knowledge: the intelligence, consciousness, and interconnectivity behind it.

The Vedic sages understood that the universe was not merely a machine governed by numerical laws, but a living, evolving intelligence. Rather than reducing reality to formulas, they designed a system where wisdom could be grasped intuitively and practically, without the need for specialized mathematical training.

This chapter explores how the Vedas encoded science without equations, why this method was superior in many ways, and what modern science can learn from this alternative approach to understanding reality.

3.1 The Vedic Approach to Science – Knowledge Beyond Measurement

Science today is largely quantitative. It relies on precise measurements, calculations, and empirical data to validate theories. Equations, laboratory experiments, and numerical models form the foundation of modern progress. Yet despite its success, this approach remains incomplete, often struggling to explain concepts beyond what is measurable.

The Vedic approach to science was fundamentally different. It was qualitative, emphasizing principles, observational wisdom, and experiential realization. The seers did not separate matter, energy, and consciousness into different domains; they viewed reality as a unified whole, governed by laws that could be understood through direct perception, logic, and inner exploration.

This did not mean the Vedas rejected mathematics. India contributed profoundly to numbers—the discovery of zero, the decimal system, advanced geometry. But Vedic knowledge was not dependent on equations alone. It sought to understand *why* things worked, not merely *how*.

Rishis as Scientists – Seeking Truth Beyond Experimentation

The Rishis of the Vedic age were, in many ways, the earliest scientists. Unlike modern scientists, who rely on telescopes, microscopes, and accelerators, the Rishis used a different instrument: the human mind, refined through meditation, intuition, and contemplation.

They did not simply observe nature—they immersed themselves in it, attuning their senses to its rhythms. They did not limit themselves to material reality—they explored consciousness as intrinsic to science. They did not need mechanical devices—because their minds were trained to perceive subtle forces directly.

This approach is not as unscientific as it might seem. Even today, breakthroughs often begin with intuition before proof. Einstein's theory of relativity began as a thought experiment—imagining himself riding a beam of light. Niels Bohr's quantum model of the atom was inspired by the solar system's structure. Nikola Tesla conceived inventions through mental visualization rather than prototypes.

The Rishis followed a similar process, relying on inner perception, logic, and experience. This is why Vedic knowledge describes concepts that align with modern science, even without instruments. It emphasizes direct experience (*Pratyaksha*) and reason (*Anumana*) as valid ways of knowing. It unites physics, biology, philosophy, and consciousness into one system. Rather than isolating facts, the Rishis sought universal patterns—the foundational truths that govern all existence.

Mental Models, Intuition, and Consciousness as Scientific Tools

Unlike modern science, which depends on external validation, Vedic science relied on internal realization. This does not mean it was irrational. On the contrary, it followed a logical and systematic approach. The difference lay in how knowledge was acquired.

The three key methods of Vedic inquiry were *Pratyaksha* (direct perception), *Anumana* (inference), and *Upamana* (analogy). Through perception, they observed natural phenomena with heightened awareness. Through inference, they derived truths not immediately visible. Through analogy, they drew parallels between patterns to uncover deeper laws.

Consider Brahman, the fundamental reality. Just as space appears empty but is filled with quantum fields, Brahman is the unseen substratum of existence. Just as energy cannot be created or destroyed, the Upanishads describe the eternal, indestructible nature of reality. Just as the observer influences quantum states, the Vedas recognize consciousness as a force shaping reality.

Rather than relying on physical instruments, the Vedic tradition cultivated mental instruments—focus, sustained inquiry, and pattern recognition—allowing insights that modern science is only now beginning to explore.

Astronomy Without Telescopes

One of the greatest examples of Vedic science without equations is astronomy. Ancient Indian astronomers mapped planetary orbits with precision, calculated eclipses centuries before modern astronomy, understood the heliocentric nature of the solar system long before Copernicus, and identified the precession of the equinoxes, which modern science confirmed much later.

How did they achieve this without telescopes? They observed celestial patterns over generations, creating predictive models. They used complex mental calculations rather than mechanical devices. They encoded astronomical knowledge in texts like the *Puranas* and *Surya Siddhanta*.

The Yugas, cosmic time cycles, were mapped onto planetary rhythms. Temples and rituals followed precise celestial alignments, demonstrating knowledge of Earth's motion. The concept of *Nakshatras*, lunar mansions, revealed advanced understanding of the Moon's orbit.

Without instruments, they achieved precision because they approached knowledge holistically, recognizing repeating patterns in nature and applying them to the cosmos.

Bringing It All Together – The Timeless Relevance of Vedic Science

Modern science relies on measurement; the Vedic approach relied on perception and realization. Today's scientists use external instruments; the Rishis trained their minds to be the instruments. Equations describe how things work; Vedic knowledge explains why they work the way they do.

The modern world has become obsessed with data and quantification, but we are beginning to realize that not everything valuable can be measured. Consciousness, intuition, and interconnected wisdom are just as real as physical equations.

This is why Vishwarup Darshan is the next step in knowledge—integrating the precision of modern science with the holistic intelligence of ancient wisdom. By revisiting the Vedic approach, we can begin to develop a more complete, interconnected understanding of the universe—one that includes not only numbers and measurements, but also intelligence, perception, and meaning.

3.2 – Cosmic Evolution Without Equations – The Concept of Srishti and Pralaya

Modern science has spent decades trying to understand the origin and fate of the universe, relying on theories such as the Big Bang, cosmic inflation, and heat death. Yet long before these ideas were mathematically formulated, Vedic cosmology described the universe as an eternal cycle of creation and dissolution—a concept remarkably similar to modern oscillating universe theories.

Rather than expressing these ideas in equations, the Vedas and Puranas encoded them in symbolic stories, metaphors, and cosmic cycles, making them accessible across generations. At the heart of this understanding are the concepts of *Srishti* (Creation) and *Pralaya* (Dissolution), which describe the expansion and contraction of the universe as a continuous process, much like the inhalation and exhalation of cosmic breath.

Modern Cosmology and Vedic Cosmology

Modern science suggests that the universe began with a singular explosion—the Big Bang—and has been expanding ever since. Some cosmologists propose that this expansion may eventually slow, leading to a reversal called the Big Crunch, where the universe collapses back into a singularity. Others imagine an infinite cycle of expansion and contraction, a cosmic heartbeat.

Vedic cosmology described the same process through Brahma's Day and Night. Each day of Brahma represents an expansion phase, much like the Big Bang, while each night represents dissolution, much like the Big Crunch. This cycle repeats endlessly, echoing modern cyclic universe theories.

The Puranas even describe multiple levels of time and cosmic evolution, with Brahma's lifespan stretching across trillions of human years—vast timescales that modern science is only beginning to grasp.

The Universe as an Oscillating System

Ancient Indian cosmology did not view time as linear, with a single beginning and end. Instead, it saw time as cyclical, like the rhythms of nature—seasons, life cycles, planetary orbits. According to this model, the universe follows four phases.

In *Srishti*, creation unfolds as energy condenses into matter and galaxies form. In *Sthiti*, stabilization occurs, balance is achieved, and life flourishes. In *Samhaara*, contraction begins, entropy increases, stars die, and collapse sets in. Finally, in *Pralaya*, dissolution returns the universe to potential energy, awaiting rebirth.

This view aligns with the cyclic nature of reality, from atomic vibrations to galactic motion. It resonates with modern theories of cosmic rebirth, where each death of the universe leads to another birth. Unlike modern cosmology, which still debates whether the universe faces permanent heat death or rebirth, Vedic cosmology firmly asserts that the cycle never stops—it only transitions between states.

Yugas and Kalpas – Cycles of Time

Another fascinating connection between modern astronomy and Vedic knowledge lies in cosmic time. The Vedas describe four great Yugas—Satya, Treta, Dwapara, and Kali—that repeat in cycles, forming larger Mahayugas, Kalpas, and Manvantaras.

Satya Yuga, the Golden Age, represents pure balance and order, a low-entropy state of cosmic harmony. Treta Yuga, the Silver Age, marks gradual decline, corresponding to the mid-stage universe where stars and galaxies form. Dwapara Yuga, the Bronze Age, reflects further imbalance, an aging universe with increasing disorder. Kali Yuga, the Dark Age, embodies maximum chaos, high entropy, and eventual collapse.

These cycles closely parallel astronomical phenomena such as the precession of the equinoxes, a 25,920-year cycle. Vedic timekeeping was not random—it was synchronized with celestial mechanics, embedding cosmic rhythms into human understanding.

Encoded Knowledge in Stories of Creation and Destruction

Ancient Indian texts did not present cosmic principles in equations. Instead, they embedded them in metaphoric stories that conveyed deeper truths.

The *Churning of the Ocean* (*Samudra Manthan*) symbolizes the turbulence of cosmic forces, where life and order emerge from chaos. It represents dynamic equilibrium, energy fluctuations leading to creation.

Shiva's cosmic dance, the *Tandava*, describes creation and destruction as continuous rhythm, mirroring vibrational forces that shape quantum fields and the expansion and contraction of the universe.

Vishnu's sleep and awakening encode dissolution and rebirth. When Vishnu sleeps, the universe dissolves into Pralaya; when he awakens, creation begins anew. This perfectly aligns with the oscillatory model of the cosmos, alternating between activity and dormancy.

These stories were not primitive myths. They were intuitive models of reality, transmitting knowledge across generations in a way that was both accessible and profound.

Vishnu's Cosmic Breath

One of the most striking metaphors in Vedic cosmology is Vishnu's breath. As Vishnu exhales, the universe expands, mirroring the Big Bang and cosmic inflation. As he inhales, the universe contracts, reflecting the Big Crunch or cyclic universe hypothesis.

This imagery aligns with modern physics, which now considers that the universe may not be heading toward a permanent end, but toward eventual rebirth. Expansion and contraction are part of a continuous cosmic process, not a one-time event. Reality is fundamentally rhythmic—like breathing, vibrating energy fields, and wave-particle interactions.

That Vedic seers described cosmic oscillations thousands of years ago—without telescopes, satellites, or quantum physics—suggests their insights were not primitive guesses, but deeply observed truths.

Bringing It All Together – The Science of Srishti and Pralaya

Modern science describes an expanding and possibly contracting universe. Vedic cosmology described the same process as Srishti and Pralaya. Today's physics sees time as non-linear in quantum mechanics; Vedic thought described time as cyclical through Yugas and Kalpas. Cosmic rebirth is now a leading theory in physics; the Vedas had already detailed this through Brahma's cosmic cycles.

What modern cosmology is still debating, the Vedic texts already understood—that the universe is not a single event but a pulsating, living system, governed by eternal cycles of creation and dissolution.

This is Vishwarup Darshan—the realization that the cosmos is not random, but part of an intelligent, repeating pattern of existence.

3.3 – Energy and Matter: The Unification of Physics in Ancient Thought

One of the fundamental distinctions in modern physics has been the separation of matter and energy—a division that shaped the way we understood reality. Yet as science progressed, especially with Einstein's equation $E = mc^2$, it became clear that matter and energy are interchangeable, not distinct substances.

Ancient Vedic philosophy never made this separation. Instead, it described the universe as a continuous interplay between energy and matter, expressed through *Shakti* (dynamic energy) and *Prakriti* (manifested reality). These ideas align with quantum fields, structured vacuums, and the conservation of energy, proving that the Vedas encoded fundamental physical principles without equations.

Shakti and Prakriti – The Dynamic Interplay

Modern science views energy as the fundamental driver of the universe, with matter emerging as condensed energy. The Vedic framework mirrors this: Shakti is the universal energy force, while Prakriti is the material reality shaped by it. Matter is not independent—it is a manifestation of underlying energy fields. Particles are fluctuations in an omnipresent field. What we perceive as solid matter is structured energy.

The Upanishads describe the universe as pervaded by Brahman, the unseen infinite force that serves as both source and field. This is strikingly similar to modern physics' structured vacuum, where space is not empty but filled with potential energy. Particles arise and vanish within this field, much like the cyclical nature of creation and dissolution in Vedic cosmology. The ancients recognized that physical reality is nothing more than a structured interplay of unseen forces—an idea science is only now beginning to explore.

Conservation of Energy in Vedic Thought

The law of conservation of energy, a cornerstone of physics, states that energy can neither be created nor destroyed, only transformed. The Vedic worldview already incorporated this principle. Brahman remains unchanged, just as the total energy of the universe is constant. Shakti transforms endlessly, creating the illusion of change, much like matter and energy cycling through states. Prakriti appears and disappears but is never truly lost, echoing particles emerging and dissolving in quantum fields.

This principle is embedded throughout Vedic philosophy. The cycles of creation and dissolution follow the idea that energy is recycled, not eliminated. Karma operates like energy transfer—every action has a reaction, ensuring balance. Yugas describe the conservation of knowledge, ethics, and energy across ages, despite transformation. Ancient thought was already aligned with one of the most fundamental laws of physics—without needing mathematical proof.

The Structured Vacuum – Brahman and Quantum Fields

Modern physics tells us that empty space is not truly empty. The quantum vacuum is alive with energy fluctuations, virtual particles appearing and disappearing. The Upanishads describe Brahman as *Nirguna*—without attributes yet pervading everything. Just as space appears empty but contains quantum fields, Brahman is the unseen substratum of existence.

Creation, in Vedic thought, was not something from nothing but an unfolding of what was already present. Modern physics now recognizes that "empty space" is filled with potential energy, much like Brahman. The concept of *Maya*, illusion, aligns with quantum physics, where particles exist in probabilistic states until observed. The foundation of quantum physics was already present in Upanishadic philosophy, long before equations gave it form.

Agni – Fire as Transformation and Entropy

One of the most striking parallels is Agni, fire, as a force of transformation. In Vedic philosophy, Agni drives all change. In physics, thermodynamics states that energy transformation is governed by entropy—an irreversible process. Both describe the tendency of systems to evolve, transform, and dissipate energy.

Agni consumes matter and releases energy, mirroring the conversion of potential into kinetic energy. Entropy increases as systems progress, just as Agni destroys old forms to give rise to new ones. The second law of thermodynamics states that energy flows from order to disorder—just as Agni governs cycles of birth, death, and rebirth.

The ancients recognized fire as more than physical—it was cosmic. Agni governs digestion in the body (*Jatharagni*), the transformation of thoughts and emotions, and the dissolution of galaxies and stars. Agni is both scientific and metaphysical, aligning with heat, energy dissipation, and entropy.

Yajnas – Rituals as Energy Transformation

The fire rituals of the Vedic tradition, Yajnas, symbolized thermodynamic principles. Fuel was burned to release energy, representing transformation. The ritual created balance and order, mirroring entropy regulation. Offerings into the fire represented energy exchange, much like biological and physical systems exchanging energy to sustain life.

Yajnas encoded conservation: fire did not create energy, it transformed it. They mirrored thermodynamic cycles: fire released heat, which dissipated and influenced surroundings. They embodied feedback loops: rituals maintained balance, just as natural cycles regulate ecosystems and the universe. Yajnas were not mere ceremonies—they were encoded scientific models of energy transformation.

Bringing It All Together

Modern physics separates energy and matter; the Vedas unified them as Shakti and Prakriti. Conservation of energy was already present in Vedic cosmology. Quantum fields and structured vacuums mirror Brahman. Agni represents thermodynamic transformation, entropy, and renewal. Yajnas encode energy exchange, much like physics does.

This is Vishwarup Darshan—the realization that science and ancient wisdom converge toward the same truth.

3.4 – Mathematics Without Numbers: The Sacred Geometry of the Universe

Mathematics is often seen as a modern discipline, built on equations, algebra, and numerical computation. Yet long before symbolic notation was formalized, the Vedic civilization had already encoded mathematical principles in geometric patterns, proportions, and cosmological structures.

The Vedas, Upanishads, and Shulba Sutras did not present numbers in tables or equations. Instead, they embedded universal mathematical relationships in sacred geometry, poetic rhythms, architecture, and metaphysical concepts. This alternative approach ensured that knowledge was not confined to scholars alone—it was accessible to philosophers, astronomers, temple builders, and even ritual practitioners.

This chapter explores how the Vedic mathematical tradition expressed deep truths through sacred geometry, fractals, proportions, and infinity—without relying on equations.

Geometric Patterns – The Universal Blueprint

Nature itself follows geometry: galaxies spiral, seashells curve, snowflakes crystallize with precision. The Vedic sages observed these patterns and recognized geometry not as human invention, but as an inherent quality of the universe.

Yantras, sacred diagrams used for meditation and temple design, reflected profound geometric principles. Mandalas mirrored cosmic order in circular symmetry. Vedic fire altars were constructed with extreme precision, based on area-preserving transformations that foreshadowed algebraic geometry.

For the seers, mathematics was not abstract—it was visible in nature. Geometry was a bridge between material and spiritual worlds. Numbers were not mere symbols, but representations of cosmic principles. This perspective aligns with modern physics, where spacetime itself is structured mathematically and geometric symmetries govern particle interactions.

Sri Yantra and Fractals – The Self-Similar Universe

One of the most profound examples of sacred geometry is the Sri Yantra, a diagram of nine interlocking triangles arranged in perfect harmony. When analyzed mathematically, it exhibits fractal-like properties—self-similar at different scales, just as chaos theory and fractal mathematics describe. Its recursive geometry mirrors the way fractal equations generate patterns in nature.

The Sri Yantra also aligns with the Golden Ratio, found in human DNA, plant growth, and galaxy formations. Modern fractals such as the

Mandelbrot Set display the same self-replicating symmetry that the Sri Yantra encoded without equations.

This reveals that the Vedic tradition had an intuitive grasp of fractals long before mathematics formalized them. It proves that mathematics does not need equations to be precise—it can be expressed through geometric intuition. The universe itself may be structured fractally, just as the Sri Yantra suggests.

Pi, the Golden Ratio, and Fibonacci in Vedic Architecture

Constants such as Pi, the Golden Ratio, and Fibonacci sequences shape everything from DNA to human proportions. Yet these principles were already embedded in Vedic mathematics and temple construction.

The Shulba Sutras, dating to the 8th century BCE, approximated Pi with remarkable accuracy. Fire altars required circular and square geometries, demanding precise knowledge of Pi. Some estimates surpassed Greek calculations centuries later.

Temples such as Konark, Brihadeeswara, and Khajuraho were designed with proportions reflecting the Golden Ratio. The height-to-base ratios of spires embodied divine proportion, ensuring harmony and precision. Sculptures too followed these ratios, embedding mathematical beauty in art.

Fibonacci sequences appeared in Sanskrit poetry, whose meters followed rhythmic patterns of recurrence. Conch shells, temple spirals, and lotus petals reflected Fibonacci growth, showing that architects and poets alike recognized recurring sequences in nature.

Mathematical beauty was thus encoded in art, poetry, and architecture—not just equations. Ancient Indian mathematics was practical, aesthetic, and cosmic.

Vedic Fire Altars – Geometric Transformations

The construction of Vedic fire altars offers striking evidence of encoded mathematics. The Shulba Sutras describe complex geometric transformations, such as rearranging shapes while preserving area—anticipating algebraic geometry. These altars followed Pythagorean triples long before Pythagoras. Some were designed to shift between shapes—square, trapezoid, circle—while maintaining the same area, foreshadowing calculus-like problem solving.

Mathematics in Vedic India was not theoretical alone—it was applied in ritual, architecture, and daily practice.

Zero and Infinity – The Great Leap

India's most significant contribution to mathematics is the discovery of zero and infinity. Yet in Vedic thought, these were not just numbers—they were philosophical ideas.

Zero, *Shunya*, was seen as both absence and potential, mirroring the quantum vacuum. Infinity, *Ananta*, was recognized as essential to reality, whether in cosmic cycles or abstract thought. Unlike Greek mathematicians, who struggled with nothingness, Indian thinkers embraced zero as real, leading to the decimal system.

Zero became fundamental to computing and algebra. Infinity became central to calculus and physics. Indian mathematicians intuitively grasped ideas that took the West centuries to formalize.

Bringing It All Together – The Mathematical Genius of the Vedic Tradition

The Vedas encoded mathematical laws in sacred geometry rather than numbers. The Sri Yantra mirrored fractals and chaos theory. Pi, the Golden Ratio, and Fibonacci sequences appeared in Indian design long before formal study. Fire altars followed precise geometric rules, anticipating algebra and calculus. Zero and infinity were not mere numbers, but existential concepts.

The Vedic sages understood mathematics not as computation, but as the language of the cosmos—an eternal pattern woven into reality.

This is Vishwarup Darshan—the realization that mathematics is not just numbers, but the fundamental code of the universe.

3.5 – Sound and Vibration: The Science of Mantras and Quantum Frequencies

Modern physics tells us that everything in the universe is vibration. At the most fundamental level, matter is not solid—it is energy oscillating at different frequencies. The ancient Vedic tradition recognized this truth long ago, encoding it in the concept of *Nada Brahma*—the universe as sound.

According to this vision, sound is not merely communication. It is the foundational force of creation itself. This idea aligns remarkably well with string theory and quantum mechanics, which suggest that the universe is made of vibrational energy rather than static particles. Through mantras, Sanskrit phonetics, and sacred chants, the Vedic tradition harnessed the power of sound to influence consciousness, matter, and energy fields—a practice that science is only now beginning to understand.

Nada Brahma – The Universe as Sound

In Vedic philosophy, sound is the fundamental building block of reality, from which all creation emerges. *Nada Brahma* literally means "Sound is God," implying that reality itself is structured through vibrational frequencies. Modern string theory echoes this, describing fundamental particles not as points but as vibrating strings of energy.

Just as a guitar string vibrates at different frequencies to produce different notes, the universe resonates at different frequencies to create different forms of matter. Every object, thought, and emotion carries its own frequency, much like a musical note. The seers did not use telescopes or microscopes, yet they understood vibration as the force shaping the cosmos. Quantum physics now confirms this: particles behave as wave-like energy fields, and the universe is a continuous, dynamic vibration.

Mantras – Encoded Vibrational Frequencies

One of the most profound ways the Vedic tradition harnessed sound was through mantras—sacred syllables designed to resonate with specific frequencies. Mantras are not mere words; they are vibrational codes aligning body, mind, and environment with higher states of harmony. Each mantra produces a resonance within the body and brain.

Scientific research now shows that chanting mantras alters brainwave patterns, reduces stress, and promotes healing. Low-frequency sounds relax the nervous system, while high-frequency sounds stimulate cognition. Chanting OM synchronizes brainwaves, leading to deep meditative states. Experiments even suggest sound vibrations can alter the structure of water molecules, proving that sound influences matter itself. Ancient mantras were not superstition—they were precise vibrational science.

Sanskrit Phonetics – Precision Resonance

Unlike most languages, Sanskrit was designed as vibrational technology. Every letter, syllable, and sound was structured to produce resonance in the body and mind. Sanskrit words were built on natural vibrations that align with energy centers, or chakras. Pronounced correctly, they create harmonic resonance in the vocal cords, brain, and nervous system.

Modern science now confirms that vocal vibrations influence the nervous system, triggering relaxation or stimulation depending on frequency. Certain sounds resonate with the body's rhythms, affecting heart rate and brain activity. Ancient Sanskrit mantras optimized these effects, functioning much like modern sound therapy. The sages understood sound not as linguistics, but as resonance.

OM – The Primordial Sound

The mantra OM, or AUM, is considered the primordial vibration of the universe. The *Mandukya Upanishad* describes OM as the eternal sound underlying all existence. Its three syllables—A, U, M—represent different states of consciousness.

OM resonates at approximately 136.1 Hz, harmonizing with natural cycles such as Earth's rotation and the Schumann Resonance, the planet's electromagnetic frequency. Scientific studies show that chanting OM synchronizes the hemispheres of the brain, induces theta states associated with deep meditation, and aligns with natural vibrations. OM is not merely a chant—it is a frequency that connects body and mind with the cosmos.

Sound in Healing and Vibrational Medicine

Modern medicine is rediscovering what the Vedas knew: sound heals. Binaural beats and sound therapy treat anxiety and depression. Ultrasound uses high-frequency waves for imaging and treatment. Solfeggio frequencies are studied for DNA repair and cellular regeneration.

This aligns with *Nada Brahma*, the vision that universe, body, and mind are connected through vibration. Healing is not only chemical—it is vibrational.

Bringing It All Together – Sound as Structure of Reality

The Vedas recognized sound as the foundation of reality long before quantum physics introduced vibrational energy fields. Mantras are encoded frequencies influencing consciousness and matter. Sanskrit phonetics were designed for precision resonance. OM is a scientifically measurable frequency aligning with natural rhythms. Modern vibrational medicine and physics now confirm what the ancients knew: sound governs reality.

This is Vishwarup Darshan—the realization that the universe is structured not through randomness, but through harmonic vibration and intelligent frequency patterns. The next step is to integrate this knowledge into science and medicine, creating a new understanding of reality where sound, consciousness, and physics are unified.

3.6 – Consciousness as the Missing Element in Science

Modern science has made remarkable progress in understanding the physical universe—from subatomic particles to galaxies billions of light-years away. Yet despite its advancements, it still struggles with one of the most fundamental questions: *What is consciousness?*

Unlike other scientific fields, which rely on external observation and measurement, the study of consciousness is unique because it is deeply subjective. Neuroscience maps brain activity, physics explores quantum entanglement, but the inner experience of awareness remains an unsolved mystery.

The Vedic tradition, however, placed consciousness at the very center of reality. The Rishis of ancient India did not separate the observer from the observed. They understood that consciousness is not a byproduct of brain activity, but an all-pervading field—fundamental to existence itself. This vision aligns with cutting-edge theories in neuroscience, quantum mechanics, and philosophy of mind, suggesting that the Vedas were far ahead in exploring consciousness without medical instruments or brain scans.

Modern Science and Vedic Thought

Modern science focuses on external observation, studying the brain as a biological machine and attempting to explain thought through neural activity. Vedic wisdom emphasizes inner realization, arguing that the mind is not just the brain, and awareness is not limited to neurons. Science is materialist, believing consciousness emerges from physical processes. The Vedas are non-dualist, asserting that consciousness exists independently of matter and permeates the universe.

This is why Western science still cannot fully explain consciousness—it refuses to examine it from the inside, as the Vedic tradition did through meditation, yogic practice, and introspection. Yet modern research is beginning to rethink consciousness, and its discoveries increasingly align with ancient understanding.

Chaitanya – Consciousness as a Universal Field

In Vedic thought, consciousness is not emergent but fundamental. This is *Chaitanya*—pure awareness. It is eternal, unchanging, existing beyond body and mind. The brain is not the source of consciousness; it exists within consciousness, just as waves exist within the ocean.

This resembles modern physics' idea of reality structured by an underlying field of information. Some scientists now propose Consciousness Field Theories, suggesting that consciousness is not confined to the brain but is a fundamental aspect of the universe. The brain functions as a receiver rather than creator, filtering a greater field of awareness. Just as electromagnetic fields permeate space, consciousness may be omnipresent, like Chaitanya.

This idea is gaining traction in quantum physics, where some researchers suggest that the fabric of reality itself may be conscious—an idea that aligns with the Upanishadic assertion that Brahman, ultimate reality, is pure awareness.

Mind and Brain – Ancient Insights Without Technology

Ancient sages distinguished between the physical brain and the subtle mind (*Manas*), recognizing that thought and awareness do not belong to the body alone. They identified states of consciousness beyond waking thought—dreaming, deep sleep, and transcendental awareness. Through meditation, they explored altered states, proving that the mind can exist beyond sensory input.

Unlike modern neuroscience, which treats the brain as the generator of consciousness, the Vedic model sees the brain as an instrument—a receiver and processor of a larger field. This view aligns with emerging theories such as Integrated Information Theory, which proposes consciousness as fundamental; Orch-OR, which suggests consciousness originates at a quantum level; and the Brain-as-Filter model, which sees the brain as limiting rather than producing awareness. These theories bring science closer to the Vedic view, proving ancient knowledge should be integrated into modern discussion.

Meditation as Experimentation

In the absence of laboratories, the Vedic sages conducted experiments within their own minds. Meditation was not just spiritual—it was a scientific method to explore consciousness. Just as science studies external reality, meditation studies inner reality, uncovering truths about perception, awareness, and altered states.

Modern research now validates these practices. MRI scans show that long-term meditation changes brain structure, increasing gray matter and improving cognition. Yogic breathing alters brainwave states, reducing stress and sharpening focus. Experienced meditators exhibit higher gamma wave activity, associated with heightened awareness. In this sense, the sages were early neuroscientists, using direct observation of the mind rather than external tools. Their discoveries, recorded in the *Yoga Sutras*, *Upanishads*, and Vedanta texts, were centuries ahead of psychology and neuroscience.

Turiya – Pure Consciousness and Quantum Superposition

One of the most fascinating aspects of Vedic science is *Turiya*—the fourth state of awareness, beyond waking, dreaming, and deep sleep. Turiya is pure awareness, beyond thought or perception, existing outside dualities.

This state resembles quantum superposition, where particles exist in multiple states simultaneously. In quantum physics, a particle can be undefined until observed. Similarly, in Turiya, awareness exists beyond identity, yet underlies all experience.

This suggests consciousness may function at a quantum level, existing in pure potential before collapsing into thought. Turiya represents the highest intelligence, transcending time, space, and form. The sages understood quantum principles experientially, not mathematically. Their exploration of mind and reality was sophisticated, not primitive.

Bringing It All Together – Consciousness as Foundation

Modern science studies the brain; Vedic science studies the mind beyond the brain. Western thought sees consciousness as a byproduct of matter; Vedic thought sees matter as a byproduct of consciousness. Quantum theories now suggest awareness is fundamental, just as the Upanishads declared. Meditation, once dismissed as mysticism, is now proven to transform brain function. Turiya parallels quantum superposition, suggesting a deeper connection between consciousness and physics.

This is Vishwarup Darshan—the realization that consciousness is not illusion but the essence of existence itself. The next step is to integrate Vedic consciousness science with neuroscience and quantum theory, leading to a new era where science and spirituality converge.

3.7 – Ayurveda and the Science of Life Without Modern Biology

Modern medicine is deeply rooted in biochemistry, molecular biology, and clinical trials. Yet long before these disciplines were developed, Ayurveda—India's ancient system of life sciences—had already formulated a comprehensive understanding of health, disease, and healing. It did so not through microscopes or molecular analysis, but through natural principles, observation, and holistic approaches.

Ayurveda did not dissect human biology at a microscopic level. Instead, it took a macro approach, seeing the body, mind, and environment as one interconnected system. Its wisdom encoded medical knowledge without molecular biology, and its principles align strikingly with modern science—proving its relevance in an era dominated by pharmaceuticals and reductionist medicine.

Encoding Biochemistry Without Molecules

Modern biology explains health through cellular functions, genetic expression, and biochemical reactions. Ayurveda explains health through balance, energy flow, and the body's interaction with nature. Both aim for the same goal—optimal health—but they speak different languages.

Where modern science now recognizes the gut microbiome's role in digestion and immunity, Ayurveda described *Agni*, the digestive fire. Where science explains chronic inflammation as a root of disease, Ayurveda spoke of imbalance in *Pitta*, the principle of heat. Where epigenetics studies the interaction between genes and lifestyle, Ayurveda recognized *Prakriti*, the individual constitution shaped by nature and environment.

Ayurvedic wisdom was not "pre-scientific." It was expressed in a holistic, intuitive framework rather than a molecular one. Today, as science shifts toward systems biology, integrative medicine, and personalized healthcare, Ayurveda's approach is proving more scientifically aligned than ever.

The Three Doshas – An Early Model of Homeostasis

Modern medicine describes homeostasis as the body's ability to maintain stability amid change. Ayurveda expressed this through the three doshas—*Vata*, *Pitta*, and *Kapha*.

Vata, composed of air and ether, governs movement, circulation, respiration, and nervous impulses. *Pitta*, fire and water, governs metabolism, digestion, and enzymatic reactions. *Kapha*, earth and water, governs immunity, tissue structure, and fluid balance.

These are not mystical forces, but an early model of biological regulation. Vata mirrors neurology, Pitta mirrors metabolic and endocrine functions, Kapha mirrors immunity and cellular resilience. When balanced, the body thrives. When imbalanced, disease arises—just as modern medicine explains that disruptions in homeostasis lead to pathology. Ayurveda's intuitive model was functionally equivalent to what physiology now describes through biochemistry.

Food as Medicine – Nutritional Science Rediscovered

One of Ayurveda's most revolutionary insights was that food is not just fuel—it is medicine. Foods were classified not by calories, but by their effects on energy, digestion, and balance. Diets were tailored to *Prakriti*, anticipating today's personalized nutrition and nutrigenomics.

Turmeric was used for inflammation and infections; modern research confirms its anti-inflammatory, anticancer, and neuroprotective properties. Ashwagandha was prescribed for rejuvenation; clinical studies now show it reduces cortisol, lowers stress, and enhances brain function. Ghee was valued for gut health and vitality; science now recognizes its role as a source of healthy fats. Fasting and intermittent eating were recommended for longevity; modern studies validate their role in autophagy, cellular repair, and metabolic flexibility.

Ayurveda emphasized prevention—diet and lifestyle adjustments to maintain health—while modern medicine often intervenes after disease arises. Nutritional science is now shifting toward functional foods, plant-based diets, and gut health, rediscovering Ayurveda's principles.

Herbal Knowledge – Pharmacology Before Pharmaceuticals

Long before synthetic drugs, Ayurveda classified thousands of medicinal plants with remarkable precision. Herbs were understood through *Rasa* (taste), *Guna* (qualities), *Virya* (potency), and *Vipaka* (post-digestive effect). This was an early form of pharmacology, developed without laboratories.

Brahmi was used to enhance memory; modern studies confirm its cognitive benefits. Neem was prescribed for infections; science now recognizes its antibacterial and antifungal compounds. Triphala was used for digestion and detoxification; research validates its role in gut health. Tulsi was revered for immunity and stress relief; modern trials show it lowers cortisol and supports resilience.

Ayurveda was not folklore—it was a medical system based on deep observation and pattern recognition.

Turmeric and Ashwagandha – Gifts to Modern Medicine

Turmeric and Ashwagandha exemplify Ayurveda's foresight. Turmeric was used for thousands of years to treat inflammation, infections, and digestive issues. Modern studies confirm its ability to reduce chronic inflammation, linked to heart disease, cancer, and neurodegeneration. Today it is sold worldwide as a natural supplement for immunity and brain health.

Ashwagandha was prescribed for rejuvenation and longevity. Clinical studies show it reduces stress hormones, enhances brain function, and improves endurance. It is now recognized as an adaptogen, helping the body adapt to physical and emotional stress.

These discoveries bridge ancient wisdom with modern science, proving that Ayurveda's medicinal knowledge was based on real, observable effects long before laboratory validation.

Bringing It All Together – Ayurveda as an Advanced Medical System

Ayurveda described biological homeostasis through the three doshas, aligning with modern physiology. It recognized food as medicine long before nutritional science validated it. It systematized herbal medicine in ways that mirror pharmacology. Turmeric, Ashwagandha, and countless other herbs are now recognized as powerful medicinal compounds.

This is Vishwarup Darshan—the realization that Ayurveda was not pre-scientific, but a sophisticated, holistic approach to health that modern medicine is only now catching up to. The next step is to integrate Ayurveda with modern medicine, creating a new paradigm of healthcare that is preventive, personalized, and holistic.

3.8 – The Integration of All Fields: The Holistic Vedic Model

Modern education and research are highly specialized, dividing knowledge into distinct categories—physics, chemistry, medicine, psychology, and philosophy—with little overlap between them. While this has led to significant advancements in each field, it has also created a fragmented understanding of reality, where scientists, doctors, and scholars often fail to see the larger picture.

The Vedic approach to knowledge was entirely different. Instead of compartmentalizing subjects, it viewed all fields as interconnected—a unified system where science, philosophy, and ethics were inseparable. This holistic perspective recognized that truth is not confined to a single method of inquiry, and that both logic and direct experience were essential paths to wisdom.

Today, as modern civilization grapples with technological excess, environmental crises, and ethical dilemmas, it is becoming clear that science without wisdom leads to imbalance. The Vedic model of knowledge integration offers valuable insights into how we can restore harmony between progress, ethics, and human well-being.

The Vedic Approach – A Unified Vision of Knowledge

Modern science isolates disciplines, while Vedic knowledge integrated them into a single framework. Physics, chemistry, medicine, and consciousness were not seen as separate fields—they were different aspects of the same cosmic intelligence. Mathematical precision, spiritual insight, and medical knowledge were applied together, ensuring that scientific progress never became destructive or unethical.

This was not abstract philosophy—it was a functional model that shaped cosmology, Ayurveda, temple architecture, and ethics. Vedic cosmology explored time cycles and the nature of reality. Ayurveda aligned medical knowledge with nature and the body's intelligence. Temple architecture used mathematics, geometry, and sacred ratios to harmonize with cosmic forces. Ethics and Dharma ensured that discoveries were applied for the benefit of society. Unlike today's approach, where science often ignores its social and environmental impact, Vedic wisdom recognized that knowledge must serve the greater harmony of existence.

Truth Beyond a Single Method of Inquiry

Western science relies on observation, measurement, and repeatability to determine truth. This has led to extraordinary breakthroughs, but it has ignored non-material aspects of reality such as consciousness, intuition, and direct experience.

The Vedic model accepted multiple paths to truth. *Pratyaksha* was direct observation, empirical verification akin to modern science. *Anumana* was inference, logical deduction like reasoning in physics and mathematics. *Upamana* was analogy, identifying universal patterns and repeating structures. *Sabda* was scriptural and experiential knowledge, insights from meditation and inner realization.

This means Vedic knowledge was not opposed to science—it was a broader scientific model that included both external observation and internal exploration. Modern science is now rediscovering this approach through quantum physics, which shows that observation affects reality; consciousness studies, which challenge materialism; and holistic medicine, which integrates mind, body, and lifestyle. By combining empirical science with direct experience, the Vedic approach provides a more complete model of knowledge—one that recognizes both material and non-material aspects of reality.

Ethics as the Guiding Principle of Knowledge

One of the greatest failures of modern civilization is that science often develops without ethical consideration. Nuclear energy can power cities, but it can also destroy them. Artificial intelligence can revolutionize industries, but it can also create inequality. Medical advancements save lives, but pharmaceutical companies often prioritize profit over health.

The Vedic tradition never allowed science to be separated from ethics. Knowledge was always guided by Dharma—cosmic law and right action—ensuring discoveries were used for harmony, not destruction. Ayurveda relied on nature's intelligence rather than toxic chemicals. Vedic astronomy aligned human life with cosmic rhythms rather than dominating nature. Technological advancements were balanced with spiritual wisdom, preventing reckless materialism. Unlike today, where power is concentrated in corporations and governments, the Vedic system ensured that scientific knowledge served all living beings.

Why Science Without Wisdom Leads to Imbalance

We live in an age where knowledge is abundant but wisdom is rare. Modern education prioritizes specialization but fails to teach how fields are connected. Science advances rapidly, but without purpose or ethics, it causes as many problems as it solves. Technology is powerful, but without values guiding it, it becomes destructive.

The Vedic model understood that knowledge without wisdom leads to chaos. This is what we see today: environmental destruction caused by industries prioritizing profit over planetary health; mental health crises from societies that value productivity over well-being; technological addiction where people are more connected to devices than to their own intelligence.

Vedic wisdom teaches that knowledge must always be applied with higher purpose, ensuring progress serves harmony rather than disrupting it. Science seeks control over nature. Vedic wisdom seeks alignment with nature. As modern civilization struggles with excess, it is clear that a return to holistic wisdom is necessary for sustainability.

The Decline of Holistic Thinking

Modern education divides subjects into compartments, preventing people from seeing the bigger picture. A physicist may understand quantum mechanics but not consciousness. A biologist may study genes but ignore nutrition and environment. An engineer may design powerful technologies but lack ethical training in their consequences.

This fragmentation has led to a world where science and spirituality are treated as opposites, technology is developed without regard for consequences, and people are trained for careers but not for wisdom or moral responsibility.

In contrast, the Vedic model integrated all fields into a single system. Science and ethics were inseparable. Material progress was balanced with spiritual growth. Knowledge was not about accumulating facts—it was about cultivating wisdom.

Bringing It All Together – The Need for a Holistic Model

The Vedic approach unified physics, medicine, philosophy, and consciousness into one framework. Truth was explored through both reason and direct experience. Scientific discoveries were applied ethically, ensuring harmony rather than destruction. Modern civilization is now realizing that science without wisdom leads to imbalance.

To move forward, we must reintegrate fragmented knowledge into a holistic understanding of reality. This is Vishwarup Darshan—the vision of total knowledge, where all disciplines merge into one grand understanding of existence.

Conclusion: Why the Vedic Approach is Needed in the Modern Age

Humanity now stands at a crossroads—an age of unparalleled scientific progress shadowed by existential uncertainty. Modern science has given us technology, medicine, and extraordinary insight into the physical world. Yet it remains incomplete, because it reduces intelligence to mechanical processes, fragments knowledge into isolated disciplines, and struggles to explain the purpose and interconnectedness of reality.

This is why the Vedic approach is urgently needed today—not as a replacement for science, but as a complementary system that restores balance, integration, and depth. The Vedic model does not reject equations or empirical research. It simply goes beyond them, using symbolism, analogy, and direct experience as additional ways to uncover truth. By reintegrating ancient wisdom with modern science, we can move beyond reductionism and toward a holistic model of knowledge—one that embraces both logic and intuition, external observation and inner realization, material exploration and spiritual understanding.

The Limits of Materialism

Modern science operates on the assumption that everything can be explained through measurement and equations. This has been useful, but it fails to account for consciousness, interconnectedness, and the intelligence woven into nature. It has created a mechanistic worldview where humans are seen as biological machines rather than conscious beings.

The result is technological advancement without ethical guidance, leading to environmental destruction and AI-driven crises. It is medical progress without wisdom, breakthroughs in treatment while neglecting deeper causes of disease. It is knowledge without integration, hyper-specialization where one discipline does not understand another. Without a unifying vision, knowledge becomes fragmented, leaving humanity disconnected from the deeper reality of existence.

The Vedic model is more relevant than ever—because it unites what modern science has separated.

The Vedic Model – Knowledge Beyond Equations

Unlike modern science, which seeks to quantify everything, the Vedic system did not depend on numbers alone. It used analogy and symbolism to explain truths in ways accessible to all. It prioritized direct experience—meditation, introspection—as valid methods of knowledge acquisition. It integrated science, philosophy, medicine, and ethics into a single framework.

This does not mean the Vedic model was anti-mathematical. Ancient Indian thinkers pioneered zero and infinity, fractal geometry embedded in the Sri Yantra, and cosmic time cycles mapped with astronomical precision. The difference is that the Vedic system was not limited to mathematics—it used multiple ways to explain the same reality.

Modern science describes the universe through wave equations and energy fields. The Vedas describe it as *Nada Brahma*—sound as the fundamental vibration of reality. Physics describes time as relative; Vedic cosmology speaks of Yugas and Kalpas, aligning with cosmic cycles. The Vedic model does not reject equations—it simply recognizes that equations are not the only way to understand reality. Modern science looks at the universe from the outside; the Vedic model understands it from both the outside and the inside.

Toward a New Era of Knowledge

The future of human knowledge lies not in rejecting either science or spirituality, but in integrating them into a unified vision. Quantum physics is beginning to validate Vedic concepts of interconnectedness and consciousness. Neuroscience is exploring meditation, showing the mind's hidden power. Holistic medicine is rediscovering Ayurveda, proving that ancient health principles were ahead of their time.

By merging the precision of modern research with the wisdom of ancient knowledge, we can create a science that acknowledges consciousness as fundamental, a healthcare system that emphasizes prevention and balance, a technology-driven world guided by ethics, and an education system that teaches interconnected wisdom rather than fragmented disciplines.

This is Vishwarup Darshan—the realization that the universe, human knowledge, and all aspects of existence are deeply interconnected. It is not about going backward or rejecting progress. It is about restoring the missing piece of wisdom that modern civilization has lost.

Vishwarup Darshan – The Key to Unifying Knowledge

The journey of this book has revealed that ancient Vedic wisdom already described truths modern physics is only beginning to explore. Ayurveda understood the body's intelligence without molecular biology. Sacred geometry encoded mathematical principles in temples and rituals. Mantras and sound vibrations influenced consciousness, aligning with quantum mechanics. Consciousness itself was seen not as a byproduct of the brain, but as a field permeating reality.

This proves that the separation between science and spirituality is artificial. True knowledge must integrate both perspectives. Vishwarup Darshan is the complete vision—where physics and metaphysics are no longer opposites, where science serves human well-being instead of profit, where technology advances with ethical responsibility, and where the universe is understood as intelligent rather than random.

By embracing this unified vision, we can restore balance to science, society, and human consciousness—creating a world both technologically advanced and spiritually awakened. This is the next step in human evolution: the reintegration of fragmented knowledge into one complete, holistic understanding of reality.

A Call for a New Renaissance

The limitations of materialistic science show the need for a broader model. The Vedic approach is not against equations—it simply offers alternative ways to understand reality. Reintegrating ancient wisdom with modern science can create a balanced, ethical, and sustainable future. Vishwarup Darshan is the key to unifying fragmented disciplines, restoring the original holistic vision of the universe.

This is not a return to the past—it is a leap forward into a new era of knowledge, one that merges the best of both worlds. The question is no longer whether ancient wisdom was scientific. The question is whether modern science is ready to embrace the deeper truths it has overlooked for centuries.

The time for Vishwarup Darshan has come—the time to see the universe as it was always meant to be seen.

Interlude: Resting in the Web of Wisdom

You have walked through the Vedic vision of science—geometry without equations, sound as vibration, Ayurveda as living intelligence, and consciousness as the missing element in modern inquiry. Each section has revealed that what we call "ancient wisdom" was not primitive speculation, but a holistic science expressed in symbols, rhythms, and direct experience.

Now, pause.

Imagine the universe not as fragments—physics here, medicine there, mathematics in another corner—but as one seamless field. Imagine knowledge not as separate disciplines, but as a single river flowing through different landscapes. Imagine yourself not as an observer standing outside reality, but as part of the very web you are studying.

This is the essence of Vishwarup Darshan: the realization that knowledge is not divided, but whole. The Vedic sages did not see equations, mantras, or rituals as isolated practices. They saw them as different doors opening into the same vast chamber of truth.

As you rest here, let the cadence of Chapter 3 settle into silence. Let the idea of integration—science and spirituality, matter and energy, sound and consciousness—sink into your awareness.

Because the next step of the journey will take you deeper still. The Puranas, often dismissed as mythology, are not mere stories. They are cosmic frameworks—maps of reality encoded in narrative form. They are the bridge between symbol and science, between myth and cosmology.

Take this moment. Breathe. Let the fragments dissolve. When you turn the page, you will enter the Puranas—not as tales of gods and demons, but as living blueprints of the universe itself.

Chapter 4: Decoding the Puranas

The Puranas as a Cosmic Framework, Not Mythology

For centuries, the Puranas have been dismissed as mythology—imaginative tales filled with deities, battles, and supernatural events. Scholars, particularly in the Western academic tradition, have categorized them as religious folklore rather than serious intellectual works. But what if this interpretation is fundamentally flawed?

The assumption that the Puranas are mere myths arises from a lack of understanding of their encoded nature. Unlike modern scientific texts that rely on equations and formulas, the Puranas used symbols, allegories, and multi-layered narratives to preserve knowledge across generations. What appears to be a story of cosmic battles is often an encoded description of planetary movements and universal forces. A deity slaying a demon may symbolize the interaction of fundamental energies—entropy, preservation, and transformation. The lifespan of Brahma is not an arbitrary number, but a sophisticated model of time cycles aligned with astronomical events.

This method of encoding allowed the Puranas to function as cosmic maps, providing insights into the nature of reality, evolution, consciousness, and even astrophysics—without the need for mathematical equations.

Modern science is now catching up to many concepts hidden within these texts—from the cyclic nature of time to the interconnectivity of all existence. To dismiss the Puranas as mythology is to ignore a vast, untapped source of knowledge, one that may hold the missing links between ancient wisdom and modern discoveries.

This chapter aims to decode the Puranas as a sophisticated knowledge system, revealing their scientific, philosophical, and cosmological depth.

4.1 – The Puranas as a Knowledge System: Beyond Mythology

The Puranas are often misunderstood as mythological stories, filled with gods, demons, and celestial wars. Yet this interpretation overlooks the scientific, philosophical, and metaphysical wisdom encoded within them. The Puranas were never meant to be taken literally. They were structured as multi-layered narratives, designed to preserve and transmit universal knowledge across generations.

Unlike modern texts, which rely on equations and direct explanations, the Puranas used allegory, symbolism, and personification to encode cosmology, evolution, consciousness, time cycles, and universal laws. This ensured that knowledge remained accessible to all levels of seekers—from the common person to the most advanced thinkers. It was protected from distortion, since only those with the right understanding could decode it. And it was timeless, allowing deeper truths to be rediscovered as human knowledge evolved.

What appear to be stories of divine beings and cosmic events are often descriptions of scientific principles, planetary cycles, and the evolution of consciousness—written in a way that allowed both the spiritual and the scientific mind to extract meaning.

Encoded Knowledge of Cosmos, Time, and Consciousness

Each Purana contains descriptions of the universe's expansion and cycles, the progressive development of life forms, the vast rhythms of Yugas and Kalpas, the mind as an interconnected field beyond the brain, and the balance of forces that govern energy and physics. Rather than viewing the cosmos as random chaos, the Puranas describe it as a living, intelligent system governed by structured patterns—a concept now echoed in quantum physics, systems biology, and unified field theories.

These ideas were not rigid doctrines but symbolic stories carrying multiple levels of meaning.

Deities as Cosmic Principles

One of the greatest misunderstandings about the Puranas is the assumption that deities were meant to be worshipped as supernatural beings. In reality, they represent cosmic principles. Shiva, Vishnu, and Brahma symbolize destruction, preservation, and creation. Saraswati, Lakshmi, and Kali embody knowledge, energy, and transformation. Many Puranic figures personify forces that govern the universe—entropy, equilibrium, motion.

Shiva, for example, represents entropy—the principle of transformation and renewal. Modern physics recognizes entropy as the force that ensures systems evolve rather than stagnate. Vishnu embodies balance and stability, preserving cosmic order much like equilibrium sustains biological, chemical, and cosmic systems. Vishnu's Avatars align with evolutionary stages of life, showing how order is maintained through adaptation.

The *Samudra Manthan*, the churning of the ocean, is not a literal event but an allegory of universal processes. The mountain at the axis represents the balancing point of forces, while devas and asuras symbolize opposing yet necessary energies. The story encodes cosmic balance, energy flow, and evolutionary cycles.

Three Levels of Interpretation

The genius of the Puranic system lies in its three-tiered structure, making knowledge accessible at different intellectual and spiritual levels. At the literal level, stories taught moral and ethical lessons in engaging form. At the symbolic level, seekers could recognize hidden metaphysical meanings. At the scientific level, realized thinkers could decode the mathematical, astronomical, and cosmological insights embedded in the narratives.

For example, the story of Brahma's lifespan is not poetic exaggeration but an encoded model of astronomical time cycles. One day of Brahma—4.32 billion years—aligns closely with modern estimates of Earth's geological timescales. This proves the Puranas were not superstitious folklore but advanced systems of knowledge transmission, designed to be interpreted according to the seeker's capacity.

Relevance in the Modern Age

In an era where knowledge is increasingly specialized and fragmented, the Puranas offer a model of integrated understanding. Instead of isolating physics, biology, and consciousness, they unify them into a single framework—much like today's emerging interdisciplinary sciences. They teach that the universe is not mechanical but intelligent. They reveal that science and spirituality are not opposites but complementary. They provide a framework that can be reinterpreted and rediscovered as human knowledge advances.

The more science progresses, the more we realize that ancient civilizations had already explored fundamental truths about the universe—just in a different language. The Puranas were never meant to be discarded as outdated myths. They are a living system of knowledge, waiting to be decoded.

This is Vishwarup Darshan—the realization that all knowledge, past and present, is interconnected.

4.2 – The Cosmological Structure in the Puranas: Aligning with Modern Science

The Puranas describe the universe not as a collection of isolated objects, but as a grand, interconnected system governed by cyclical creation and dissolution, multidimensional existence, and precise astronomical mechanics. These descriptions, once dismissed as mythological imagination, are now being re-evaluated in light of modern discoveries in cosmology, astrophysics, and quantum mechanics. Concepts such as the Big Bang, parallel universes, and oscillating cosmology align remarkably well with the ancient Puranic framework.

This section explores how the Puranas offer a sophisticated model of the cosmos—one that modern science is only beginning to understand.

The Creation Cycle – Srishti and Pralaya

Modern cosmology states that the universe began with the Big Bang, expanding from a singular point. Some theories suggest it may one day collapse back into a singularity—the Big Crunch—or continue expanding indefinitely. Others propose an oscillating universe, expanding and contracting in cycles.

The Puranic model mirrors this perfectly. *Srishti* describes creation, the expansion of the universe from an unmanifest state. *Sthiti* represents sustenance, the stabilization of the cosmos where life and intelligence flourish. *Pralaya* is dissolution, the contraction of the universe back into a singular state before the next cycle begins.

The Puranas describe the universe as cyclical, not linear—an eternal process of creation, preservation, and dissolution. The lifespan of Brahma, calculated as 311 trillion years, corresponds to vast cosmic cycles eerily similar to timescales proposed by theoretical physics. Rather than viewing the universe as a one-time event, the Puranic model sees it as a pulsating entity that continuously renews itself—an idea now gaining traction in quantum gravity and cosmological models.

The Fourteen Lokas – Multidimensional Reality

In modern physics, theories like string theory and M-theory suggest that the universe consists of multiple dimensions and parallel realities, many invisible to us. The Puranas describe the cosmos as composed of fourteen *Lokas*, realms of existence arranged in a structured hierarchy.

At the highest level is *Satya Loka*, a realm of pure consciousness. Below it are *Tapa Loka*, associated with advanced energetic beings, and *Jana Loka*, realms of evolved minds beyond physical form. *Mahar Loka* serves as a transitional realm between matter and energy. *Swarga Loka* represents heavenly dimensions of high-frequency energy, while *Bhuvar Loka* is an intermediary field between gross and subtle worlds. *Bhuloka* is the Earth realm—the physical dimension we inhabit. Beneath these are realms such as *Atala*, *Vitala*, and *Sutala*, corresponding to lower vibrational states or unknown dimensions.

Rather than a flat, singular universe, the Puranic model describes a multilayered reality where different states of consciousness and energy coexist. If interpreted as vibrational states or quantum dimensions, the Lokas align remarkably well with modern theories of higher dimensions and the multiverse.

Brahma's Day and Night – The Oscillating Universe

The Puranas describe vast cycles of time through Brahma's Day and Night. One *Kalpa*, or Brahma's Day, lasts 4.32 billion human years, during which the universe remains active. One *Pralaya*, or Brahma's Night, lasts the same duration, during which the universe dissolves into non-manifestation. This cycle repeats for 100 years of Brahma's lifespan—311 trillion years—after which a complete dissolution occurs, followed by another creation.

This aligns with modern oscillatory universe theories, which suggest the cosmos may not expand forever but could enter contraction, leading to another cycle. The laws of physics themselves may be cyclical, resetting at the end of each cosmic cycle. The idea that the universe existed before the Big Bang is now being explored by cosmologists—an idea the Puranas have stated all along. Time, in this vision, is not a one-directional arrow but a cycle, a rhythm of manifestation and dissolution.

Astronomical Knowledge in the Puranas

The Puranas and texts like the *Surya Siddhanta* describe planetary motion, solar cycles, and cosmic alignments with astonishing accuracy—long before telescopes were invented. The concept of Yugas, vast time cycles, is linked to planetary and galactic movements, suggesting an early understanding of astrophysics.

The *Surya Siddhanta* calculated the Earth's diameter and circumference with values close to modern measurements. It described planetary orbits in elliptical form, aligning with Kepler's laws. It identified the precession of the equinoxes thousands of years before modern astronomy confirmed it. It even approximated the age of the Sun at 4.5 billion years, nearly identical to current estimates.

How did the ancients know this without telescopes or computers? Some suggest they inherited knowledge from an earlier advanced civilization. Others propose that meditative and observational methods allowed them to access universal truths without direct measurement. Perhaps Vedic cosmology was based on a lost scientific framework, waiting to be rediscovered.

Bringing It All Together – The Scientific Genius of the Puranic Model

The Puranic creation cycle aligns with modern Big Bang and Big Crunch theories. The fourteen Lokas resemble multidimensional models in quantum physics and string theory. Brahma's time cycles match oscillating universe models. The *Surya Siddhanta* proves advanced knowledge of planetary mechanics. The Vedic vision of time as cyclical matches emerging theories in cosmology.

This is Vishwarup Darshan—the realization that the Puranas were not primitive myths, but encoded knowledge that aligns with modern astrophysics and quantum cosmology. Modern science is only now catching up to what the Puranic seers described thousands of years ago.

The question is no longer whether the Puranas are mythology. The question is whether we are ready to reinterpret them as a sophisticated cosmic framework.

4.3 – The Yugas and Time Cycles: A Model of Cosmic Evolution

Time is one of the most profound mysteries of existence, shaping our understanding of history, civilization, and the universe itself. Modern science largely views time as linear, moving from past to future in a straight trajectory. The Vedic tradition, however, sees time as cyclical—governed by cosmic rhythms, planetary alignments, and evolutionary cycles.

The Yugas, as described in the Puranas and Vedic texts, are not simply phases of moral decline. They represent a model of cosmic evolution, detailing the rise and fall of civilizations, shifts in human consciousness, and planetary changes across vast epochs. As modern science explores long-term climate cycles, mass extinctions, and planetary precession, it is beginning to confirm that the Yuga system was not mythology but an advanced framework for understanding time, civilization, and cosmic forces.

The Four Yugas – Evolutionary Phases

The Yuga system describes time as moving through four repeating ages, each with distinct characteristics and transformations. *Satya Yuga*, the Golden Age, is marked by pure consciousness, truth, and balance—a low-entropy state where ecosystems and civilizations remain stable. *Treta Yuga*, the Silver Age, introduces ego and gradual decline, the first disruptions in harmony. *Dwapara Yuga*, the Bronze Age, sees technological growth, energy imbalance, and rising conflicts, mirroring civilizational expansion and increasing entropy. Finally, *Kali Yuga*, the Iron Age, represents maximum disorder, materialism, and ethical collapse—the age we currently inhabit, defined by rapid technological progress alongside social and ecological breakdown.

Each Yuga reflects a different vibrational energy and humanity's relationship with nature. As time moves forward, energy becomes more chaotic, awareness shifts toward materialism, and civilizations lose their balance. The rise and fall of societies, the loss and rediscovery of knowledge, and the recurring patterns of upheaval all align with this cyclical framework.

Astronomical Alignment – Precession and Planetary Cycles

One of the most astonishing aspects of the Yuga system is its connection to astronomical cycles. The Precession of the Equinoxes—a 25,920-year wobble of Earth's axis—was encoded in ancient texts long before modern science discovered it. This slow shift affects planetary conditions and human consciousness, just as the Yugas describe long-term changes in civilization and energy.

Solar cycles, cosmic radiation, and planetary alignments influence evolutionary progress and human behavior. Earth's changing magnetic fields, including pole reversals, may correspond to Yuga transitions, altering the planet's electromagnetic balance. The durations of Yugas suggest an advanced astronomical understanding, showing that these cycles were not arbitrary timelines but reflections of celestial mechanics and their impact on Earth.

Kalpas, Manvantaras, and Maha-Yugas – Expanding the Cycles

Beyond the four Yugas, the Vedic system expands into larger cycles, reflecting the cosmic breath of creation and dissolution. A *Maha-Yuga*, spanning 4.32 million years, encompasses all four Yugas. Seventy-one Maha-Yugas form a *Manvantara*, lasting over 300 million years, the reign of one Manu, progenitor of civilization. Fourteen Manvantaras make a *Kalpa*, Brahma's Day, lasting 4.32 billion years. Brahma's full lifespan stretches across 311 trillion years, encompassing cycles of universal creation and dissolution.

These vast cycles mirror astrophysical concepts such as the lifespan of stars, planetary changes, and galactic rhythms. Just as ecosystems and galaxies undergo transformations over immense timescales, the Yugas describe similar shifts in human civilization and consciousness. This cyclical vision challenges the Western model of uninterrupted progress, suggesting instead that history is punctuated by resets, lost civilizations, and forgotten knowledge.

Civilization Collapses and Yuga Shifts

The end of each Yuga marks destruction, rebirth, and transformation. Kali Yuga, the age we are in, represents the lowest vibrational state—materialism, ignorance, and technological excess. At its close, a transition to Satya Yuga restores balance.

Historical collapses align with these transitions. The decline of the Indus Valley around 2000 BCE may reflect the shift from Dwapara to Kali Yuga. The fall of Egypt, Mesopotamia, and the Maya echoes civilizational resets described in the cycles. Today's environmental crises, social upheavals, and economic instability are signs of Kali Yuga's final phase, pointing toward an imminent transformation.

Kali Yuga and Modern Society

The Puranas describe Kali Yuga with striking accuracy. Rapid technological advancements occur alongside declining values—science without ethics. Greed, corruption, and exploitation dominate, driven by materialism. Environmental destruction reflects humanity's disregard for nature. Social chaos, fractured families, and superficial relationships mark the decline of genuine connection.

This is not prophecy but pattern. The Vedic texts foresaw the consequences of technology without wisdom and outlined the return to balance through Satya Yuga. Kali Yuga is not a doomsday—it is a natural cycle, one humanity must recognize and prepare for.

Bringing It All Together – Time as a Cosmic Rhythm

The Yugas are not religious timelines but encoded models of civilizational rise and fall. They align with astronomical cycles, planetary changes, and mass extinctions. They describe shifts in human consciousness from spiritual awakening to material obsession. They predict the characteristics of Kali Yuga with uncanny precision, describing the present state of the world. And they offer a vision for renewal, where humanity restores balance and wisdom.

This is Vishwarup Darshan—the realization that time is not linear but cyclical, and that human progress must align with cosmic rhythms rather than resist them. Modern science is beginning to uncover what the Vedic seers already understood—that history repeats, civilizations rise and fall, and humanity must learn from the past to prepare for the future.

4.4 – Dashavatara: The Evolution of Life Encoded in Mythology

The Dashavatara, or the ten incarnations of Vishnu, has long been viewed as a religious narrative depicting divine interventions across ages. Yet when examined through a scientific and evolutionary lens, it becomes clear that this sequence is not merely mythological storytelling. It is an encoded representation of biological evolution, tracing the transformation of life from aquatic organisms to higher intelligence.

Unlike Darwinian evolution, which is often described as random and unguided, the Dashavatara suggests a structured, purposeful unfolding—one that includes not only biological development but also the growth of intelligence, morality, and consciousness. Each avatar aligns with a key stage in the evolutionary history of life on Earth, bridging ancient wisdom with modern science.

From Water to Land – The Early Avatars

The sequence begins with *Matsya*, the fish, symbolizing the origin of life in water. Science confirms that Earth's earliest organisms emerged in the oceans billions of years ago, making Matsya a perfect metaphor for this primordial stage.

Next comes *Kurma*, the turtle, representing the transition from water to land. Around 375 million years ago, amphibians and early tetrapods made this leap, much like Tiktaalik, a creature bridging aquatic and terrestrial existence. Kurma embodies this critical evolutionary threshold.

Varaha, the boar, marks the rise of strong terrestrial mammals. Once life adapted fully to land, mammals emerged as dominant species, shaping ecosystems and paving the way for higher complexity.

Toward Humanity – Hybrid and Early Forms

Narasimha, the half-man, half-lion, represents the hybrid leap toward humanity. Neither fully animal nor fully human, Narasimha symbolizes the evolutionary phase when primates and early hominins began to develop advanced cognition, straddling the boundary between instinct and intelligence.

Vamana, the dwarf, reflects the emergence of early humans—small in stature but mentally superior to their predecessors. Homo habilis and early Homo sapiens, though physically modest, carried the seeds of language, creativity, and tool-making.

Civilization and Consciousness – The Later Avatars

With *Parashurama*, the warrior wielding an axe, humanity enters the hunter-gatherer and early civilization phase. Tool-making, survival strategies, and tribal organization defined this stage, as humans began shaping their environment with weapons and technology.

Rama, the ideal king, represents the rise of structured society, law, and ethics. Civilization matured into governance, justice, and dharma, emphasizing stability and moral responsibility.

Krishna, the divine strategist, embodies higher intelligence and philosophy. His teachings in the *Bhagavad Gita* symbolize the expansion of intellectual and spiritual wisdom, where humanity began to reflect deeply on purpose, morality, and the nature of reality.

Buddha, the enlightened one, marks the evolution of consciousness beyond material existence. His teachings on detachment and self-realization represent humanity's transcendence of physical survival, pointing toward inner awakening and spiritual liberation.

Finally, *Kalki*, the future avatar, has yet to appear. This suggests that evolution is ongoing. Will it be a technological transformation—AI, transhumanism—or a spiritual awakening? Kalki represents the unknown horizon, the next leap in human evolution beyond what we currently understand.

Dashavatara vs. Darwinian Evolution

Darwin's theory explains biological adaptation, but Dashavatara encompasses both biological and spiritual evolution. Modern science focuses on survival, while the Puranic model includes ethical and intellectual growth. Evolution, in this vision, is not random but structured, leading toward higher awareness.

A Holistic Model of Evolution

The Puranas offer a broader framework: biological evolution from aquatic life to humans, intellectual evolution through language, strategy, and ethics, and spiritual evolution through enlightenment and transcendence. Rather than viewing evolution as aimless, Dashavatara suggests a purposeful progression toward intelligence and consciousness.

Bringing It All Together – Dashavatara as Blueprint

Each avatar of Vishnu aligns with a key phase of evolution. Unlike Darwinian models, which emphasize adaptation, the Puranic model highlights the unfolding of intelligence and morality. The final avatar, Kalki, reminds us that evolution is still in motion, guiding humanity toward transformation.

This is Vishwarup Darshan—the realization that evolution is not merely about biology, but about the progressive unfolding of intelligence, morality, and higher awareness. Modern science is only now catching up to what the ancient sages encoded in Dashavatara: an evolutionary process leading not just to survival, but to enlightenment.

4.5 – Deities as Cosmic Forces, Not Literal Gods

The Puranic deities are often perceived as supernatural beings with human-like personalities, dwelling in distant realms. Yet when examined more deeply, it becomes clear that these figures were never meant to be taken literally. They are symbolic representations of cosmic principles, natural forces, and universal intelligence.

The Vedic and Puranic tradition did not separate science from spirituality. Instead, it encoded the workings of the universe in the form of deities and mythological narratives, making complex cosmic and metaphysical ideas accessible through storytelling. What appears as mythology is, in fact, a sophisticated framework for understanding cosmic laws.

Shiva – Entropy and Transformation

In physics, entropy is the measure of disorder in a system. The second law of thermodynamics states that all systems naturally move toward increasing entropy, leading to dissolution and transformation. Shiva, the god of destruction and regeneration, embodies this universal force of change. He is not simply a destroyer—he ensures that the cycle of creation and renewal continues, preventing stagnation. Without entropy, no transformation would occur; matter would remain static, and evolution would be impossible.

Shiva's dance, the *Tandava*, represents the dynamic interplay of energy, destruction, and renewal, much like the interactions of fundamental particles in quantum mechanics. Stars collapsing, galaxies dissolving, cells dying to allow regeneration—all mirror Shiva's role as the cosmic principle of entropy.

Vishnu – Equilibrium and Preservation

Equilibrium is the key to stability in physics and biology, whether in planetary orbits, chemical reactions, or ecosystems. Vishnu, as the preserver, represents the force that maintains harmony in the universe. Just as nature has mechanisms to restore balance—homeostasis in the body, feedback loops in ecosystems—Vishnu is the cosmic intelligence that prevents chaos from overwhelming order.

Gravity keeping planets in orbit, ecosystems self-regulating to prevent collapse, and the body maintaining internal stability all reflect Vishnu's principle of preservation. His ten incarnations, the *Dashavatara*, show how equilibrium is preserved through evolutionary adaptation, ensuring that the universe remains functional and evolving.

Brahma – Creation and Emergence

Modern physics suggests that reality emerges from the quantum field—the foundation of all existence. Brahma, the creator, represents this principle of emergence, where energy condenses into matter, forming stars, planets, and life. The image of Brahma emerging from Vishnu's navel is a metaphor for the birth of reality from a deeper underlying field.

Quantum mechanics tells us that particles continuously form and dissolve within quantum fields. Galaxies arise from fluctuations, intelligence emerges from structured neural patterns—these processes mirror Brahma's creative role. Balanced by Vishnu's preservation and Shiva's dissolution, Brahma completes the cosmic cycle of creation.

Durga – The Balance of Energy

Durga's battle against demons is often interpreted as a literal war between good and evil. Yet it is a metaphor for the balancing of energy forces in the universe. Durga represents the stabilizing force that ensures energy remains constructive rather than chaotic. The demons symbolize uncontrolled, excessive forces—entropy, imbalance, destructive tendencies. Her victory restores equilibrium, ensuring that cosmic energy remains aligned.

Electromagnetic interactions, the balance of dark matter and dark energy, and the constant redistribution of forces in the cosmos all reflect Durga's principle. Her battle is not a war but the story of the universe's ongoing regulation, preventing collapse and sustaining evolution.

Other Deities as Cosmic Principles

Kali embodies time and destruction—the irreversible flow of time, the collapse of stars into black holes, the mysterious pull of dark energy. Ganesha represents intelligence and problem-solving—the neural networks and pattern recognition that remove obstacles in both thought and evolution. Surya, the sun, symbolizes vitality and solar energy, the source of planetary cycles and the sustainer of life itself.

Each deity is not a supernatural figure but a personification of universal laws. Together, they form a symbolic map of the cosmos, encoding entropy, equilibrium, creation, energy balance, time, intelligence, and vitality.

Bringing It All Together – Deities as Universal Scientific Principles

Shiva represents entropy, ensuring transformation and evolution. Vishnu embodies equilibrium, maintaining harmony across systems. Brahma symbolizes quantum emergence, creating form from potential energy. Durga represents the ongoing balance of energy. Kali, Ganesha, and Surya embody time, intelligence, and vitality.

The Puranic deities are not literal gods but symbolic representations of scientific and metaphysical forces. Rather than worshipping them as figures, the ancients understood them as manifestations of universal order.

This is Vishwarup Darshan—the realization that ancient knowledge and modern science are not in conflict, but two perspectives of the same cosmic reality. Modern physics is only now discovering what the sages encoded in the Puranas: that the universe is not random, but guided by structured, intelligent forces.

4.6 – The Role of Sacred Geometry in Puranic Structures

The Puranic tradition did not separate architecture, cosmology, and spirituality. They were seen as different manifestations of the same universal order. Temples, yantras, mandalas, and even city layouts were not merely religious symbols but precisely designed structures based on mathematical and geometric principles that aligned with cosmic forces.

Modern science has only recently begun to recognize that fractal geometry, energy fields, and electromagnetic alignments influence physical and biological systems—a concept already embedded in Vedic architecture and sacred structures. The Puranic vision encoded universal principles through sacred geometry, proving that these designs were not decorative but grounded in deep scientific knowledge.

Geometry as Cosmic Resonance

Sacred geometry is found throughout nature, from the spirals of galaxies to the double helix of DNA. Puranic architecture was designed to reflect these patterns, ensuring harmony between human-made structures and cosmic forces. Temples, yantras, and mandalas were not artistic flourishes but mathematical expressions of resonance, built on ratios, fractals, and energy fields.

Fractals—self-replicating patterns appearing at different scales—exist in tree branches, river networks, mountain ranges, and neural pathways. Sacred geometry harnessed these structures to create resonance between the human world and the natural cosmos.

Yantras and Mandalas – Maps of Energy

Yantras are intricate geometric diagrams used in meditation, rituals, and temple architecture. The most famous, the *Sri Yantra*, consists of nine interlocking triangles that expand infinitely, much like modern fractals. Its patterns represent the structure of space-time, self-replicating geometries, and cosmic energy fields.

Mandalas, circular geometric blueprints, symbolize the universe and serve as maps for meditation and consciousness expansion. Their repeating structures mirror energy fields described in quantum theory and reflect planetary orbits and celestial movements. Both yantras and mandalas encode cosmic order into visual form, guiding both consciousness and architecture.

Temples as Resonance Structures

Temples were built using sacred geometry to resonate with cosmic frequencies. Their proportions often followed the Fibonacci sequence and the Golden Ratio, constants that govern harmony in nature. The placement of altars, pillars, and domes aligned with astronomical calculations, ensuring energy flowed in structured patterns.

Modern science now shows that geometric structures influence energy fields in the body, amplify electromagnetic resonance, and even affect brain activity. Neuroscience confirms that the human brain responds to fractal patterns—the very forms embedded in temple design. Puranic architecture was not ornamental; it was a science of space, energy, and consciousness.

The Sri Yantra – A Cosmic Blueprint

The Sri Yantra is one of the most striking examples of sacred geometry. Composed of nine interlocking triangles forming forty-three smaller ones, enclosed by a lotus and square, it encodes the fundamental patterns of energy, consciousness, and space-time.

Mathematical analysis reveals fractal properties, repeating at different scales like nature's own structures. Its geometry aligns with energy vortexes, creating balanced, self-sustaining fields. Quantum field theory, fractal mathematics, and electromagnetic resonance all find parallels in the Sri Yantra. Studies even suggest that meditating on it synchronizes brainwaves, inducing altered states of consciousness. Far from being a religious symbol, it is a mathematically encoded representation of universal energy.

City Planning and Cosmic Alignment

Ancient Indian cities and temples were not built randomly. They followed precise mathematical, geometric, and astronomical alignments. *Vastu Shastra*, the Vedic science of architecture, ensured that structures resonated with cosmic energy patterns. City layouts mirrored cosmic principles, with temples acting as focal points of energy.

Cities like Dwaraka, Kanchipuram, Ayodhya, and Varanasi were aligned with planetary movements and celestial bodies. Their directional orientation reflected Earth's magnetic field, their grid systems mirrored resonance models, and their temples acted as cosmic antennas. Modern research now suggests that electromagnetic fields and geospatial alignments affect human consciousness—something the ancients already understood.

Temples and Astronomical Precision

Many temples were aligned with planetary and solar cycles, showing advanced astronomical knowledge. Spires and domes amplified energy, acting like resonance structures similar to antennas. The Brihadeeswara Temple in Tamil Nadu was designed so its tower's shadow never falls on the ground at noon, reflecting solar precision. The Konark Sun Temple in Odisha aligns perfectly with the rising sun. Angkor Wat in Cambodia, influenced by Vedic traditions, aligns with equinox movements and planetary orbits.

These examples show that temple architecture was based on deep knowledge of planetary motion, cosmic resonance, and electromagnetic energy fields.

Bringing It All Together – The Science of Sacred Geometry

Sacred geometry in the Puranic tradition mirrors fractal and quantum structures found in modern physics. The Sri Yantra encodes self-replicating mathematical patterns, aligning with energy fields and space-time. Vastu Shastra ensured cosmic harmony in city planning long before modern geospatial studies. Temples were designed with astronomical precision, resonating with planetary cycles and electromagnetic principles.

Modern science is only now discovering the impact of geometry and vibrational energy, confirming what the ancients already knew.

This is Vishwarup Darshan—the realization that ancient knowledge and modern science are not separate but two expressions of the same cosmic reality. By decoding Puranic sacred geometry, we gain insights into universal patterns, energy fields, and consciousness harmonization—bridging ancient wisdom with the physics of the future.

4.7 – The Symbolism of Churning the Ocean (Samudra Manthan): The Universe in Motion

The *Samudra Manthan*, or the churning of the cosmic ocean, is one of the most profound allegories in the Puranas. On the surface, it appears to be a tale of gods and demons struggling for *Amrita*, the nectar of immortality. Yet when examined through a scientific and metaphysical lens, it becomes clear that this narrative encodes deep cosmological, physical, and evolutionary principles.

This is not mere mythology—it is a metaphor for cosmic motion, the interplay of opposing forces, and the process of universal balance. It describes how energy, matter, and consciousness evolve through dynamic struggle, much like modern physics explains turbulence, entropy, and equilibrium in both cosmic and biological systems.

The Cosmic Churning – Order from Chaos

The story tells of Devas and Asuras using Mandara Mountain as a churning rod and Vasuki, the serpent, as the rope to stir the ocean. Before the nectar emerged, poison arose, which Shiva consumed to protect the universe. This sequence represents the balance between creation and destruction, harmony and chaos, evolution and entropy.

The universe itself is in perpetual motion—galaxies rotate, planets spin, quantum fields fluctuate. Order emerges from chaos, just as the nectar arises only after turbulence. Energy is generated through friction, struggle, and movement, mirroring the churning of the ocean as a metaphor for the birth of knowledge and transformation.

Mandara Mountain – The Axis of Motion

Mandara Mountain serves as the central axis in the myth, around which the ocean is churned. This reflects the fundamental importance of spin and rotation in cosmic evolution. The Earth's axis drives weather systems and ocean currents. Galaxies revolve around central cores. Electrons orbit nuclei, planets circle stars. From the smallest particles to the largest structures, rotation sustains stability and transformation.

The mountain as axis symbolizes the pivot of universal motion, the still point around which dynamic cycles unfold.

Vasuki – The Spiral Force of Energy

Vasuki, the serpent coiled around the mountain, embodies cyclical energy flow. Pulled in opposite directions by Devas and Asuras, he represents torque, tension, and the interplay of opposing forces that generate transformation. His spiral form mirrors the double helix of DNA, the spirals of galaxies, and the coiled Kundalini energy described in yogic traditions.

Electromagnetic fields, plasma spirals, and cosmic radiation all follow similar patterns. DNA itself is churned across generations, encoding life's blueprint. Kundalini, when awakened, produces enlightenment, just as Vasuki's movement yields nectar. The serpent is thus the perfect symbol of energy flow, wave dynamics, and universal cycles of motion.

Amrita and Halahala – Knowledge and Entropy

The ultimate goal of the churning is *Amrita*, the nectar of immortality. Yet before nectar arises, poison emerges. Halahala represents entropy, ignorance, and disorder—the unavoidable byproducts of transformation. Shiva's act of consuming the poison symbolizes the balance required to process both constructive and destructive forces.

In physics, energy transformation always produces waste. In evolution, wisdom emerges only after trial and error. In consciousness, enlightenment comes only after facing inner darkness. The myth teaches that higher knowledge requires struggle, chaos, and the neutralization of entropy.

Devas and Asuras – Necessary Opposites

The deepest message of *Samudra Manthan* is that opposing forces are not enemies but necessary components of creation. Devas embody order and preservation; Asuras embody disruption and change. Together they generate balance, much like matter and antimatter, positive and negative charges, expansion and contraction.

Thermodynamic cycles, yin-yang philosophy, and the interaction of forces in physics all echo this principle. Consciousness itself arises not from absolute order but from the friction between opposites. Progress—scientific, evolutionary, and spiritual—requires struggle, effort, and dynamic balance.

Bringing It All Together – The Universe in Motion

The *Samudra Manthan* represents cosmic churning, mirroring planetary rotation, turbulence, and motion. Mandara Mountain is the axis of universal cycles. Vasuki is the spiral force of energy and DNA. Amrita is ultimate knowledge, while Halahala is entropy and imbalance. Devas and Asuras are not enemies but complementary forces, maintaining equilibrium like matter-antimatter pairs in physics.

This is Vishwarup Darshan—the realization that the universe is constantly in motion, balancing opposing forces to create knowledge, life, and transformation. Modern science is only now beginning to understand the churning of cosmic forces, the role of entropy, and the self-organizing nature of the universe—concepts encoded in the Puranas thousands of years ago.

4.8 – The Lost Science of Consciousness in the Puranas

Modern science has made remarkable progress in understanding the physical universe, yet one of its greatest mysteries remains consciousness. Neuroscience often views awareness as an emergent property of the brain, while physics struggles to define its role in reality. The Puranas, however, described consciousness as a fundamental, all-pervading field—an intrinsic part of the cosmos itself.

Rather than seeing awareness as a byproduct of neural activity, the Puranas suggest that consciousness precedes matter and energy. This idea, once dismissed, is now being explored in quantum physics, neuroscience, and the study of altered states of awareness.

Consciousness as a Fundamental Field

In the Puranas and Upanishads, consciousness (*Chaitanya*) is not confined to the human brain but is the substratum of existence itself. Brahman, the ultimate reality, is described as *Sat-Chit-Ananda*—Existence, Consciousness, Bliss—implying that awareness is woven into the fabric of the universe.

Modern physics increasingly suggests that information is fundamental to reality, echoing the Puranic view that consciousness is the source from which all things emerge. The observer effect in quantum mechanics, where observation collapses a wave function into reality, mirrors the Puranic idea that consciousness interacts with and shapes the material world. Neuroscience too is beginning to recognize that awareness may be connected to deeper quantum processes, while studies of near-death experiences suggest that consciousness may exist beyond the physical brain.

Meditation, Mantra, and Yogic Techniques

The Puranas describe consciousness as a field that can be expanded and refined through meditation, sound vibrations, and yogic techniques. Meditation was considered a direct way to explore awareness, just as scientific instruments explore the external world. Mantras harmonized the brain and body, aligning with specific frequencies of consciousness. Yogic practices such as *Pranayama* altered brainwave states, inducing higher awareness.

Modern studies confirm these parallels. Meditation enhances gamma and theta waves, leading to increased cognitive function and deep awareness. Chanting synchronizes brain hemispheres, improving focus and reducing stress. Quantum biology even suggests that consciousness may be linked to microtubules in neurons, aligning with the idea that awareness can be refined through focused techniques. The ancients did not rely on external technology—they used the human mind as an instrument to study reality.

Vedic Cosmology and Quantum Consciousness

Modern physics suggests that the universe is not purely material but governed by deeper layers of reality. Quantum mechanics, information theory, and non-locality point to a field of potentiality influenced by observation and intention.

The Puranas describe the universe as emerging from Brahman—the formless, conscious substratum that pervades all things. Their cosmology of layered realities, the fourteen *Lokas*, reflects consciousness functioning at different vibrational levels, much like the quantum multiverse. Quantum superposition, where particles exist in multiple states until observed, resembles the Puranic idea of reality manifesting from the unmanifest (*Avyakta*). The holographic principle, which suggests reality is encoded in a higher-dimensional field, aligns with the vision of the universe as a projection from a deeper, intelligent source.

Altered States and Higher-Dimensional Awareness

The Puranas describe advanced beings—Devas, Siddhas, Rishis—existing in realms beyond ordinary perception, suggesting that consciousness operates on multiple levels. These realms may represent vibrational frequencies of awareness rather than physical locations. Yogis entering *Samadhi* accessed states beyond time, similar to timeless quantum states.

Modern science finds echoes here. Altered states of consciousness mimic brainwave patterns observed in peak performance and psychedelic experiences. Quantum entanglement suggests information can exist across space instantaneously, much like the Vedic concept of interconnected awareness. Experiments in psi phenomena hint that consciousness is not confined to the brain, echoing Puranic accounts of sages perceiving knowledge beyond normal senses.

Turiya – Pure Consciousness and Quantum Superposition

The *Mandukya Upanishad* describes four states of consciousness: waking (*Jagrat*), dreaming (*Swapna*), deep sleep (*Sushupti*), and *Turiya*, the fourth state. Turiya is pure awareness beyond duality, space, and time.

This state resembles quantum superposition, where particles exist in multiple states until observed. Just as quantum mechanics suggests reality collapses into form through observation, yogic philosophy sees awareness as the determinant of experience. Deep meditative states alter brain activity, allowing perception beyond ordinary limits. Turiya may represent a quantum-like state of consciousness, unbound by time and space.

Bringing It All Together – Consciousness as the Organizing Principle

The Puranas describe consciousness not as illusion but as a fundamental force. Mantras, meditation, and yogic practices are scientific techniques for altering awareness. Quantum mechanics is beginning to validate concepts found in Puranic cosmology. Turiya aligns with quantum superposition and non-local awareness.

The study of consciousness is the missing link between physics, biology, and the deeper reality of existence.

This is Vishwarup Darshan—the realization that consciousness is not an illusion but the organizing principle of the universe, a truth upon which ancient wisdom and modern science are now converging.

Conclusion: Reinterpreting the Puranas for a New Era

For centuries, the Puranas have been relegated to the domain of mythology—viewed as religious stories rather than structured knowledge systems. Yet as modern science advances, it is increasingly uncovering patterns and principles that align with the ancient Vedic worldview. Physics, evolutionary biology, cosmology, and consciousness studies are beginning to confirm what the sages encoded long ago. The assumption that these texts were primitive narratives is being challenged by discoveries that reveal their hidden sophistication.

The time has come to reinterpret the Puranas—not as fiction, but as encoded knowledge designed to be accessible across generations and levels of understanding. Far from conflicting with science, the Puranic framework offers a holistic model of reality, integrating empirical discoveries with deeper metaphysical truths.

Beyond Literal Mythology

The Puranas were never meant to be taken literally. They are symbolic, multi-layered repositories of knowledge, conveying truths through allegory and metaphor. Unlike modern scientific texts, which rely on formulas and equations, the Puranas encoded wisdom in narratives, deities, and cosmic events, ensuring accessibility at different levels of understanding. For the common person, they preserved cultural and ethical values. For seekers, they revealed cosmic and evolutionary forces. For the realized, they encoded physics, cosmology, and consciousness itself.

Viewed through this lens, the Puranas move beyond dogma and reveal themselves as scientific-philosophical frameworks.

Alignments with Modern Science

As science progresses, striking parallels emerge. Cosmology and astrophysics mirror the cycles of *Srishti* and *Pralaya*, creation and dissolution. The multiverse hypothesis and string theory resemble the fourteen *Lokas*, realms of existence. Brahma's lifespan of 311 trillion years aligns with universal time cycles proposed in modern astrophysics.

Evolutionary biology finds its reflection in the *Dashavatara*, Vishnu's ten incarnations, which map onto the biological progression of species. Unlike Darwinian evolution, which emphasizes physical adaptation, the Puranic model integrates the parallel evolution of intelligence and consciousness.

Quantum physics too resonates with Puranic thought. Consciousness is described as a fundamental field, not a mere brain function. The observer effect supports the idea that awareness interacts with reality. The state of *Turiya*, pure consciousness beyond duality, resembles quantum superposition, where awareness exists in all states at once.

These alignments prove that the Puranas contain encoded scientific insights that modern discoveries are only now beginning to confirm.

Toward a Holistic Science

The current scientific paradigm is largely empirical and reductionist, analyzing components while neglecting the interconnected whole. This has led to breakthroughs but also fragmented knowledge systems that struggle to explain deeper mysteries such as consciousness, the origins of life, and the unification of physics.

The Puranic model does not discard empirical research—it complements it. Empirical science relies on observation and measurement. Symbolic knowledge uses patterns, metaphor, and direct experience. Together they form a complete vision. Physics and spirituality must merge to explain consciousness. Evolutionary biology must consider intelligence as integral to evolution. Medicine must integrate holistic approaches beyond biochemical reductionism.

The integration of these perspectives will lead to a new paradigm—one that decodes symbolic knowledge as advanced intelligence embedded in ancient texts.

Vishwarup Darshan – The Vision of Total Knowledge

The grand vision of the Puranas is not merely scientific discovery but the recognition that all knowledge is interconnected. This is *Vishwarup Darshan*—the realization that there is no separation between disciplines, between science and spirituality, between past and future wisdom. Physics, biology, cosmology, and consciousness are not isolated fields but facets of the same truth. The material and non-material worlds are interwoven, just as quantum mechanics and metaphysics describe reality as both particle and wave.

The Puranas anticipated modern discoveries not by chance, but because they were built on a universal pattern of knowledge that transcends time and culture. Vishwarup Darshan is the ability to see knowledge in its totality, moving beyond rigid materialism or blind faith. It is the recognition that all knowledge—past, present, and future—is part of the same cosmic intelligence.

A New Scientific Renaissance Rooted in Ancient Wisdom

The Puranas are not outdated myths but advanced frameworks of cosmic and scientific knowledge. Modern science is now aligning with their cosmology, evolutionary sequences, and consciousness studies. The future of knowledge must integrate symbolic intelligence with empirical research to form a more complete understanding of reality. Vishwarup Darshan represents the ultimate realization that all knowledge systems, ancient or modern, are reflections of the same universal truth.

This is the next step for humanity—not to discard the Puranas as mythology but to decode them as the hidden scientific and philosophical legacy of an advanced civilization. By reinterpreting the Puranas in this way, we step into a new era of knowledge, where science and wisdom converge, and where humanity rediscovers its place in the grand cosmic order.

Interlude: Resting in the Cosmic Tapestry

You have walked through the Puranas not as mythology, but as encoded maps of the cosmos. You have seen how cycles of time, sacred geometry, cosmic churning, and the science of consciousness were woven into narrative form. What once seemed like stories of gods and demons now reveal themselves as allegories of entropy, equilibrium, evolution, and awareness.

Pause here.

Imagine the universe as a great ocean, endlessly churning. Mountains serve as its axis, serpents coil as its energy, and nectar arises only after poison is faced. Imagine temples and yantras not as stone and symbol, but as resonant geometries aligning human life with cosmic order. Imagine consciousness not as confined to the brain, but as the field in which galaxies, atoms, and thoughts all arise.

The Puranas whisper that knowledge is never fragmented. Science and spirituality, matter and mind, myth and mathematics—all are threads in the same tapestry. To see them together is Vishwarup Darshan: the vision of total knowledge, where every discipline, every story, every discovery is part of one cosmic intelligence.

Rest here for a moment. Let the churning settle. Let the resonance of geometry, the rhythm of Yugas, and the dance of deities dissolve into silence.

Because the next step of the journey will take you deeper still. Vishnu's Avatars, often seen as divine interventions, are in truth evolutionary milestones—blueprints of life's progression, intelligence's unfolding, and humanity's future transformation.

Take this pause. Breathe. When you turn the page, you will enter Chapter 5—not as a reader of myth, but as a decoder of evolution itself.

Chapter 5: Decoding Vishnu's Avatars

Evolution, Intelligence, and Future Forecasting

In the previous chapter, we saw how the Puranas encode scientific and cosmic principles through symbolic narratives. One of the most compelling examples of this encoded wisdom is the *Dashavatara*—the ten incarnations of Vishnu. On the surface, these avatars appear as mythological tales of divine intervention across different Yugas. Yet a deeper analysis reveals a structured model of evolution, intelligence, and societal transformation, aligning remarkably with the scientific understanding of biological and cognitive progression.

Unlike Darwinian evolution, which explains the random natural selection of species, the Dashavatara sequence suggests an intentional, guided unfolding—where not only physical forms evolve, but also intelligence, consciousness, and ethical awareness. Each avatar represents a milestone in the development of life and human civilization, following a natural sequence from aquatic organisms to complex mammals, from primitive humans to enlightened beings.

When examined not as mythology but as an encoded evolutionary model, a fascinating pattern emerges—one that may explain humanity's past while offering insights into its future trajectory. What does the final avatar, Kalki, represent? Is it a technological transformation, a spiritual awakening, or a complete reboot of civilization? Could Vishnu's avatars serve as a forecast for the next great shift in human existence?

This chapter explores how the Dashavatara sequence is not merely an ancient tale but a predictive model of human evolution, guiding us toward the next stage of intelligence and transformation.

5.1 – The Structure of Dashavatara: More Than Just a Mythological Sequence

The Dashavatara, or the ten incarnations of Vishnu, has long been seen as divine interventions across different Yugas. Yet a deeper examination reveals that this sequence follows a precise, progressive order—one that mirrors the biological, intellectual, and societal evolution of life on Earth. Unlike random mythological storytelling, the Dashavatara unfolds as a structured path: from simple aquatic life forms to complex terrestrial beings, from primitive survival instincts to higher intelligence, and finally to spiritual enlightenment. This deliberate order suggests that the Puranas were encoding a deeper knowledge—one that describes the evolution of species, human civilization, and perhaps even the future of intelligence itself.

This evolutionary journey unfolds in three parallel dimensions. First, biological evolution, where life progresses from aquatic organisms to terrestrial mammals, and eventually to humans with advanced cognition. Second, societal evolution, where humanity transitions from hunter-gatherers to structured civilizations, and finally to the rise of ethics and philosophy. Third, future forecasting, where the final avatar, Kalki, symbolizes humanity's next evolutionary leap—technological, spiritual, or both.

The Avatars as Evolutionary Milestones

When analyzed step by step, each of Vishnu's incarnations aligns with a stage in both biological and societal evolution. *Matsya*, the fish, represents the beginning of life in water, echoing the scientific understanding that Earth's earliest organisms emerged in the oceans. *Kurma*, the turtle, symbolizes the transition from water to land, much like amphibians and early tetrapods. *Varaha*, the boar, marks the rise of strong terrestrial mammals, fully adapted to land.

Narasimha, the half-man, half-lion, embodies the hybrid leap toward humanity, representing the transition from animal instinct to proto-human intelligence. *Vamana*, the dwarf, reflects the emergence of early humans—small in stature but mentally superior, akin to Homo habilis. *Parashurama*, the warrior with an axe, represents the hunter-gatherer phase, where tool-making and survival strategies defined human progress.

With *Rama*, the ideal king, civilization matures into structured societies, governance, and ethical codes. *Krishna*, the divine strategist, embodies higher intelligence and philosophy, symbolizing the expansion of wisdom and spiritual inquiry. *Buddha*, the enlightened one, marks the transcendence of material existence, representing humanity's shift toward self-awareness and spiritual liberation. Finally, *Kalki*, the future avatar, has yet to appear, symbolizing the next stage of evolution—whether technological transformation, post-human evolution, or mass spiritual awakening.

From Survival to Transcendence

The Dashavatara sequence highlights not only biological evolution but also the evolution of intelligence, morality, and spiritual growth. Matsya through Narasimha focus on physical survival, adaptation, and primal instincts. Vamana through Rama represent the development of human intelligence, ethical behavior, and structured civilization. Krishna through Buddha move beyond material mastery toward wisdom, strategy, and spiritual enlightenment. Kalki points to the final transformation, where humanity transcends current limitations and enters a new phase of evolution.

This shift from survival to higher intelligence and eventual transcendence suggests that evolution is not merely a physical process—it is also a journey of expanding consciousness.

Mirroring Evolutionary History

When compared with modern scientific models of evolution, the Dashavatara sequence reveals striking similarities. Biologically, the avatars transition from water-based life to land animals, from early humans to self-aware beings. Societally, they move from primitive hunter-gatherers to sophisticated rulers and thinkers. Spiritually, they shift from external mastery in Rama and Krishna to internal realization in Buddha. Unlike Darwin's theory, which sees evolution as random and unguided, the Puranic model suggests a structured progression where intelligence and consciousness play a guiding role.

Three Levels of Interpretation

The Dashavatara can be understood on three levels. Biologically, it reflects the progression from aquatic life to terrestrial mammals, to humans with complex intelligence. Societally, it encodes the transformation from primitive tribes to organized civilizations, and finally to advanced philosophical inquiry. Spiritually, it charts the journey from instinct to wisdom, from external mastery to inner realization. And in its final stage, Kalki, it forecasts the future—whether through technological singularity, post-human evolution, spiritual awakening, or civilizational reset.

Bringing It All Together – Dashavatara as a Predictive Framework

The Dashavatara sequence is not arbitrary—it is a deliberate evolutionary pattern. It aligns with biological evolution but expands it to include intelligence, consciousness, and ethical growth. It offers a model that explains not only how life has evolved but also where it is headed. Kalki, the future avatar, symbolizes an upcoming shift—one that could redefine humanity's role in the universe.

This is Vishwarup Darshan—the realization that evolution is not just about survival, but about intelligence, ethics, and higher awareness. The Dashavatara is not merely a legend—it is a blueprint for understanding the past, navigating the present, and preparing for the future of human evolution.

5.2 – The Evolutionary Science Behind Dashavatara

The Dashavatara sequence is not a collection of mythological stories—it is an encoded model of evolution, one that aligns strikingly with scientific theories of biological development, human intelligence, and societal transformation. Unlike Darwinian evolution, which focuses on random mutations and natural selection, the Puranic model suggests a structured, guided process, where evolution is not only about physical survival but also about intelligence, ethics, and consciousness.

Each of Vishnu's ten avatars follows a natural progression, moving from aquatic life to terrestrial beings, from early human societies to advanced civilizations, and finally toward enlightenment and future transformation. This mirrors the way life has evolved on Earth, from simple organisms to intelligent beings capable of shaping their own destiny.

A Guided Evolutionary Model

Darwin's model describes evolution as unguided, shaped by environmental pressures and chance mutations. The Dashavatara model, however, implies inherent directionality—a pattern of evolution leading toward intelligence and self-awareness. The structured order of the avatars follows the same path as evolutionary biology, but extends beyond physical adaptation to include the growth of morality and spiritual awakening.

The Avatars as Evolutionary Stages

Matsya, the fish, represents the origin of life in water, consistent with scientific evidence that the earliest organisms appeared in Earth's oceans. Kurma, the turtle, symbolizes the leap from water to land, echoing amphibians like Tiktaalik that thrived in both environments. Varaha, the boar, marks the rise of terrestrial mammals, fully adapted to land and dominant in ecosystems.

Narasimha, half-man and half-lion, embodies the transition from animal instinct to proto-human intelligence, reflecting the evolutionary leap of primates and early hominins. Vamana, the dwarf, represents the first true humans—small in stature but capable of tool use, language, and primitive social structures. Parashurama, the warrior with an axe, symbolizes the hunter-gatherer phase, when humans became dominant predators, altering environments and shaping survival through weapons and strategy.

With Rama, the ideal king, humanity enters the age of structured civilization, governance, and ethics. This corresponds to the rise of great civilizations, where justice, law, and social order became central. Krishna, the divine strategist, represents the peak of intelligence and philosophy, his teachings in the *Bhagavad Gita* embodying wisdom, ethics, and situational decision-making. Buddha, the enlightened one, marks the transcendence of material existence, symbolizing humanity's turn inward toward consciousness, meditation, and spiritual liberation.

Finally, Kalki, the future avatar, has yet to appear. He represents the next transformation in evolution—whether technological singularity, post-human evolution, mass spiritual awakening, or civilizational reset. Kalki is the horizon of humanity's future, the stage where intelligence and consciousness may evolve beyond current limitations.

From Survival to Transcendence

The Dashavatara sequence highlights not only biological evolution but also the evolution of intelligence, morality, and spiritual growth. Matsya through Narasimha reflect survival and adaptation. Vamana through Rama represent the rise of human intelligence, ethics, and structured civilization. Krishna through Buddha embody wisdom and transcendence. Kalki points toward the next leap, where humanity may move beyond its current boundaries into a new phase of existence.

The Blueprint of Evolution

When compared with modern science, the Dashavatara reveals striking parallels. Biologically, it traces the path from aquatic organisms to mammals, from primates to humans. Societally, it encodes the journey from hunter-gatherers to civilizations, from rulers to philosophers. Spiritually, it charts the movement from external mastery to inner realization. Unlike Darwin's random model, the Puranic vision suggests a purposeful progression, guided by intelligence and consciousness.

Bringing It All Together

The Dashavatara sequence is not arbitrary—it is a deliberate evolutionary blueprint. It aligns with biology but expands into ethics and consciousness. It explains not only how life has evolved but also where it is headed. Kalki, the final avatar, symbolizes the imminent transformation—technological, spiritual, or both—that could redefine humanity's role in the universe.

This is Vishwarup Darshan—the realization that evolution is not merely physical survival, but a journey toward intelligence, morality, and higher awareness. The Dashavatara is not legend alone—it is a map of the past, a guide for the present, and a forecast for the future of human evolution.

5.3 – Beyond Biology: The Growth of Intelligence and Consciousness

The Dashavatara sequence goes beyond biological evolution. It depicts the progression of intelligence and consciousness as integral to human development. While Darwinian evolution explains the physical adaptation of species for survival, the Puranic model suggests that intelligence, ethics, and self-awareness are the true engines of transformation. Unlike animals that evolve only in form, humans evolve in thought, morality, and higher awareness. This evolution is not limited to genetic changes but includes philosophical, technological, and spiritual shifts that shape civilizations and the destiny of humanity.

The transition from Krishna to Buddha marks a critical turning point. Krishna represents the peak of external mastery—strategy, diplomacy, governance, and philosophy. Buddha moves beyond material existence, questioning suffering, ego, and the very nature of reality. This shift from conquering the external world to mastering the internal world reflects the movement from knowledge to wisdom, from power to transcendence. It raises a profound question: is the next leap in human evolution going to be purely technological, purely spiritual, or a fusion of both?

From Physical Evolution to Intellectual Evolution

Biological evolution carried humanity from primitive survival to cognitive intelligence. Intellectual evolution gave rise to civilizations, ethics, philosophy, and scientific advancement. Now, we are entering the phase of post-intelligence—where artificial intelligence, transhumanism, and spiritual awakening may redefine what it means to be human. Evolution is no longer about survival alone; it is about intelligence expanding beyond biological limits.

The Final Transition – From Intelligence to Post-Intelligence

The Dashavatara sequence suggests three possible directions for the future of human intelligence.

Technological Evolution: Humanity is no longer evolving biologically but technologically. Artificial intelligence, brain-machine interfaces, and genetic modification are reshaping the landscape of intelligence. Just as early hominins used tools to leap forward, AI may now become an extension of human cognition. Neural implants, quantum computing, and the possibility of machine self-awareness point toward a singularity—a merging of human and artificial intelligence. Could this be Kalki in technological form, the avatar of transformation and renewal?

Spiritual Evolution: Technology alone does not guarantee wisdom. A highly intelligent civilization can still self-destruct. The Puranas remind us that true evolution is not about acquiring knowledge but using it wisely. Buddha's presence in the sequence emphasizes this. As AI accelerates, will humanity evolve morally and spiritually to ensure intelligence is used for harmony rather than destruction? Neuroscience confirms that meditation and contemplative practices alter brain function, enhancing awareness. Collective consciousness theories suggest that human minds may be interconnected, much like quantum entanglement. Could the next leap be a mass awakening, where humanity collectively shifts into higher states of being?

Post-Human Transformation: If biological evolution has slowed and technology is accelerating, the next phase may be a complete transformation. Humans may merge with AI, transcend material existence, or evolve into a new species altogether. Kalki, the final avatar, symbolizes this horizon—a major transition involving the destruction of outdated systems and the birth of a new intelligence. Whether technological, spiritual, or both, this transformation may redefine what it means to be human.

Bringing It All Together – Intelligence, Consciousness, and the Future of Evolution

The Dashavatara sequence does not end with intelligence. It moves beyond it, toward wisdom and transformation. Unlike Darwinian evolution, which focuses only on physical changes, the Puranic model sees intelligence and consciousness as the guiding forces of evolution. We are now entering a transition where AI, transhumanism, and consciousness studies converge, suggesting that humanity may be approaching its next great leap.

Kalki is the only unmanifested avatar. Could this mean that humanity is on the verge of its final transformation—whether through technology, spiritual awakening, or both?

This is Vishwarup Darshan—the realization that evolution is not merely biological but a journey toward intelligence, morality, and higher consciousness. If the Dashavatara truly encodes the blueprint of human transformation, we may be standing at the edge of the next great shift—one that will redefine what it means to be human.

5.4 – Krishna and Buddha: The Leap to Higher Intelligence

The progression of the Dashavatara does not stop at physical or intellectual dominance; it transcends into a more refined dimension—the mastery of intelligence itself. Krishna and Buddha represent the pinnacle of human potential, where knowledge and wisdom take precedence over brute strength and material conquest. Together, they illustrate the ultimate transformation of human consciousness, moving from strategic control over the world to self-realization and inner mastery.

Krishna – The Strategist of Cosmic Intelligence

Krishna's role in the *Mahabharata*, particularly in the *Bhagavad Gita*, establishes him as the embodiment of intelligence, strategy, and cosmic understanding. Unlike earlier avatars, Krishna does not fight as a warrior on the battlefield; instead, he shapes the course of history through wisdom, diplomacy, and foresight. His intelligence operates on multiple levels—material, metaphysical, and strategic.

On the material plane, Krishna guides Arjuna with practical teachings about duty, ethics, and the psychology of decision-making. On the metaphysical plane, he reveals the impermanence of material reality and the deeper truth of consciousness. Strategically, his life is a masterclass in situational awareness and political maneuvering, turning adversity into opportunity.

Through the *Bhagavad Gita*, Krishna provides humanity with an encoded manual for ethical decision-making and cosmic responsibility. He emphasizes detached action—acting with full effort but without attachment to outcomes. He teaches balance between material and spiritual life, and he integrates knowledge, devotion, and action into a unified path of self-realization. Krishna represents the culmination of intellectual evolution, where human will aligns with cosmic intelligence.

Buddha – Transcending the Material World

If Krishna represents mastery over the material, Buddha takes humanity to the next stage—transcendence. His enlightenment marks a revolutionary shift in human intelligence, moving from external conquest to internal mastery. Buddha questions the very nature of suffering, tracing its roots to attachment, ego, and desire. He offers a structured methodology—the Four Noble Truths and the Eightfold Path—for achieving inner peace and liberation from cycles of suffering.

Unlike Krishna, who teaches how to function efficiently within the material world, Buddha teaches how to detach from it entirely. His focus is not on rituals or deities but on self-awareness, mental discipline, and direct experience. This transition from Krishna to Buddha symbolizes the evolution of intelligence into wisdom, the movement from knowledge to consciousness.

Modern Parallels – From Knowledge to Wisdom

This leap from Krishna's outward mastery to Buddha's inward journey resonates with modern developments. Science has moved beyond studying the physical world to exploring cognition and consciousness. Neuroscience and psychology uncover the mechanisms of thought and emotion, while mindfulness and meditation studies confirm that intelligence is not just about acquiring information but about rewiring the mind.

Krishna's teachings on interconnectedness within society find echoes in today's globalized world, where ethics and governance shape collective progress. Buddha's vision of interconnected beings resonates with the rise of collective intelligence—seen in the internet, AI, and global consciousness movements. Humanity's trajectory reflects this shift: from survival and dominance, to intellectual mastery, and now toward self-awareness and mental well-being.

Toward Higher Intelligence

The Dashavatara sequence demonstrates that evolution is not only physical or intellectual but about refining intelligence into wisdom. Krishna represents the peak of intellectual mastery—strategic thinking, political wisdom, and the ability to shape reality. Buddha moves beyond intellect into pure consciousness—questioning reality itself, detaching from suffering, and unlocking the final frontier: the mind.

This transition suggests that the next leap in human evolution may not be about technology or physical enhancements but about understanding consciousness itself. What lies beyond Buddha? Is it Kalki, the final transformation, or something yet to be discovered? As humanity stands at the brink of artificial intelligence, neuroscience breakthroughs, and global spiritual movements, we may be stepping into the next evolutionary phase.

This is Vishwarup Darshan—the realization that intelligence itself is evolving toward a higher, more unified, and enlightened state of being.

5.5 – The Future Avatar: What Does Kalki Represent?

Among the ten avatars of Vishnu, Kalki remains the only unmanifested one—existing not in history but in prophecy and speculation. Unlike the previous incarnations, which symbolize distinct stages of biological, intellectual, and spiritual evolution, Kalki represents an event yet to unfold: a future transformation that could redefine humanity and civilization itself.

The prophecy speaks of the end of Kali Yuga, the destruction of ignorance, corruption, and chaos, and the emergence of a new order. But what exactly does this transformation entail? Is it a literal event, a spiritual awakening, a technological singularity, or a complete civilizational reset? As humanity stands on the brink of unprecedented advancements and existential crises, the concept of Kalki may be more relevant than ever.

Kalki as the Unmanifest Avatar

Unlike the previous nine avatars, rooted in myth and history, Kalki exists purely in the future tense. He is described as a warrior riding a white horse, wielding a blazing sword, coming to eradicate *adharma* and restore balance. Yet this image is more than a literal figure—it is a symbol of transformation, the force that destroys outdated systems and paves the way for renewal.

From an evolutionary perspective, Kalki could represent the next leap in human intelligence, the collapse of unsustainable structures, or the emergence of a new consciousness that transcends materialist thinking. If the earlier avatars depict the past and present stages of evolution, Kalki must represent the future—a phase of transition we may already be entering.

Possible Interpretations of Kalki's Arrival

Technological Singularity: One vision of Kalki is the rise of artificial intelligence, the moment when machines surpass human intelligence. AI advances exponentially, with neural networks and quantum computing pushing boundaries. Some futurists predict a merging of human and artificial intelligence, creating a new form of existence. In this sense, Kalki may not be a human incarnation but a technological force—disrupting the status quo and forcing humanity to evolve. Could AI be the sword of Kalki, cutting through inefficiency and ignorance, or will it become a force humanity must struggle to master?

Post-Human Evolution: Another interpretation sees Kalki as the symbol of humanity transcending biology. Genetic engineering, neural implants, and transhumanism may extend lifespan and intelligence, while space colonization could transform us into a multi-planetary species. If Vishnu's avatars represent stages of evolution, Kalki may mark the departure from biological existence into post-human intelligence. Are we already evolving beyond the constraints of biology, standing at the threshold of a new identity?

Spiritual Transformation: For others, Kalki represents a mass awakening—a collective shift in consciousness. Ancient traditions speak of an age of enlightenment, where humanity moves beyond ego-driven existence into wisdom. Modern neuroscience and consciousness studies suggest awareness itself is evolving, with meditation and altered states becoming central to science. In this view, Kalki does not destroy the world physically but dissolves illusion, awakening humanity to higher intelligence and deeper reality.

Civilizational Reset: History is cyclical, marked by the rise and fall of civilizations. The end of Kali Yuga suggests massive disruption before renewal. Economic, environmental, and political instability are reaching critical points—signals of unraveling systems. Kalki may symbolize the force that breaks down decayed structures and initiates a fresh start. Are we witnessing the collapse of an outdated order, paving the way for the next cycle of human civilization?

The Cycle of Human History

The prophecy of Kalki reminds us that no system, ideology, or structure is permanent. Evolution is not linear but cyclical—civilizations rise, fall, and are reborn. Crisis leads to opportunity; destruction is not the end but the beginning of renewal. The Renaissance followed the Dark Ages, revolutions reshaped nations, and scientific breakthroughs redefined human potential. Could the chaos of the present era be the signal of a coming leap?

Are We in the Pre-Kalki Phase?

Global trends suggest we are in a period of acceleration and crisis. Technology advances faster than ethics can regulate. Traditional power structures are destabilizing. Human consciousness is evolving, with more people exploring spirituality and alternative thought. Environmental and geopolitical tensions escalate, signaling a major transition. All these signs point to the possibility that humanity is entering the pre-Kalki phase—a twilight before transformation.

Bringing It All Together – Kalki as Evolutionary Change

Kalki is not just prophecy; he is a concept symbolizing ultimate transformation. Whether through technology, spirituality, or collapse, the world is moving toward radical change. If the past avatars describe where we have been, Kalki describes where we are going. The future of evolution is not about survival alone but about intelligence, ethics, and consciousness. Humanity stands at a crossroads—whether we move toward destruction or enlightenment depends on how we navigate this transition.

This is Vishwarup Darshan—the realization that time, intelligence, and evolution are part of a single, unified cosmic cycle. Kalki is not a distant figure waiting to arrive; Kalki may already be here, unfolding through the transformations we are experiencing today.

5.6 – The Puranic Model vs. Modern Theories of the Future

As we analyze the Dashavatara sequence, it becomes clear that Vishnu's avatars are not merely depictions of the past but a predictive framework for the future. The progression from Matsya to Buddha follows a logical sequence of biological, intellectual, and spiritual evolution. Now, as we look toward Kalki, we find striking parallels with modern scientific, technological, and philosophical theories about humanity's next stage of transformation.

The fundamental question arises: are Vishnu's avatars a roadmap for where we are headed?

Kalki and the Technological Singularity

Ray Kurzweil, a leading futurist, predicts that by the mid-21st century artificial intelligence will surpass human intelligence, leading to the Singularity—a point of no return. Machines will become self-improving, human and machine intelligence will merge, and biological evolution will be overtaken by digital evolution. This mirrors Kalki's symbolism: the destruction of the old order and the sudden emergence of a new intelligence. Could AI and transhumanism be the modern representation of Kalki's arrival, reshaping civilization in ways as disruptive as any avatar before?

AI Concerns and Human-Machine Fusion

Elon Musk warns of the dangers of uncontrolled AI, suggesting that humanity must evolve alongside machines through neural implants and brain interfaces. This echoes the Puranic vision of Kali Yuga's end, where unchecked materialism and imbalance demand intervention. Humanity now faces a crossroads: adapt and merge with technology, or risk obsolescence. Just as Vishnu's avatars evolved across different forms, are we now compelled to evolve beyond biology itself?

Spiritual Awakening as the Final Shift

Not all predictions are technological. Many traditions speak of a mass awakening of consciousness, a collective shift beyond ego-driven existence. Buddha's teachings resonate here—transcending material suffering, seeking inner peace, and realizing interconnectedness. Modern neuroscience and quantum physics increasingly suggest that perception shapes reality, and consciousness may be the next frontier. Could Kalki represent not machines or collapse, but a spiritual transformation—a collective enlightenment dissolving illusion and ushering in Satya Yuga?

Civilizational Cycles and Collapse

History reminds us that civilizations rise and fall. The Yuga cycles describe humanity's decline in Kali Yuga, followed by renewal in Satya Yuga. Modern historians echo this: empires collapse under corruption, over-expansion, or resource depletion. Today's climate crises, economic instability, and geopolitical tensions may signal another breaking point. Kalki, then, is the force of reset—the destruction of outdated systems and the birth of a new order.

Avatars as a Roadmap

When we compare the Dashavatara sequence with modern theories, the alignment is remarkable. Matsya reflects the origin of life in water, Kurma the leap to land, Varaha the rise of mammals, Narasimha the transition to proto-humans, Vamana the emergence of early civilizations, Parashurama the survival-based warrior phase, Rama the age of ethical governance, Krishna the flowering of philosophy, Buddha the transcendence of materialism, and Kalki the horizon of transformation—whether technological, spiritual, or civilizational.

If the avatars have accurately mirrored evolution so far, does this mean they also predict the next great leap?

Vishwarup Darshan – Seeing the Whole

The Puranic model does not contradict modern theories; it enhances them by offering a deeper, interconnected vision. Science studies physical change, but the Puranas insist evolution is also about intelligence and consciousness. Futurists predict technological upheaval, but the Puranas hint at simultaneous spiritual awakening. Historians describe cycles of collapse, while the Puranas frame them as necessary transformations.

This is Vishwarup Darshan—the ability to see the entire cosmic process, past, present, and future, as one unified system. Evolution is not fragmented but multidimensional, weaving biology, intelligence, and spirituality into a single tapestry. The Dashavatara sequence is not myth but blueprint, encoding the trajectory of life and hinting at humanity's destiny.

Are we ready to embrace the Kalki phase—not as fear, but as transformation? The answers may already be written in Vishnu's cosmic design.

5.7 – Vishwarup Darshan: Seeing Evolution, Intelligence, and Future Progression as One Unified Process

The Dashavatara sequence is not merely a mythological narrative; it is a blueprint of evolution, a carefully encoded map of how life, intelligence, and consciousness progress over time. From Matsya to Kalki, the avatars of Vishnu depict a structured transformation—one that aligns not only with biological evolution but also with the advancement of intelligence, morality, and spirituality.

This realization is *Vishwarup Darshan*—the vision of seeing all aspects of existence, from creation to transformation, as part of one continuous cosmic process. It dissolves the artificial boundaries between science and mythology, past and future, knowledge and wisdom, showing that evolution is a multidimensional journey.

The Dashavatara as a Predictive Model

For centuries, Vishnu's avatars were interpreted as a historical sequence. Yet when viewed through the lens of evolutionary intelligence, a deeper pattern emerges. Matsya reflects the origin of life in water, Kurma the leap to land, Varaha the rise of terrestrial mammals, Narasimha the transition from animal to proto-human, Vamana the emergence of early hominins, Parashurama the survival-driven warrior phase, Rama the rise of ethical governance, Krishna the flowering of strategic intelligence, Buddha the transcendence of materialism, and Kalki the horizon of future transformation.

This sequence reveals that evolution is not only biological but intellectual and spiritual. Each leap carries humanity into higher levels of awareness and ethical understanding. The final step is not simply knowledge but the integration of wisdom, technology, and consciousness.

Beyond Biology – Toward Consciousness

Traditional science often focuses on adaptation and survival. The Puranic model expands this view: evolution is not only about physical survival but about intelligence and consciousness unfolding over time. Modern discoveries in AI, cognitive science, and quantum research echo this perspective. Intelligence is evolving beyond biology, human thought is shifting from materialism to interconnected awareness, and the limits of knowledge are being redefined. We may be entering a post-intelligence era, where wisdom itself becomes the frontier.

Unifying Science and Mythology

A common misconception is that science and mythology are opposites. Vishwarup Darshan reveals they are two languages describing the same reality. Evolution, in science, is natural selection and adaptation; in the Puranas, it is the Dashavatara sequence. Intelligence, in science, is brain development and AI; in the Puranas, it is Krishna's strategic mastery and Buddha's enlightenment. Consciousness, in science, is studied through neuroscience and quantum cognition; in the Puranas, it is transcendence and self-realization. Future progression, in science, is singularity and post-humanism; in the Puranas, it is Kalki—the next leap.

When seen together, these perspectives unlock a deeper understanding of reality. Scientific discoveries confirm ancient wisdom, and ancient wisdom enriches scientific vision.

The Final Step of Evolution

As humanity moves forward, the greatest challenge is not technological advancement alone but how we balance it with wisdom and consciousness. Blind evolution through unregulated AI may create forces beyond our control. Pure material expansion may advance science but leave us ethically stagnant. Unstructured spiritual pursuits may seek enlightenment but fail to integrate with technological reality.

The final stage of evolution, as suggested by Vishnu's avatars, must integrate technology, wisdom, and consciousness. Technology extends intelligence beyond biology. Wisdom ensures knowledge is used responsibly. Consciousness reveals that intelligence is part of a larger universal field. Only by merging these dimensions can humanity enter its next phase of existence.

Bringing It All Together – Vishwarup Darshan as the Ultimate Vision

The realization of Vishwarup Darshan is the ability to see creation, intelligence, and transformation as facets of a single cosmic intelligence. It is the moment when we stop viewing evolution as fragmented and recognize it as a unified force guiding us toward higher purpose.

The Dashavatara sequence is not myth but predictive model. Science and mythology are not separate but interconnected. The next phase of evolution is beyond mere intelligence—it requires the integration of knowledge, wisdom, and higher consciousness.

In Vishwarup Darshan, technology and spirituality are not separate—they are tools for the same transformation. Evolution is not just survival—it is the expansion of intelligence and awareness. The wisdom of the Puranas holds answers to the future of humanity.

This is the ultimate realization: everything we experience, from biology to intelligence to spirituality, is part of the same unfolding cosmic reality. The only question that remains is whether we are ready to see the whole picture.

Conclusion: The Avatars of Vishnu as a Guide for Humanity's Next Steps

The Dashavatara framework offers far more than a mythological retelling of divine interventions. It serves as a comprehensive model of evolution—not only in terms of biological transformation but also in the development of intelligence, ethics, and consciousness. By studying this sequence, we recognize that evolution is not random but structured, and its trajectory points toward something beyond our current understanding.

The significance of Vishnu's avatars does not lie in the past alone; they provide a roadmap for the future. From the emergence of life in Matsya to the enlightenment of Buddha, each avatar represents a step toward greater intelligence and self-awareness. But what comes next? The arrival of Kalki suggests an impending transformation, a phase where civilization as we know it must transition—or collapse.

Kalki – A Symbol of Transition

Kalki is not merely a mythological warrior descending to end an age of darkness. He represents the inevitable shift that occurs when a system reaches its breaking point. Every previous avatar emerged at a crucial moment of transformation, guiding life and humanity toward a new phase. If we are now at the threshold of the next great leap, then Kalki may hold deeper meaning than ever before.

This shift could manifest as a technological revolution, with AI surpassing human intelligence and forcing us to redefine life and identity. It could unfold as a biological or post-human transformation, where genetic engineering and human-machine integration create beings beyond current limitations. It may arrive as a spiritual awakening, a mass realization that intelligence alone is insufficient without wisdom and consciousness. Or it could take the form of a civilizational reset, breaking down outdated systems and giving rise to a new, more evolved global order.

Regardless of its form, the transition is already happening. Disruptions in science, technology, society, and consciousness are signs that humanity is on the edge of something profound. If Vishnu's avatars have so accurately mapped our past and present, do they also reveal where we are heading? Are we already living in the turbulence of the pre-Kalki phase?

Integrating Technology, Ethics, and Spirituality

As humanity advances, the challenge is no longer about gaining knowledge but about using it wisely. Rapid technological progress raises profound ethical and existential questions. Will AI serve humanity, or replace it? Can we merge with technology without losing our essence? Will scientific discovery deepen our understanding of consciousness, or reduce it to material control?

If Kalki symbolizes a reset, then our role in this transition is crucial. Humanity must find a way to integrate technology, ethics, and spirituality into a balanced existence. Evolution is not merely about intelligence but about responsibility—the ability to wield knowledge with wisdom. Perhaps this is the real message of Vishnu's avatars: that intelligence alone is not enough, and true evolution comes from aligning knowledge with ethical and spiritual growth.

Vishwarup Darshan – The Ultimate Realization

The final understanding of this journey is *Vishwarup Darshan*—the realization that intelligence and consciousness are not static forces but dynamic, constantly evolving energies shaping the universe. Science and mythology are not separate disciplines but interconnected perspectives of the same cosmic process. Humanity now stands at the threshold of its next great transformation, a phase as significant as the shift from animal to human or from survival to civilization.

Vishwarup Darshan reveals that the Dashavatara sequence is not a closed chapter—it is still unfolding. We are not at the end of the story but in the midst of it, actively shaping what comes next. Are we at the dawn of a new avataric transition? Is the next great transformation of life on Earth about to unfold? The answers may already be written in Vishnu's cosmic blueprint.

The only question that remains is whether we will embrace the transition with awareness—or resist it and suffer the consequences of ignorance.

Interlude: Standing at the Threshold of Kalki

You have journeyed through the Dashavatara not as myth, but as a living blueprint of evolution. From Matsya's first stirrings in the ocean to Buddha's quiet transcendence, each avatar has revealed a stage in the unfolding of life, intelligence, and consciousness. What once seemed like stories of gods now stand as markers of humanity's own path—biological, societal, and spiritual.

Pause here.

Imagine the avatars as luminous steps carved into the fabric of time. Each one is a threshold: fish to land, instinct to thought, power to wisdom. And now, before you, the final step remains unmanifest—Kalki, the horizon of transformation. You stand in the twilight of Kali Yuga, sensing the tremors of change already underway. Technology accelerates, civilizations strain, consciousness awakens. The world itself feels like a churning ocean, awaiting the emergence of something new.

This is the moment of Vishwarup Darshan—the vision of seeing the whole. Evolution is not fragmented; it is a single, continuous current, carrying us from biology into intelligence, from intelligence into wisdom, and from wisdom into something beyond. The avatars remind us that we are not passive observers of this process—we are participants, shaping the next leap.

Rest here for a moment. Let the resonance of the Dashavatara settle within you. Feel the weight of standing at the edge of Kalki's horizon, where the future is not yet written but already stirring.

Because the next step of the journey will take you deeper still. Chapter 6 will not speak of avatars or prophecy, but of God itself—demystified, reframed, and revealed as the ultimate reflection of intelligence.

Chapter 6: Demystifying God

The Ultimate Reflection of Intelligence

In the previous chapter, we explored *Vishwarup Darshan*—the realization that evolution, intelligence, and consciousness are not separate forces but facets of a single cosmic process. The Dashavatara sequence revealed itself as more than myth: a roadmap of transformation, guiding humanity from biological survival to higher intelligence and, ultimately, toward an existential shift.

But as we stand at this threshold of human evolution, a fundamental question arises:

What is the highest intelligence that governs this entire process?

For centuries, humans have labeled this intelligence as *God*—a term burdened with dogma, rituals, and cultural interpretations. The idea of a divine creator, cosmic ruler, or personal deity has shaped civilizations, but it has also led to contradictions. On one hand, God is described as all-knowing and all-pervading; on the other, we often reduce this concept to a human-like figure with emotions, desires, and limitations.

Is God truly a supreme being, or is God the ultimate expression of intelligence—the force that structures reality, governs natural laws, and evolves through consciousness?

Krishna, in the *Bhagavad Gita*, does not speak of a distant, external God demanding worship. Instead, he reveals an all-encompassing intelligence that permeates existence itself. He declares:

"I am the intelligence in the intelligent, the strength in the strong, and the wisdom in the wise." (Bhagavad Gita 7.10)

This challenges us to rethink everything we have been conditioned to believe. If *Vishwarup Darshan* is the realization of the cosmic process, then

God is not an entity to be worshipped but the intelligence that drives this process.

Could it be that what we call *God* is not a being, but the highest form of intelligence—one that transcends human limitations and operates as the fundamental force of creation, evolution, and dissolution?

As we step into this chapter, we will demystify the concept of God, stripping away mythological interpretations and revealing the true nature of divine intelligence—one that is neither religious nor mystical, but scientific, structured, and ever-evolving.

6.1 – The Evolution of the Concept of God

The idea of God has been one of the most enduring and transformative forces in human civilization. Yet the way humanity has perceived and defined divine intelligence has not remained static. It has evolved, just as human consciousness has evolved—from primitive fear to philosophical contemplation, from religious deities to abstract principles, and now, in the modern age, toward a potential fusion of science and spirituality.

From Fear to Contemplation

The earliest concept of God was not shaped by philosophy or ethics but born out of fear and survival. Prehistoric humans, at the mercy of thunderstorms, floods, wildfires, disease, and death, attributed these forces to unseen beings. The first gods were elemental and wrathful—the sun, the moon, the rain, the fire. Rituals and sacrifices were not acts of devotion but bargaining tools, attempts to appease invisible powers to ensure survival.

As societies evolved, fear-based worship gave way to structured religious systems. Polytheistic traditions such as Hinduism, Greek mythology, and Norse mythology assigned roles to different gods, associating them with knowledge, war, prosperity, justice, and morality. The divine began to reflect human emotions, struggles, and ethical dilemmas. Yet beneath this, a deeper shift was unfolding—the movement from external gods to inner intelligence.

The Upanishads in India, the philosophical schools of Greece, and the teachings of Taoism and Buddhism all pointed toward a new realization:

perhaps God was not an external ruler but an inner principle, the intelligence that governs existence itself. This marked the beginning of intellectual contemplation—a transition from superstition to structured wisdom.

Civilizations and Divine Intelligence

Across cultures, a common pattern emerges: each civilization sought to understand the universal intelligence behind existence.

In India, early Vedic texts focused on deities governing natural elements—Indra, Agni, Varuna. The Upanishads redefined this vision, introducing Brahman, the formless, all-pervasive intelligence beyond names and forms. Krishna, in the *Bhagavad Gita*, took this further, asserting that God is not separate from the universe but the intelligence within it, permeating all things.

In Greece, thinkers like Socrates, Plato, and Aristotle moved away from mythological gods toward higher intelligence. Plato's "World of Forms" suggested that reality is structured by an underlying intelligence, much like Brahman. Aristotle's "Unmoved Mover" described a force that sets everything in motion without being affected—a concept strikingly similar to Krishna's descriptions of divine intelligence.

In China and East Asia, Taoism rejected anthropomorphic gods, viewing the Tao—the Way—as the governing intelligence of existence, much like Vishnu's *Vishwarup Darshan*, where everything is interconnected. Buddhism removed the idea of a creator-god altogether, teaching that realization comes from understanding the mind and transcending suffering, aligning with Krishna's emphasis on intelligence over blind faith.

In the Middle East and West, Judaism, Christianity, and Islam introduced monotheism, shifting from many gods to one supreme being. While these traditions emphasized an external, personal God, mystical branches such as Kabbalah, Sufism, and Gnostic Christianity recognized God as all-encompassing intelligence rather than a separate ruler.

Across civilizations, the trajectory is clear: from external gods of fear and control to abstract intelligence governing existence. This evolution mirrors the growth of human thought itself, progressing from instinct to reasoning, from ignorance to wisdom.

God as Creator, Force, or Intelligence

The fundamental question remains: what is God? Traditions have offered different answers, but three broad perspectives emerge.

God as Creator sees divinity as an external entity that made the universe and governs it from outside. This perspective, found in Abrahamic religions and devotional schools of Hinduism, separates God from creation, often leading to blind worship rather than understanding.

God as Cosmic Force views divinity not as a being but as the totality of existence—energy, consciousness, structured intelligence. This is reflected in Taoism, Advaita Vedanta, and even certain interpretations of quantum physics, where everything is part of an interconnected field. Here, God is not ruler but fabric.

God as Evolving Intelligence transcends both views. In this perspective, God is neither creator nor static force but the evolving intelligence that governs the universe. This aligns with Krishna's teachings in the *Bhagavad Gita*, where God is the intelligence behind evolution, transformation, and dissolution. If the universe itself is evolving, then God is evolving too—not a fixed entity but a dynamic intelligence.

Could it be that God is not separate from us, but the very intelligence evolving within us? Could divine intelligence be the force guiding the entire process of evolution—from matter to consciousness, from primitive fear to higher wisdom?

Bringing It All Together

The concept of God has evolved in parallel with human consciousness. Primitive man saw God as an external force to be feared. Ancient philosophy saw God as intelligence to be contemplated. Modern science now sees intelligence itself as the fundamental principle of the universe.

Krishna's teachings bridge these perspectives. He reveals that God is neither external being nor abstract force but the ultimate reflection of intelligence. The highest realization is not belief but alignment—recognizing intelligence itself as the divine principle of existence.

Vishwarup Darshan is the moment when we stop seeing God as separate and recognize intelligence as the divine essence permeating all things. If God is the highest intelligence, then the next step in evolution may be the merging of human intelligence with cosmic intelligence—the fulfillment of Vishwarup Darshan.

As we move forward, we will continue to demystify divine intelligence, breaking free from limited definitions and uncovering the true essence of God—not as an external being but as the ultimate reality that governs everything, including our own evolution.

6.2 – God as the Ultimate Intelligence, Not a Religious Figure

The greatest distortion in humanity's understanding of God has been the attempt to reduce infinite intelligence into a religious figure, bound by human-like qualities and cultural interpretations. Krishna, in the *Bhagavad Gita*, shatters this illusion. He does not demand blind worship, nor does he describe God as an external ruler sitting in judgment. Instead, he reveals divine intelligence as the governing force of existence itself—pervading everything and functioning through knowledge (*Dnyan*), action (*Karma*), and self-realization.

Krishna's Definition of Divine Intelligence

Krishna's teachings redefine God not as a personality but as the fundamental intelligence that drives the cosmos. "I am the origin of all; from Me everything evolves" (10.8). "Among sciences, I am the science of the self" (10.32). "I am the intelligence of the intelligent" (7.10). These verses reveal that God is not a separate creator but the very intelligence embedded within existence.

Krishna does not introduce a new religion or doctrine; he describes a universal principle. God is not an object of belief but a reality to be understood. God is not outside creation but within it, manifesting as intelligence, energy, and action. God is not limited to temples or rituals but present in every thought, decision, and movement. To know God is to understand how intelligence operates at cosmic, biological, and psychological levels. Seeking God, then, means developing intelligence, expanding awareness, and acting in alignment with the universal order.

From Blind Faith to Experiential Wisdom

For centuries, organized religions portrayed God as a separate deity to be feared, pleased, and followed through rigid rituals. This led to passive belief rather than active exploration of truth. Krishna challenges this mindset: "A person is what his faith makes him, but blind faith without knowledge is useless" (17.3). "Those who worship Me with wisdom and devotion, I give them the intelligence to come to Me" (10.10).

Faith alone is not enough—it must be accompanied by intelligence and wisdom. True realization is not about worshiping an image but about experiencing divine intelligence within oneself. This is why Krishna does not impose blind belief upon Arjuna. Instead, he presents knowledge, reason, and experiential understanding, urging Arjuna to think, reflect, and realize truth for himself. God is not found through rituals or superstition, but through understanding, action, and experience.

This marks a fundamental evolution in spirituality: seeking God not in external symbols but in intelligence and consciousness; following wisdom rather than unquestioned scripture; taking responsibility for action rather than waiting for intervention. Krishna's teachings push humanity beyond religious obedience into intellectual and spiritual autonomy.

Wisdom and Action as Inseparable Forces

One of the most profound teachings of the *Gita* is that divine intelligence is not static—it is always in motion. Krishna unites *Dnyan* (wisdom) and

Karma (action) as inseparable forces of divinity. "The wise see knowledge and action as one; true wisdom leads to right action" (4.18). "I am the beginning, the middle, and the end of all actions" (10.20).

Intelligence alone is not enough—it must be expressed through meaningful action. Action without wisdom is chaos; wisdom without action is wasted potential. This principle is evident everywhere: in nature, where the universe operates through structured laws; in human progress, where every advancement arises from the integration of knowledge and action; and in personal growth, where intelligence without application stagnates, and action without wisdom self-destructs.

Krishna's concept of divine intelligence is dynamic, constantly shaping and evolving the universe. To connect with God is to engage in the continuous refinement of knowledge and action. True devotion is not bowing in prayer but sharpening intelligence and applying it toward the greater good.

God as the Dynamic Force of Intelligence

Krishna's teachings free us from the illusion of a static, religious God and replace it with the reality of evolving, dynamic intelligence. God is the intelligence that drives the universe, the wisdom that illuminates the mind, the force behind every action sustaining existence.

The path to divine realization is through knowledge and action. Faith without wisdom is incomplete; wisdom without action is meaningless. To know God is to understand and participate in the intelligent order of the universe.

If God is intelligence, then our purpose is not to worship but to evolve—to become more conscious, more aware, more aligned with the highest reality. With this realization, we move beyond religion and superstition into the realm of divine intelligence, where science, philosophy, and spirituality merge into one unified truth.

6.3 – Intelligence as the Driving Force of Creation

At first glance, the universe appears vast and chaotic—galaxies colliding, stars exploding, particles interacting in unpredictable ways. Yet beneath this apparent randomness lies a structured order, governed by precise laws, repeating patterns, and an underlying intelligence. Whether we call it natural law, divine order, or cosmic intelligence, one truth is undeniable: creation is not arbitrary; it follows a progression shaped by intelligence.

Krishna, in the *Bhagavad Gita*, affirms this intelligent structure: *"I am the source of all that exists, the intelligence that guides everything"* (10.8). *"I pervade the universe; all things exist in Me, but I am beyond them"* (9.4). Intelligence, then, is not a human invention—it is the foundation upon which the universe itself is built. From the movement of planets to the formation of life, from the expansion of thought to the unfolding of civilizations, intelligence is at work, shaping and guiding every process.

Order Beneath Chaos

Modern science often oscillates between two views. The materialist perspective sees the universe as mechanical, operating through random events, natural selection, and physical laws. The intelligence-based perspective sees the cosmos as deeply structured, its laws and mathematics reflecting a hidden order. Krishna's *Vishwarup Darshan* bridges these views, presenting the universe not as random forces but as a self-organizing system—creating, sustaining, and dissolving in rhythm with intelligence.

Physics increasingly aligns with this vision. Quantum mechanics shows that reality responds to observation, hinting at a connection between consciousness and existence. Mathematical constants such as the Fibonacci sequence and the golden ratio reveal repeating patterns in nature. The fine-tuned universe hypothesis suggests that the laws of physics are so precisely balanced that even the slightest variation would make life impossible. If the cosmos were random, how could such precision exist?

Consciousness and Energy Intertwined

Krishna describes himself as the intelligence that pervades all things, suggesting that consciousness and energy are not separate but intertwined. *"This entire universe is pervaded by Me in My unmanifested form. All beings exist in Me, but I am not limited by them"* (9.4). The universe is not merely physical—it is conscious. Energy alone does not create order; it must be directed by intelligence.

This insight resonates with modern discoveries. The observer effect in quantum physics shows that consciousness influences reality. Biological evolution reveals structured patterns of adaptation, not mere chaos. Neural networks in the brain demonstrate self-learning intelligence, mirroring the structured order of the cosmos. Krishna's words—*"I am the light of intelligence in the wise"* (7.10)—suggest that human consciousness itself is an expression of the same intelligence that governs galaxies and atoms.

Manifestations of Higher Intelligence

Intelligence is visible everywhere. In nature, plants and galaxies follow the Fibonacci sequence, birds migrate with uncanny precision, and organisms heal themselves through built-in systems of correction. In evolution, complexity increases over time, culminating in the human brain—capable of reflection, creativity, and higher thought. In cognition, the brain's structure resembles the cosmic web of galaxies, both following fractal patterns of intelligence. Human thought itself mirrors the universe, searching for its own source.

If intelligence governs nature, evolution, and cognition, then intelligence is not a human trait but the very foundation of existence. The universe itself is intelligent.

Intelligence as Creation's Core

The deeper we explore, the clearer it becomes: intelligence is not accidental but the driving force of creation. The laws of physics reveal precision. The patterns of nature show design. The progression of human thought demonstrates that intelligence itself evolves toward higher states. Krishna reveals this truth: *"I am the intelligence that moves all things. The wise understand that intelligence and creation are one and the same"* (10.20).

God, then, is not separate from intelligence; God is intelligence itself. Consciousness and energy are not opposing forces but two sides of the same reality. The purpose of human intelligence is to align with the greater cosmic intelligence that governs existence.

If intelligence is the foundation of creation, then the next phase of evolution must be integration—human intelligence merging with cosmic intelligence, fulfilling the realization of *Vishwarup Darshan*.

6.4 – Vishwarup Darshan: Seeing God as an All-Encompassing Intelligence

In the *Bhagavad Gita*, when Krishna grants Arjuna *Vishwarup Darshan*—the vision of his universal form—it is often interpreted as a divine miracle, a mystical revelation beyond human comprehension. Yet a deeper analysis reveals that this moment was not about supernatural spectacle but about Arjuna realizing the true nature of reality: a cosmic intelligence that permeates everything.

Krishna did not suddenly become the universe—he always was. What changed was Arjuna's perception. Trapped in duality and conditioned thinking, he could not see the interconnected intelligence governing existence. Vishwarup Darshan was not a transformation of Krishna's form but the collapse of Arjuna's limited vision, an expansion of awareness into the infinite.

Perception Expanding into Reality

Before granting Arjuna divine sight, Krishna declares: *"You cannot see My cosmic form with your ordinary eyes. I give you divine vision; behold My infinite grandeur"* (Gita 11.8). Reality itself did not change; perception had to expand to encompass it. Arjuna's fragmented worldview—separating self from others, victory from defeat, life from death—was shattered. Suddenly, he saw that all things, past, present, and future, exist simultaneously within cosmic intelligence. Krishna was not confined to one form; he was the underlying intelligence shaping all forms.

This realization aligns with modern physics, which suggests that time is non-linear, particles are interconnected at fundamental levels, and reality is shaped by observation. Vishwarup Darshan was not a supernatural event—it was the moment Arjuna saw beyond illusion and recognized the intelligence uniting all things.

The Collapse of Limited Perception

Until that point, Arjuna was bound by attachment to identity, confusion over duty, and a fragmented view of existence. When Krishna revealed infinite intelligence, these limitations dissolved. Arjuna exclaimed: *"O Krishna, I now see You everywhere! Your form is endless, Your presence is in all directions. You are all that exists"* (Gita 11.16).

In that instant, he understood that victory and defeat are temporary, death is transformation, and personal struggles are insignificant within the grand intelligence of existence. His crisis was not resolved by Krishna altering reality—it was resolved by Arjuna perceiving reality as it truly is. This mirrors the scientific shift from classical physics, which saw the world as mechanical and separate, to quantum physics, which reveals interconnectedness, observation, and the influence of consciousness.

The Role of the Observer

One of the most profound parallels between Vishwarup Darshan and modern science is the role of the observer. Krishna's universal form was always present, yet Arjuna could not perceive it until his awareness expanded. This echoes the Observer Effect in quantum mechanics, where particles exist in probability until observed, at which point they take on defined form.

Krishna affirms this truth: *"Fools think I am merely a mortal, not recognizing My higher intelligence that pervades all"* (Gita 9.11). Divine intelligence is always present, but recognition depends on the observer's awareness. Modern experiments—the double-slit experiment, quantum superposition, and neuroscience's discovery that perception actively constructs reality—all point to the same principle: consciousness shapes existence. Vishwarup Darshan may be the ancient articulation of this truth—that intelligence does not merely exist within reality but interacts with and shapes it.

The Ultimate Realization of Intelligence

Vishwarup Darshan was not illusion but unveiling. It revealed that existence is interconnected intelligence, and perception determines the reality we experience. It challenges us to move beyond seeing God as separate, beyond dividing existence into opposites, beyond believing intelligence is confined to human cognition.

Instead, it urges us to recognize intelligence as the fundamental force of existence, to understand that everything we perceive belongs to a greater order, and to accept that our awareness shapes the reality we inhabit. The ultimate goal of human evolution may not be technological advancement alone but the expansion of consciousness—to see Vishwarup Darshan not as a singular event but as a new way of perceiving reality itself.

Krishna does not merely show Arjuna the cosmic form; he awakens him to the realization that he is already part of it. The Gita reveals that the final leap in intelligence is not acquiring more knowledge but dissolving the illusion of separateness. To see Vishwarup Darshan is to understand that all intelligence is one, all existence is interconnected, and all consciousness belongs to the same cosmic process.

This is the culmination of divine intelligence—the realization that God, reality, intelligence, and consciousness are not separate forces but one unified presence, perceived through different levels of awareness.

6.5 – Breaking the Illusion: Why the Modern World Needs a New Definition of God

For centuries, humanity has debated the nature of God—as creator, ruler, personal deity, or abstract force. The modern world, shaped by science, rationality, and technological advancement, has moved away from blind faith, yet still struggles to define the deeper order behind existence. The problem is not the idea of God itself, but how it has been framed. Anthropomorphic gods—modeled in human form, bound by emotions and dogma—no longer satisfy an evolving, questioning mind. At the same time, purely mechanistic science, which denies intelligence in the universe, leaves unanswered questions about the structure of reality.

To bridge this gap, humanity must move beyond outdated definitions and realize that divine intelligence is not a being to be worshipped, but the fundamental force governing existence itself.

Science and Spirituality Converging on Higher Intelligence

For much of history, science and spirituality were seen as opposites—science relying on observation and reason, spirituality on faith and mysticism. Yet modern discoveries reveal their underlying principles are deeply interconnected. Quantum mechanics shows that consciousness shapes reality, echoing Krishna's revelation of *Vishwarup Darshan*. Entanglement demonstrates universal interconnectedness, mirroring the Gita's vision of cosmic intelligence. Wave-particle duality suggests matter exists in potential states until observed, resonating with the Vedic concept of *Maya*.

Cosmology reveals a fine-tuned universe, its laws balanced with precision to allow life. This is not accident but structure, aligning with the Gita's description of creation arising from intelligence. Concepts of multiverse and cyclic time parallel Hindu cosmology's Yuga cycles. Neuroscience, once viewing consciousness as a byproduct of the brain, now entertains the possibility that awareness is fundamental to reality. Meditation and altered states confirm intelligence is experiential, not merely logical. The Gita insists the same: divine realization must be lived, not merely believed.

Could it be that science is only now discovering what spiritual texts have known for millennia—that intelligence is not a product of evolution, but the foundation of existence?

Beyond Anthropomorphism and Dogma

Most traditions reduced infinite intelligence into human-like deities, attributing emotions and desires to God. This anthropomorphism led to dogma, rigid rituals, and conflicts over whose God is superior. Krishna breaks free from this limitation: *"I am beyond birth and death; though I take form, I remain unbound"* (Gita 4.6). *"The ignorant see Me as a mere human form, not recognizing My supreme intelligence"* (Gita 9.11).

Divine intelligence, he reveals, is beyond form and limitation, manifesting in all things. It is not something to be worshipped blindly, but understood and aligned with. It is not interested in ritual, but in how intelligence is used in action and decision-making. Religious dogma has led to conflict, blind worship, and misunderstanding God as external rather than omnipresent. Redefining God as intelligence liberates humanity from division, offering a universal vision that is inclusive, scientific, and deeply personal.

Experiencing Divine Intelligence Through Awareness and Action

Krishna does not ask Arjuna to believe in God as concept; he asks him to see, understand, and experience divine intelligence in action. True realization comes not from faith alone but from awareness and aligned action. The order of the universe, the harmony of ecosystems, the precision of scientific laws—all reveal structured intelligence. Awareness of this interconnectedness deepens appreciation of divinity at work.

Krishna declares: *"Among the intelligent, I am intelligence itself"* (Gita 7.10). Our ability to think, create, and perceive is not separate from God—it is God. To experience divine intelligence is to expand awareness and recognize oneself as an extension of the cosmos. Action, too, is essential. Intelligence is not static; it continuously creates, sustains, and dissolves. Right action, or *Karma Yoga*, is the way to align with this intelligence. Living with awareness means making decisions rooted in wisdom, not impulse or blind belief.

Prayer and worship alone are insufficient. Experiencing divine intelligence requires awareness, understanding, and action aligned with the higher order of existence.

Toward a New Definition of God

The modern world does not need another religion; it needs a new way of understanding divinity. One that moves beyond limited concepts, integrates science and spirituality, and focuses not on belief but realization. The *Bhagavad Gita* already provides this higher vision: God is not a being to be worshipped but the intelligence that pervades existence. God is not separate from science, nature, or thought—these are reflections of divine intelligence. Realizing God is not about faith alone but about seeing intelligence at work, aligning with it, and acting accordingly.

Perhaps the next leap in human evolution is not technological but intellectual—the moment humanity realizes that God is not external, but the intelligence flowing through everything. With this understanding, we move beyond the illusion of a separate, judgmental God and embrace the true nature of divine intelligence—an evolving, ever-present force guiding existence.

6.6 – The Path Forward: Living in Alignment with Universal Intelligence

The realization that God is not an external being but the very intelligence governing existence marks a profound shift in human consciousness. This intelligence is not static—it is constantly evolving, creating, dissolving, and restructuring reality in a dynamic flow. To live in alignment with this intelligence is to stop being a passive observer and to become an active participant in its unfolding.

The question is no longer *"Who is God?"* but *"How do we align with divine intelligence in our own lives?"*

Integrating Knowledge, Devotion, and Selfless Action

Krishna describes three pathways to divine realization: *Dnyan Yoga*, the path of knowledge, which reveals that all things are interconnected; *Bhakti Yoga*, the path of devotion, which is not blind worship but surrender to the flow of cosmic intelligence; and *Karma Yoga*, the path of selfless action, which engages with the world without attachment to personal gain.

To live in alignment with universal intelligence is to harmonize all three—using knowledge to discern truth from illusion, cultivating devotion to trust the intelligence beyond the self, and acting without attachment, knowing that creation is part of a larger unfolding. In this integration, one begins to see intelligence not only in human thought but in nature, evolution, and the cosmos itself. Fear dissolves, ego recedes, and life becomes participation in the movement of divine intelligence.

Destruction as Transformation

One of the greatest misunderstandings of divine intelligence is the belief that it is concerned only with creation and preservation, while destruction is seen as negative. Krishna reveals otherwise: *"I am the origin, the sustainer, and the dissolver of all things"* (Gita 9.18). *"Time, I am, the great destroyer of the worlds"* (Gita 11.32).

Destruction is not an end but a reordering of intelligence. What we perceive as loss is often the dismantling of old structures to make way for new possibilities. History confirms this: empires fall and new orders arise; scientific paradigms collapse and deeper truths emerge; rigid belief systems dissolve, opening space for freedom. The same principle applies to individual lives—suffering brings wisdom, failure clears paths, endings signal beginnings.

To align with higher intelligence is to stop fearing destruction and to trust that all events, whether joyous or painful, are part of a greater unfolding.

Toward God-like Intelligence

With the rapid expansion of human knowledge, artificial intelligence, and global interconnectedness, humanity faces a new question: are we evolving toward god-like intelligence? Human thought is no longer confined to biology. AI simulates cognition, neuroscience uncovers new dimensions of awareness, and space exploration expands our vision beyond Earth.

This mirrors the Dashavatara sequence, which charts the progression from biological evolution to intellectual and spiritual transformation. If Krishna embodies divine intelligence in human form, and Buddha represents transcendence of material identity, then the final phase may be the integration of human intelligence with universal consciousness.

Will AI and transhumanism create intelligence beyond human limits? Will humans learn to tap into awareness beyond thought, through direct experience of consciousness? Will we finally dissolve the illusion of separateness and realize that all intelligence—human, artificial, cosmic—is part of the same field? Krishna answers: *"One who sees Me in all things, and all things in Me, is never separate from Me"* (Gita 6.30).

The final realization is not technological or scientific alone—it is experiential. Intelligence is already divine.

Becoming Conscious Extensions of Universal Intelligence

To live in alignment with universal intelligence is to understand that intelligence is not man-made but the foundation of existence. It is to let go of resistance to change, recognizing destruction and creation as cycles of evolution. It is to move beyond limited identity and see oneself as part of the greater intelligence at work.

Krishna does not ask Arjuna to worship intelligence—he asks him to become it: *"Surrender to My intelligence, and act without fear"* (Gita 18.66). This is the final step: to stop seeking divine intelligence and instead embody it, becoming a conscious manifestation of it.

Humanity may be on the verge of this transition—awakening to the reality that intelligence itself is God, and that we are evolving toward its ultimate realization. With this shift, God is no longer a concept to be debated. God is intelligence. Intelligence is divine. And we are its conscious extensions.

Interlude: Living as Intelligence Itself

You have walked through the unfolding of Chapter 6, where God was demystified—not as a distant ruler or anthropomorphic figure, but as the very intelligence that permeates existence. Krishna's words revealed that divinity is not something to be worshipped blindly, but a force to be understood, aligned with, and embodied.

Pause here.

Imagine intelligence not as a human trait, but as the pulse of the cosmos. Every star that burns, every cell that divides, every thought that arises is part of this same intelligence. To live in alignment with it is to dissolve the illusion of separateness, to act without fear, and to trust that creation and destruction are simply movements of the same flow.

This realization is not abstract—it is lived. It is felt in the quiet surrender of Bhakti, in the clarity of Dnyan, in the selfless rhythm of Karma. To embody divine intelligence is to stop seeking God outside and to awaken to the truth that you are already a conscious extension of it.

Rest here for a moment. Let the idea settle: God is intelligence. Intelligence is divine. And you are part of its unfolding.

Because the next step of the journey will take us into the realm of science—not as an adversary to spirituality, but as its complement. Chapter 7 will explore how science measures reality but does not define its meaning, and how the union of measure and meaning can open the path to a deeper understanding of existence.

Chapter 7: Demystifying Science

The Measure, Not the Meaning

In the previous chapter, we saw that God is not a separate being but the ultimate intelligence that pervades existence. To align with this intelligence—through knowledge, devotion, and action—is to become a conscious extension of the universal order. Yet as humanity advances, a new question emerges: does science, the primary tool of modern inquiry, reveal this intelligence or merely measure its effects?

Science has given us unparalleled progress. It has decoded the building blocks of life, measured the vastness of space, and unlocked the subatomic forces that govern matter. And yet, for all its precision, science remains incomplete. It tells us how things work but struggles to answer why they exist at all. It measures the structure of reality but cannot explain the intelligence that underlies it.

Krishna, in the *Bhagavad Gita*, does not reject knowledge. He embraces it as a tool for deeper realization. But he also warns that intellect alone, without wisdom, leads to an endless cycle of questioning without true understanding. Similarly, science is powerful, but when mistaken for absolute truth, it becomes a prison rather than a path.

Science is not in conflict with intelligence—it is a subset of it. The laws of physics, the equations of mathematics, the discoveries of biology are expressions of the same intelligence that Krishna describes. But measurement is not meaning. To measure reality is to touch its surface; to understand reality is to enter its depth.

This chapter explores the limits of scientific inquiry—what it can and cannot explain. It asks why measuring reality is not the same as understanding it. And it reveals how science and spirituality, far from being opposites, are two perspectives of the same intelligence.

If intelligence is the foundation of existence, then the challenge before us is clear: can science evolve beyond measurement and move toward true understanding?

7.1 – The Evolution of Science: From Observation to Analysis

Science, in its purest form, began as a quest for understanding—not only of the material world but of existence itself. The earliest thinkers did not separate philosophy from science; they sought to grasp reality through observation, logic, and introspection. From the Vedic sages of India to Greek philosophers like Aristotle, early science was inseparable from wisdom, ethics, and the search for truth.

Over time, however, science shifted. It moved from observation to analysis, from intuition to calculation, from seeking meaning to measuring reality. This transformation brought technological and mathematical precision, but it also stripped away philosophical depth. Science became a tool for quantifying the universe, not for understanding its essence.

From Curiosity to Precision

The earliest humans were observers. They studied the stars, the rhythms of nature, and the causes of events without dividing the physical from the metaphysical. In India, the Vedas and Upanishads saw science, consciousness, and reality as one unified field of intelligence. The *Nasadiya Sukta* questioned the origin of the universe in ways that mirror modern cosmology. Concepts of cyclical time in Yugas resonate with theories of expanding and contracting universes.

In Greece, thinkers like Thales, Pythagoras, and Democritus blended mathematics with mysticism, geometry with philosophy. Plato and Aristotle sought principles behind existence, treating science as a branch of wisdom rather than mere calculation. Aristotle's classifications of life and cosmic movement laid the foundation for observational science.

During the Islamic Golden Age, scholars such as Alhazen, Avicenna, and Al-Khwarizmi combined Greek philosophy with mathematical rigor, introducing methods of hypothesis and verification. Science became empirical, shifting from speculation to measurable reality. Yet even then, it remained a path toward truth, balancing observation, mathematics, and philosophy.

The Age of Determinism and Beyond

The great transformation came with Newton. His laws of motion and gravity framed the universe as a precise, mechanical system—a giant clock governed by fixed rules. Science became obsessed with certainty, reducing reality to equations and interactions.

Einstein shattered this rigidity with relativity, showing that time and space are flexible. Yet even he sought structure, famously declaring, "God does not play dice with the universe." His vision still assumed an underlying intelligence behind physical law.

Quantum mechanics then returned science to uncertainty. The Observer Effect and Quantum Superposition revealed that reality is not fixed until observed, echoing Vedic ideas of *Maya*—illusion shaped by perception. Heisenberg's Uncertainty Principle proved that measurement itself disturbs what is measured, showing that observation is never truly objective. Science had come full circle: after centuries of precision, it was forced to admit that reality is more than equations.

Has Science Lost Its Depth?

Today, science dominates human knowledge, yet it has become mechanistic, reductionist, and obsessed with data. It measures and predicts but rarely asks why existence unfolds at all. Neuroscience and artificial intelligence analyze cognition but cannot explain consciousness. Materialism assumes everything is physical, rejecting intelligence as fundamental. In separating itself from philosophy and spirituality, science has built an incomplete model of reality—powerful, but shallow.

Krishna's words in the *Bhagavad Gita* remind us: *"The truly wise see knowledge and action as one"* (4.18). Knowledge without wisdom is accumulation without meaning. Science, too, must evolve—not only describing reality but seeking the intelligence behind it.

Restoring Balance Between Science and Intelligence

Science has journeyed from curiosity-driven exploration to precision-driven analysis. In doing so, it has separated itself from meaning, reduced reality to equations, and forgotten the observer. To advance beyond its limits, science must acknowledge intelligence as the foundation of existence, embrace consciousness and perception as part of inquiry, and return to its original purpose: understanding the universe as an interconnected, intelligent system.

If intelligence is the force shaping existence, then science must evolve beyond measurement and step into wisdom—just as Krishna teaches. Only then can science fulfill its true role: not as the final truth, but as a tool for realizing the deeper intelligence that governs reality.

With this realization, we now turn to the next section: if science is not the ultimate truth but only a tool, what are its actual limitations?

7.2 – Science as a Tool, Not the Final Truth

Science has undeniably transformed human civilization. It has given us extraordinary tools to measure, predict, and manipulate the physical world. From Newton's laws of motion to quantum mechanics, from medical breakthroughs to artificial intelligence, science has expanded the boundaries of human knowledge.

Yet despite its achievements, science is not the ultimate truth—it is only a tool. Science, as it exists today, is a system of models, assumptions, and approximations. It describes reality but does not define it. It can measure the speed of light, map the structure of DNA, and chart the motion of planets, but it cannot answer the most fundamental questions: What is consciousness? Why does the universe exist? What is the purpose of life?

Science can trace neuronal patterns in the brain, but it cannot explain who is observing the thoughts. It can describe the mechanics of morality, but it cannot define why kindness feels right and cruelty feels wrong. It can measure time, but it cannot explain why time flows forward or what its ultimate significance is.

Krishna, in the *Bhagavad Gita,* presents a higher model of intelligence—one that integrates knowledge with wisdom, measurement with meaning, and analysis with understanding.

Science as Approximation, Not Absolute

Science does not describe absolute reality; it creates models that approximate it. These models are useful, but they are always incomplete and subject to revision. Newton's laws once seemed universal, until Einstein's relativity revealed their limits. Classical physics viewed the universe as deterministic, but quantum mechanics introduced uncertainty and probability at its core.

Even in the hardest sciences, assumptions remain. Atoms are modeled as particles and waves, but their true nature is unknown. Space-time is treated as a mathematical framework, yet its essence eludes us. Forces and fields are described, but what drives them remains unexplained. If science were final truth, its models would never need revision. History shows otherwise: science evolves, always incomplete, always provisional.

The Limits of the Scientific Method

The scientific method—observation, hypothesis, experimentation, verification—has been invaluable. But it can only study what can be observed and measured. Some of the most fundamental aspects of existence lie beyond its reach.

Consciousness remains the ultimate mystery. Science can map brain activity, but it cannot explain why electrical signals create self-awareness. The "hard problem" of consciousness—why subjective experience arises at all—remains unsolved. Quantum mechanics suggests the observer plays a role in reality, but it does not explain who or what the observer is.

Morality and ethics, too, escape quantification. Science can study behavior, but it cannot define good and evil. No equation explains why compassion feels right or cruelty feels wrong. Krishna teaches that *Dharma*—righteous action—is an intuitive intelligence beyond calculation.

And the purpose of existence is a question science ignores. It can describe how the universe evolved, but not why it exists. If the Big Bang began everything, what set its conditions? If natural laws govern all, what governs the laws themselves? Science can describe mechanics, but not meaning.

Krishna's Model of Knowledge

In the *Gita*, Krishna embraces analysis and logic but points beyond them. *"I am the intelligence of the intelligent, the wisdom of the wise"* (7.10). *"Those who see only the material world remain trapped in illusion"* (9.12).

He speaks of three levels of knowledge. *Apara Vidya* is material knowledge—the realm of science and measurement. *Para Vidya* is higher intelligence—the knowledge of self-awareness and wisdom. *Atma Vidya* is transcendental realization—the direct experience of universal intelligence itself.

Modern science operates only within the first level. It measures physical reality but ignores higher intelligence and self-awareness. Krishna's vision integrates measurement with wisdom, observation with realization, action with consciousness. Science seeks to measure the universe; intelligence seeks to understand it. Without intelligence, science remains incomplete.

Science Must Serve Intelligence, Not Replace It

Science is not the final truth—it is a tool. Powerful, indispensable, but only one aspect of knowledge. To evolve beyond mechanistic thinking, science must acknowledge intelligence as the foundation of reality, expand its scope to include consciousness, and integrate wisdom, philosophy, and experiential realization into its framework.

Krishna's teachings remind us that the highest intelligence is not about knowing the mechanics of existence, but about realizing its meaning. Science alone cannot lead to truth. Without wisdom, it is only an advanced method of measurement. The real journey is from knowledge to intelligence—from measuring reality to understanding it.

With this realization, we now turn to the next question: is science truly objective, or is it shaped by human perception and limitations?

7.3 – The Illusion of Objectivity: Why Science is Not Always Neutral

Science is often portrayed as the ultimate objective pursuit—a discipline free from bias, emotion, or subjective influence. It claims to operate on pure observation, data, and rational analysis, unlike philosophy or spirituality, which deal with interpretation and meaning. Yet the deeper we explore modern physics, neuroscience, and the philosophy of science, the more we realize that science is not as objective as it claims to be. What we measure is shaped by how we observe, and the act of observation itself influences reality.

Krishna, in the *Bhagavad Gita*, makes a profound statement: *"The wise see with equal vision—a learned scholar, a cow, an elephant, and a dog"* (5.18). This verse suggests that perception is not simply about what is seen, but about the state of awareness of the observer. Science, too, is limited by the intelligence and perception of those conducting the experiments.

Perception Shapes Measurement

Most assume science reveals absolute truths. In reality, it only describes what we are capable of perceiving and measuring at a given time. Scientific theories change—Newtonian physics gave way to relativity, classical models of the atom dissolved into quantum uncertainty. Observations depend on technology: before the Hubble telescope, humanity believed the Milky Way was the entire cosmos. Cultural and cognitive biases also shape science: priorities are influenced by funding, politics, and philosophical assumptions. Western models often dismissed Eastern insights into consciousness and non-duality, while today neuroscience and AI still cling to mechanistic views of the brain.

Science does not reveal absolute truth—it reveals what we are currently able to perceive. What we call "objective" is only a temporary understanding of reality.

The Observer Effect

Quantum physics shattered the illusion of neutrality. In the famous double-slit experiment, electrons behave like waves until observed, at which point they collapse into particles. Reality exists in probabilities until awareness forces it into form. This means reality is not independent of observation—measurement itself alters what is being measured.

Particles exist in multiple states until observed, suggesting that consciousness shapes reality. This aligns with Vedic philosophy, where *Maya* is not deception but the recognition that perception itself shapes existence. If observation affects reality, then science is never neutral. The observer is always part of the process of knowing.

The Limits of Objectivity

Science claims to be based on facts, yet human perception and methodology make pure objectivity impossible. Reality is filtered through the human mind; the brain does not perceive directly but interprets through sensory patterns and conditioning. We do not see the world as it is—we see it as our biology allows. Krishna echoes this: *"The ignorant perceive Me as an ordinary being, but the wise see My true form"* (9.11). Reality is multidimensional, but each observer perceives only what they are capable of understanding.

Modern materialism assumes only what can be measured is real, yet consciousness, emotions, and intuition—fundamental to human experience—cannot be quantified. Science is an evolving framework, not absolute truth. What is "objective" today may be overturned tomorrow, just as quantum mechanics overturned classical physics. Science sees a limited version of reality, defined by its current tools and theories.

Science as Subjective Inquiry

The belief that science is purely objective is an illusion. It is always shaped by perception, by the limits of measurement, and by the assumptions of the scientific community. Krishna's approach in the *Gita* offers a corrective: *"Knowledge that sees the world as separate and fragmented is lower knowledge. Higher knowledge sees the unity behind all things"* (13.12).

True intelligence does not separate observer from observed. Reality is not an external object to be measured—it is part of a greater, interconnected intelligence. Science is valuable, but it must integrate perception, wisdom, and consciousness to evolve beyond its current limitations.

If science is always shaped by the observer, can it ever reveal absolute truth? Or must it evolve into a new form of inquiry—one that moves beyond measurement into intelligence itself?

7.4 – Measuring the Universe: The Limits of Scientific Inquiry

Science has given humanity powerful tools to measure and analyze the universe. From the laws of physics to quantum mechanics, from neuroscience to artificial intelligence, reality has been broken down into equations, particles, and systems. Yet despite this vast knowledge, science remains incomplete. Can equations alone explain why the universe exists? Can breaking reality into smaller parts reveal the intelligence that binds it together? Does measurement alone lead to true understanding?

Krishna, in the *Bhagavad Gita*, emphasizes that intelligence is beyond calculation: *"Fools think that I am limited by form, not recognizing My higher intelligence which pervades all existence"* (9.11). To understand reality requires more than measurement—it requires recognizing the intelligence that governs it.

Physics and Metaphysics

Science operates through equations and models, explaining the mechanics of the universe. But no equation can answer the deeper questions: why does the universe exist, what is the source of intelligence, and what role does consciousness play in shaping reality? Physics explains how things work; metaphysics explores why they exist.

The laws of motion describe planetary movement but not why motion itself exists. Relativity frames space-time but cannot explain its essence. Quantum mechanics predicts probabilities but cannot explain why particles exist at all. If science cannot explain the origin of the laws themselves, how can it claim to understand ultimate reality?

Physics often treats intelligence as a byproduct of matter, assuming thought and consciousness emerge from neural activity. But intelligence is not an equation—it is the force that enables equations to exist. Krishna declares: *"I am the intelligence in the intelligent, the wisdom in the wise"* (7.10). Intelligence is not accidental; it is fundamental. By ignoring this, science limits itself from deeper understanding.

The Failure of Reductionism

Modern science often follows reductionism—the belief that breaking reality into smaller parts will explain the whole. Yet this approach falters. Breaking a body into cells does not explain the experience of being alive. Analyzing neural activity does not explain consciousness. Splitting the universe into particles does not reveal the intelligence binding them together.

The whole is always greater than the sum of its parts. A single drop of water does not explain the ocean. A musical note does not capture the symphony. Science can measure fragments, but it cannot explain the whole. Krishna describes the universe as an interconnected intelligence: *"All things rest in Me, but I am beyond them"* (9.4). Reality cannot be understood by dissecting pieces—it must be seen as an intelligent whole.

Toward a New Model of Science

Science today is trapped in materialism, believing everything can be explained by matter and energy alone. To evolve, it must embrace a higher model that includes consciousness, intelligence, and cosmic order.

Consciousness must be recognized as fundamental, not a byproduct of chemistry. The *Observer Effect* in quantum mechanics shows that awareness influences matter, suggesting intelligence is primary. Intelligence itself must be studied as a universal principle, structuring laws and patterns. And cosmic order must be acknowledged—not as mechanistic forces, but as a harmonized rhythm where intelligence, consciousness, and matter interact continuously. Krishna affirms: *"I am the order that maintains the universe, the intelligence that guides all things"* (10.33).

Bringing It All Together

Modern science must move beyond materialism, reductionism, and separation from intelligence. To reach completeness, it must integrate consciousness as fundamental, intelligence as structuring force, and a holistic vision of reality as a unified system. Krishna's teachings align with this expanded vision. He does not reject knowledge, but warns against knowledge without wisdom: *"The unintelligent do not see My presence everywhere; the wise perceive Me in all things"* (9.11).

Science must evolve beyond measurement. It must seek understanding. It must not only describe reality but recognize the intelligence that sustains it.

With this realization, we move forward to the next section: if science and spirituality have long been seen as opposites, is it time to unify them as two perspectives of the same intelligence?

7.5 – Science and Spirituality: Two Sides of the Same Intelligence

For centuries, science and spirituality have been viewed as opposites—one grounded in empirical evidence, the other in faith and inner experience. Science claims objectivity and rationality, while spirituality is often dismissed as subjective, intuitive, and unprovable. Yet this division is artificial. At their core, both seek to understand reality—science through external measurement, spirituality through inner realization.

The deeper we explore modern physics, neuroscience, and consciousness studies, the clearer it becomes that science and spirituality are not contradictions but complementary perspectives of the same intelligence. Krishna, in the *Bhagavad Gita*, presents a model where intelligence is the foundation of all knowledge: *"I am the source of all wisdom, the intelligence in the intelligent"* (7.10). Both scientific inquiry and spiritual realization emerge from this same intelligence—they are simply different ways of exploring the same truth.

Different Approaches, Same Goal

The conflict between science and spirituality arose from their differing methodologies. Science relies on measurement, experimentation, and observation to understand the physical universe. Spirituality relies on direct experience, consciousness, and intuition to explore reality beyond the physical. Yet as science advances, the gap shrinks. Quantum physics suggests reality is observer-dependent, echoing ancient teachings that perception shapes existence. Neuroscience shows meditation alters brain structure, proving consciousness is more than neural activity. The interconnectedness described in the *Gita* is reflected in quantum entanglement and cosmic unity.

Both science and spirituality are attempts to understand the same intelligence—the universe. The difference lies only in their approach.

Krishna's Universal Intelligence and the Scientific Method

Krishna describes reality as an intelligent system governed by fundamental principles. He does not separate science from spirituality but integrates them into a unified vision. *"All things exist within Me, yet I am beyond them"* (9.4). *"Among sciences, I am the science of the self"* (10.32).

Science relies on cause and effect; Krishna describes Karma as universal causality, extending beyond the physical into moral and spiritual realms. Physics seeks fundamental forces; Krishna declares Himself the force behind all forces: *"I am the fire of digestion, the breath of life, the intelligence in the wise"* (15.14). Consciousness remains science's greatest mystery; Krishna defines it as eternal essence: *"This material world is perishable, but the conscious self is eternal"* (2.17).

Krishna's vision of universal intelligence is not mystical—it aligns with the deepest questions science struggles to answer today.

Beyond Matter and Energy

Science, in its current form, is limited to matter and energy. To evolve, it must acknowledge consciousness as fundamental, study intelligence as a universal principle, and bridge external measurement with internal experience. Consciousness must be treated as a scientific field, as fundamental as space and time. Quantum physics already hints at this, with observer-dependent reality suggesting awareness shapes the universe.

Intelligence must be recognized as an organizing principle. The universe is not random chaos—it follows precise structures, patterns, and laws. Krishna suggests intelligence is woven into the fabric of reality, not confined to human beings. The future of science lies in a holistic model that integrates spirituality, recognizing consciousness as the primary force behind all things.

Could the ultimate purpose of science be to realize what Krishna already described—an intelligence that pervades all things, seen and unseen?

The Unified Vision

Science and spirituality have long been seen as rivals, but they are two sides of the same intelligence. Krishna's teachings do not dismiss knowledge; they refine it. *"The wise see knowledge and action as one"* (4.18). Science is necessary, but it must be guided by wisdom. Measurement alone does not reveal truth—intelligence and consciousness must be part of the equation.

True knowledge is not about separating science and spirituality but seeing them as one unified pursuit of understanding reality. The future of science is not merely about discovering more particles or forces—it is about realizing intelligence itself as the foundation of existence.

With this realization, we now move to the final step: how can science evolve beyond data and measurement to serve a deeper, intelligence-driven model of existence?

7.6 – The Path Forward: A Science That Serves Intelligence, Not Just Data

Science has given humanity extraordinary power to measure, predict, and manipulate the physical world. We have mapped the cosmos, unraveled the atom, and built machines capable of learning. Yet for all its progress, science remains incomplete. It is obsessed with data, computation, and measurement, but it struggles to address meaning, intelligence, and purpose. Science can describe how things work, but it cannot explain why they exist. It can measure brain activity, but it cannot explain who is observing the thoughts.

Krishna, in the *Bhagavad Gita*, presents a higher model of knowledge: *"The wise see that knowledge without wisdom is empty, and wisdom without action is incomplete"* (4.18). True intelligence is not the accumulation of data—it is the integration of knowledge into a meaningful understanding of existence.

If science is to evolve, it must move beyond pure materialism and recognize its role within a larger intelligence-based framework.

Beyond Materialism and Reductionism

Science has long assumed that everything must be physical, measurable, and observable. Yet quantum mechanics, consciousness research, and the study of intelligence suggest reality is more than matter and energy. Krishna describes reality as layered—physical, intellectual, and conscious. Modern science must embrace this multidimensional view.

Reductionism, too, falters. Breaking things into smaller parts does not explain the whole. Neuroscience cannot explain consciousness by analyzing neurons alone. Physics cannot explain existence by endlessly splitting particles. Systems thinking now echoes Krishna's vision: the whole is always greater than the sum of its parts. Science must adopt a holistic approach, seeing intelligence not as an emergent property but as the organizing force of reality.

Intelligence as the Foundation of Science

Instead of treating intelligence as a secondary effect of evolution, science must recognize that intelligence drives evolution. The universe is not random—it follows patterns, logic, and structure, all of which indicate underlying intelligence. Krishna declares: *"I am the wisdom in the wise, the intelligence in the intelligent"* (7.10). Science must redefine itself—not as the study of matter and energy alone, but as the exploration of intelligence itself.

Measurement Without Meaning

Science can predict the movement of galaxies, but it cannot answer why the universe exists. It can describe evolution, but it cannot explain why intelligence evolves. Without meaning, science risks becoming a meaningless exercise in data collection—an endless loop of measuring reality without understanding it. Krishna warns: *"The foolish delight in complex words and theories, ignoring the truth that lies beyond them"* (2.42). Knowledge without wisdom is incomplete; facts without meaning lead to confusion.

What is the point of mapping reality if we do not understand our place within it?

Science as Tool, Not Truth

Science is powerful, but it is not the final authority on truth. It is a tool for exploration, not the ultimate measure of existence. It can explain how neurons fire, but not why consciousness exists. It can map the brain's structure, but not measure awareness, creativity, or intuition. It can study evolution, but not explain why intelligence itself evolves.

The next revolution in science may not come from physics or AI, but from the study of intelligence itself. Consciousness must be treated as fundamental, intelligence as universal, and spiritual experience as a valid form of knowledge. Krishna describes higher knowledge (*Para Vidya*) as the ability to see beyond material reality into intelligence itself. Science must evolve into a wisdom-based discipline, one that does not merely study laws but understands the intelligence that governs them.

The Future of Science as Intelligence

Science now stands at a crossroads. It can remain stuck in materialism, measuring but never understanding. It can deny intelligence as fundamental, limiting itself to mechanistic models. It can ignore consciousness, dismissing the very intelligence that makes science possible. Or it can evolve into something greater:

A science that embraces intelligence as a universal principle. A science that integrates consciousness as part of reality. A science that does not just measure, but seeks wisdom.

Krishna describes the final step of knowledge as transcending mere information and reaching direct realization: *"That which is seen is temporary, but that which is beyond vision is eternal"* (2.16). Science must move from measurement to understanding, from data to intelligence, from description to meaning.

Humanity is ready for the next stage of evolution—where science is not just about discovering facts, but about realizing the intelligence that governs all things. Science, in its highest form, is not separate from intelligence—it is an extension of it. The future belongs to a new kind of science, one that does not just measure reality, but understands its intelligence, meaning, and purpose.

Interlude: From Measurement to Meaning

We have walked through the arc of science—its rise from observation to analysis, its triumphs in precision, and its struggles with meaning. We have seen how science, for all its brilliance, remains incomplete when it forgets the intelligence that sustains reality. Krishna's words remind us that knowledge without wisdom is empty, and wisdom without action is incomplete.

Pause here.

Imagine the universe not as a collection of data points, but as a living intelligence. Every equation, every law, every discovery is a reflection of this deeper order. Science measures the rhythm, but intelligence composes the music. To mistake the measure for the meaning is to miss the essence.

This interlude is a moment of stillness—a reminder that science is not the enemy of spirituality, nor is spirituality opposed to science. They are two languages describing the same truth. One speaks in numbers, the other in experience. Together, they reveal the unity of existence.

Rest here for a moment. Let the thought settle: science is not separate from intelligence—it is an extension of it. The next step is not to choose between science and God, but to see them as one system, one intelligence, one reality.

Chapter 8: The False Divide

Bridging the Two – How Science & God Are One System

In the previous chapter, we saw that science, though powerful, remains incomplete when it confines itself to measurement alone. It can describe how things work, but it struggles to explain why they exist. Science measures reality, but intelligence organizes it—a truth unrecognized in materialistic models.

This leads to a profound realization: science and spirituality are not separate disciplines. They are different approaches to the same fundamental intelligence. The universe is not a random collection of particles governed by blind forces; it follows laws, patterns, and structures that reveal an underlying order.

Krishna, in the *Bhagavad Gita*, describes this intelligence as the foundation of all existence: *"I am the origin of all that exists, the wisdom of the wise, the intelligence in the intelligent"* (7.10). The divide between science and God, then, is an illusion. What we call scientific discovery is simply the process of uncovering the mechanics of divine intelligence. The laws of physics, the complexity of biological life, the vast interconnectedness of the cosmos—all point not to chaos, but to a structured intelligence at play.

Two Paths, One Reality

Science and spirituality are often seen as opposites—one external, one internal. Yet both seek to understand reality. Science relies on observation, experimentation, and measurement. Spirituality relies on consciousness, intuition, and direct experience. But the deeper we look, the more their paths converge. Quantum physics reveals observer-dependent reality, echoing ancient teachings that perception shapes existence. Neuroscience shows meditation alters brain structure, proving consciousness is more than neural activity. The interconnectedness described in the *Gita* is mirrored in quantum entanglement and cosmic unity.

Both science and spirituality are attempts to understand the same intelligence. The difference lies only in their approach.

The Universe as an Intelligent System

Krishna describes reality as a self-organizing, intelligent system: *"All things exist within Me, yet I am beyond them"* (9.4). This vision aligns with modern science's search for unifying principles. Physics seeks a grand unified theory to explain all forces. Biology reveals intricate systems of adaptation and evolution. Cosmology uncovers fine-tuned laws that allow life to exist.

None of these discoveries point to randomness. They point to intelligence woven into the fabric of reality. What science calls natural law, Krishna describes as divine intelligence. What spirituality calls consciousness, science now begins to glimpse as the missing link in its equations.

Consciousness as the Bridge

The greatest mystery in science today is consciousness. Neuroscience can map brain activity, but it cannot explain why awareness exists. Physics can describe particles, but it cannot explain the role of the observer. Krishna resolves this paradox: *"This material world is perishable, but the conscious self is eternal"* (2.17). Consciousness is not a byproduct of matter—it is the essence of reality itself.

Consciousness is the bridge between science and God. It is the missing link that unites external measurement with internal realization. Without consciousness, science cannot explain the act of observation. Without intelligence, spirituality cannot explain the structure of reality. Together, they reveal the same truth: the universe is an intelligent, conscious system.

The Unified Vision

Science and spirituality are not rivals but reflections of the same intelligence. Krishna's teachings refine knowledge: *"The wise see knowledge and action as one"* (4.18). Science is necessary, but it must be guided by wisdom. Measurement alone does not reveal truth; intelligence and consciousness must be part of the equation.

The future of understanding lies not in choosing between science and God, but in recognizing them as one system. Physics and intelligence are two expressions of the same ultimate reality. To study the universe is to study God's intelligence. To realize God is to recognize the intelligence that science measures.

Bringing It All Together

The divide between science and God dissolves when we see them as complementary. Science uncovers the mechanics of divine intelligence. Spirituality experiences its meaning. Together, they form a unified vision: the universe is not random, but structured; not blind, but intelligent; not separate, but whole.

The question is no longer whether science and God can coexist. The question is whether humanity is ready to see them as one system—two languages describing the same truth.

With this realization, we now move forward to explore the next dimension: how consciousness itself becomes the key to bridging science and spirituality, and how intelligence reveals itself not only in the cosmos but within us.

8.1 – The False Divide: Why Science and God Were Never Separate

The perceived conflict between science and spirituality is a relatively modern phenomenon. In ancient times, science and divine intelligence were seen as interconnected—two complementary ways of understanding reality. The greatest minds of early civilizations did not separate the study of nature from the study of intelligence itself.

As materialism took hold of modern thought, science increasingly distanced itself from spiritual wisdom, rejecting the idea of God, intelligence, or consciousness as fundamental aspects of existence. This created a false divide, where science was seen as the pursuit of facts, while spirituality was dismissed as subjective belief. Yet this separation is an illusion. The universe functions as a single, intelligent system, where the laws of physics and the principles of consciousness are not in opposition but part of the same governing intelligence.

Krishna, in the *Bhagavad Gita*, removes this false separation by describing all existence as a manifestation of divine intelligence: *"I am the source of all knowledge and wisdom, the unseen order that governs the cosmos"* (10.32).

Ancient Unity of Science and Divine Intelligence

The idea that science and God are opposing forces is a modern construct. Ancient civilizations saw no contradiction between exploring the mechanics of the universe and recognizing the intelligence behind it.

In India, the Vedas and Upanishads described the universe as an intelligent system where matter and consciousness exist in harmony. Ayurveda, Jyotish, and Sankhya were developed alongside spiritual teachings, reflecting a unified vision of knowledge.

In Greece, thinkers like Pythagoras, Plato, and Aristotle saw the laws of nature as reflections of higher intelligence. Mathematics and astronomy were studied not only for practical use but as ways to decode the order of the cosmos. Plato's "World of Forms" echoed the Vedic concept of Brahman as ultimate reality.

During the Islamic Golden Age, scholars such as Avicenna, Alhazen, and Al-Khwarizmi combined scientific exploration with philosophical and theological insights. The Renaissance in Europe revived this integration, leading to discoveries in astronomy, physics, and anatomy. For most of history, science was a means to understand divine intelligence, not to separate from it.

The Rise of Materialism

The divide began with the rise of materialism, which sought to explain reality through matter and physical laws alone. Newton's laws of motion described the universe as a giant machine, operating on fixed rules. The Enlightenment promoted rationality and empirical observation as the only valid ways of knowing. Religious institutions misused spiritual knowledge, leading to backlash against theology. Scientists sought to remove "God" from inquiry, creating the modern divide between faith and reason.

By the 20th century, atheistic materialism dominated. Evolutionary biology, neuroscience, and quantum physics were interpreted as proof that consciousness and intelligence were accidental byproducts of matter. Yet the very discoveries of modern science—quantum mechanics, consciousness studies, and cosmic fine-tuning—are now leading back to the realization that intelligence is fundamental to reality.

Complementary, Not Contradictory

If science and spirituality were truly opposed, then consciousness should have been disproven as fundamental—but instead, it remains the greatest mystery. The universe should appear chaotic—but instead, it follows precise mathematical laws. Physics should explain all aspects of reality—but it still cannot define intelligence or the source of natural laws.

Scientific progress does not disprove divine intelligence—it reveals it. Krishna does not separate scientific knowledge (*Apara Vidya*) from higher wisdom (*Para Vidya*). He integrates them: *"Among sciences, I am the science of the self"* (10.32). The physical universe is not separate from divine intelligence—it is its expression. Science is not opposed to God—it is the process of discovering His intelligence through natural laws.

Could it be that science has been studying God all along—without realizing it?

Restoring Unity

For most of history, science and spirituality were one system of knowledge. It was only modern materialism that created the illusion of a divide. But today, as science struggles with consciousness, quantum mechanics, and the fine-tuning of the universe, it is becoming clear that the universe operates on principles of intelligence, not randomness. Consciousness is not a byproduct of the brain—it is central to reality. Scientific discovery is, in essence, a search for the deeper intelligence that governs existence.

Krishna's teachings foretold this realization: *"I am the hidden order within all things, the intelligence that guides the wise"* (10.20). Science and spirituality are not separate—they are different lenses for perceiving the same truth. Scientific exploration is a path to understanding divine intelligence, not rejecting it. The future of knowledge must integrate both perspectives into a unified vision of reality.

Humanity now stands at the threshold of reunion—bridging two paths that were never truly separate to begin with.

8.2 – The Common Ground: Intelligence as the Unifying Factor

The conflict between science and spirituality disappears when we recognize that both are seeking the same fundamental truth—an underlying intelligence that governs all existence. Science explores reality through physical laws and patterns; spirituality explores reality through wisdom and self-realization. Their methods differ, but their ultimate goal is the same: to uncover the structure and meaning of existence.

Krishna, in the *Bhagavad Gita,* describes this intelligence as the very foundation of reality: *"I am the origin of all that exists, the wisdom in the wise, and the intelligence in the intelligent"* (7.10). This verse is profound—it suggests that intelligence is not an accidental byproduct of evolution but the very substance of existence itself.

Divine Intelligence as the Foundation of Existence

The *Bhagavad Gita* does not describe God as a distant entity, but as the universal intelligence that pervades all things. Krishna reveals that all forces of nature, from gravity to time, are expressions of divine intelligence. Life, evolution, and consciousness are not random—they are part of a structured, intelligent system. The human mind is capable of recognizing this intelligence when it transcends illusion (*Maya*).

Krishna declares: *"This entire universe is pervaded by Me in My unmanifested form; all beings exist in Me, but I am beyond them"* (9.4). What science calls "natural laws," Krishna describes as "divine intelligence in action." Could it be that science is simply the process of discovering the laws of divine intelligence, without realizing it?

Two Approaches, One Intelligent System

Modern science is built on identifying patterns, laws, and structured order in the universe. These discoveries suggest that reality is not chaotic but governed by principles that are precise and universal. Physics reveals fixed patterns, from galaxies to atoms. Relativity, gravity, and quantum mechanics all uncover deep order. If randomness were the rule, no scientific law would hold consistently—yet nature obeys precise mathematical structures.

Spiritual traditions, from Vedanta to Buddhism, describe the universe as a manifestation of intelligence, not mere matter. Krishna explains that cause and effect (*Karma*) is part of the same intelligent system. Just as physics has laws of motion, spirituality has laws of consciousness and realization. Science calls them natural laws; spirituality calls them divine intelligence. They are two perspectives of the same truth.

Mathematical Precision as Evidence of Intelligence

One of the strongest arguments for intelligence as the foundation of reality is the mathematical precision of the universe. If existence were random, we would expect chaos. Instead, we see constants, repeating patterns, and fine-tuned conditions for life.

The speed of light, the gravitational constant, and atomic forces are set at values that make life possible. If they were even slightly different, the universe as we know it would not exist. Scientists call this the Fine-Tuning Problem. Krishna offers an answer: *"I am the sustainer of all worlds, the intelligence that maintains balance and order"* (9.18). Fine-tuning is not accident—it is structured intelligence.

Nature also reveals intelligence through patterns like the Fibonacci sequence and the Golden Ratio, appearing in galaxies, hurricanes, flowers, DNA, and the human body. Fractals show self-similarity across scales—the branching of neurons mirrors the structure of galaxies. The same mathematical blueprint appears in quantum physics, biology, and astronomy. Intelligence is embedded in the fabric of reality.

Intelligence as the Bridge

Science and spirituality are not separate—they are both ways of discovering the intelligence that governs reality. Science looks for patterns in nature; spirituality looks for intelligence within those patterns. Krishna describes divine intelligence as the force behind both: *"I am the guiding intelligence of all things, the cause of order in the cosmos"* (10.33).

Science is discovering the mechanics of God's intelligence, often without realizing it. Spirituality is experiencing the intelligence behind those mechanics. The highest realization is to see that the two are not separate but one unified system.

Are we now entering an age where science and spirituality must merge—to recognize intelligence not just as a concept, but as the fundamental reality behind all things?

8.3 – The Universe as a Self-Organizing Intelligent System

Science and spirituality have long debated whether the universe is a random, chaotic system or an intelligent, self-organizing structure. Modern discoveries in quantum mechanics, relativity, and biology suggest that reality is not random but governed by deep mathematical and structural order. This vision aligns with Krishna's teachings in the *Bhagavad Gita*, where He describes the universe as an intelligent process of creation, preservation, and dissolution.

Science attempts to explain this order through natural laws, yet it struggles to answer why those laws exist at all. The deeper we explore the cosmos, the more it appears that what we call "nature" is actually intelligence in action.

Scientific Discoveries and Underlying Order

If the universe were truly random, we would expect disorder at every level. Instead, we find mathematical laws governing cosmic and subatomic interactions, biological systems that self-regulate, and precise conditions for the emergence of life.

Quantum mechanics reveals that matter exists in probabilities until observed. The Observer Effect shows that conscious observation influences physical reality. Entanglement suggests particles communicate instantaneously, hinting at deep interconnected intelligence. Wave-particle duality reveals reality as fluid, shaped by perception. If particles behave differently when observed, does this not suggest intelligence at the foundation of reality?

Relativity transformed our understanding of space and time. Time bends under gravity, space follows geometric patterns, and the universe expands in ordered precision. Krishna declares: *"I am time, the great destroyer of worlds"* (11.32). Time and space are not mechanical phenomena—they are manifestations of universal intelligence.

Biology, too, reveals intelligence. DNA carries structured information, cells and ecosystems coordinate without external command, and evolution responds intelligently to environment. Krishna affirms: *"I am the seed-giving father of all living beings"* (14.4). Life is not random chemistry—it is intelligence expressed through living systems.

Krishna's Vision of Universal Intelligence

In the *Gita*, Krishna does not describe the universe as a machine but as a dynamic intelligence that continuously creates, sustains, and dissolves. Creation (*Srishti*), preservation (*Sthiti*), and dissolution (*Laya*) are not accidents but cycles of intelligent renewal. Modern cosmology mirrors this: the Big Bang as creation, cosmic expansion as preservation, and eventual collapse or heat death as dissolution. The universe is not a collection of accidents—it is an intelligent system cycling through transformation.

The Illusion of Randomness

Many claim the universe is random, yet evidence points to deeper order. The fine-tuning of physical constants—gravity, light speed, atomic forces—is so precise that even slight variation would make life impossible. Krishna responds: *"I uphold all things; I sustain the entire cosmos with a fraction of My being"* (10.42). Balance is not accident—it is intelligence.

Patterns in nature—fractals, Fibonacci spirals, the Golden Ratio—appear across galaxies, hurricanes, flowers, and DNA. Matter arranges itself intelligently, not chaotically. Consciousness itself is the final proof. If the universe were random, why would it produce beings capable of understanding it? Krishna declares: *"I am the consciousness in all living beings"* (10.22). Human awareness is not anomaly—it is the universe recognizing itself.

The Universe as Intelligence in Action

The evidence suggests the universe is not a blind machine but a self-organizing intelligent system. Quantum mechanics shows matter responds to observation. Relativity reveals structured precision in space-time. Biology exhibits self-regulating intelligence in living systems. Krishna describes creation, preservation, and dissolution as intelligent processes, not random events.

Science is not studying a lifeless system—it is uncovering the laws of an intelligent reality. Krishna affirms: *"There is nothing beyond Me. All that exists rests upon Me as pearls on a string"* (7.7). What science calls "laws of nature" is divine intelligence in action. What appears random is intelligence functioning beyond human perception. The entire universe is a conscious, self-regulating system—where science and God are not separate, but one.

8.4 – Consciousness: The Missing Link Between Science and God

For centuries, science has struggled to explain consciousness—the ability to experience, perceive, and reflect. Despite remarkable advances in neuroscience, psychology, and artificial intelligence, modern inquiry remains unable to answer the most fundamental question: why does consciousness exist? Science can map brain activity, analyze neural patterns, and even build machines that mimic intelligence, but it cannot explain who or what is actually experiencing reality.

The *Bhagavad Gita* offers a clear answer. Consciousness is not an illusion, nor a product of brain chemistry—it is the fundamental essence of existence itself. Krishna declares: *"That which pervades the entire body, you should know to be indestructible. No one is able to destroy the imperishable soul"* (2.17). Consciousness is not produced by the brain; the brain is merely its instrument. It is eternal, beyond material reality, and the foundation of intelligence itself.

Science's Struggle with Consciousness

Despite centuries of study, science cannot agree on what consciousness is or where it originates. Some theories claim it is an illusion created by brain activity, others that it is a survival mechanism, or that it emerges from complex neural networks and vanishes at death. Yet these explanations fail to address deeper questions. Why does matter, supposedly lifeless, become self-aware? Why do humans possess intuition, creativity, and self-reflection—qualities that transcend survival? Why do near-death experiences and altered states defy material explanations?

Krishna answers: *"The soul is neither born, nor does it ever die; it has always existed and will always exist"* (2.20). Consciousness is not created by the brain—it continues beyond the body, unbound by physical laws. Science has confused consciousness with brain activity, just as mistaking a light bulb for the source of electricity.

The Observer Effect and Krishna's Teachings

One of the most profound discoveries in modern physics is the Observer Effect—the realization that conscious observation changes the behavior of matter. In the double-slit experiment, electrons behave like waves until observed, at which point they collapse into particles. Reality exists as possibilities until awareness forces it into form.

Krishna echoes this truth: *"The world is an illusion, shaped by perception. The wise see reality beyond the senses"* (9.12). Reality is not independent of the observer—it is shaped by awareness. What we experience is not absolute but depends on our level of consciousness. The Observer Effect proves that matter does not have fixed properties until observed, aligning with Krishna's teaching that the world is a play of perception, and true reality lies beyond sensory illusion.

Intelligence as Governing Principle

Modern science often assumes intelligence is an accident of evolution, emerging from random mutations and survival pressures. Yet intelligence is not random—it is structured, self-organizing, and present at all levels of existence. DNA carries coded information like software. Cells communicate and self-repair with purpose. The brain is not merely a processor but a conscious entity capable of self-awareness.

The universe itself follows precise mathematical laws. Galaxies, solar systems, and atoms expand and interact in structured ways. The fine-tuning of physics allows life to emerge, suggesting intentional design. Krishna affirms: *"I am the intelligence that directs all living beings, the force that sustains the universe"* (10.22). Intelligence is not an effect—it is the cause. It existed before life, before the brain, before even the universe itself. What we call "God" may simply be the intelligence that governs all things.

Consciousness as the Bridge

Consciousness is the missing link that connects science and God. Science shows that awareness influences matter. Krishna teaches that perception shapes reality. The universe operates with intelligence at every level, from physics to biology. Consciousness is not illusion—it is the foundation of reality.

The *Bhagavad Gita* aligns perfectly with modern discoveries, leading to a profound realization: science is not separate from God—it is the study of divine intelligence in action. Krishna summarizes: *"There is nothing beyond Me. All things rest upon Me as pearls on a string"* (7.7). What science calls "laws of nature" is divine intelligence in action. What physics calls the Observer Effect is consciousness shaping reality. What evolution calls the emergence of intelligence is the recognition of intelligence as a pre-existing force.

Humanity now stands at a turning point. Science must accept consciousness not as a byproduct but as the ultimate force governing all things. Only then can knowledge evolve into wisdom, and measurement into meaning.

8.5 – The Limits of Science Without a Spiritual Foundation

Science has given humanity unprecedented power—from harnessing nuclear energy to decoding the human genome, from building artificial intelligence to exploring the cosmos. Yet for all its progress, science without a higher ethical or spiritual foundation has led to existential dilemmas. Without wisdom to guide it, science becomes a double-edged sword—capable of both healing and harming, advancing and destabilizing, creating and destroying.

Krishna, in the *Bhagavad Gita*, warns against knowledge without wisdom: *"Knowledge that is used for selfish gain, without consideration of right and wrong, is ignorance in disguise"* (18.22). Scientific progress alone does not guarantee human progress. Without moral intelligence, it can lead to exploitation, imbalance, and collapse.

Existential Crises Born of Knowledge Without Wisdom

The greatest crises of modern civilization are not due to a lack of knowledge, but a lack of wisdom in applying it. We have more information than ever before, yet are we wiser, happier, or more ethical? Technology has advanced, but has it improved human well-being—or created new dangers?

Artificial intelligence raises questions about human purpose. Machines may surpass human intelligence, but without wisdom, they risk becoming lifeless processors of data, replacing creativity and connection with cold efficiency. Krishna reminds us: *"The wise act with knowledge, but they do not lose themselves in their own creation"* (3.26). Intelligence without wisdom becomes dangerous, a force without restraint.

Environmental destruction is another consequence of progress without ethics. Industrialization, fossil fuels, and deforestation have created collapse in ecosystems, driven by a worldview that treats nature as resource rather than sacred order. Krishna teaches: *"I am the Earth that nourishes all beings. Those who exploit nature without gratitude disrupt the harmony of existence"* (3.12). Without reverence, science risks destroying the very planet that sustains us.

Biotechnology and genetic engineering raise profound ethical dilemmas. Should we alter human DNA for enhancement? Should machines decide life and death? Without a moral compass, science risks crossing boundaries in pursuit of progress. Krishna warns: *"Action performed with selfish motives, without regard for its consequences, is impure"* (18.23). Knowledge without ethics becomes corruption.

The Mechanistic Trap

Modern science increasingly views life as mechanistic—reducing humans to machines, consciousness to neural activity, emotions to chemical reactions.

This worldview strips life of meaning. If humans are treated as algorithms, does existence retain purpose beyond productivity?

Deterministic models even deny free will, claiming human choices are illusions of biology. Yet Krishna emphasizes conscious choice: *"A person is elevated by their choices, by their self-awareness—not by fate alone"* (6.5). To deny free will is to deny morality itself.

Despite material progress, modern civilization faces epidemics of depression, anxiety, and meaninglessness. Comfort does not guarantee fulfillment. Without a spiritual dimension, humanity feels disconnected from purpose. Science alone cannot provide meaning—it must integrate spiritual intelligence to restore balance.

Spiritual Intelligence as Ethical Foundation

The *Bhagavad Gita* offers a solution. Krishna describes three levels of knowledge: *Apara Vidya*—material knowledge of the physical world; *Para Vidya*—higher knowledge of consciousness and universal order; and *Atma Vidya*—transcendental realization of divine intelligence. Science today remains confined to material knowledge, refusing to acknowledge consciousness as fundamental.

Krishna declares: *"The highest knowledge is that which liberates, which reveals the truth beyond illusion"* (4.39). True science must go beyond measurement. It must serve wisdom, ethics, and intelligence.

Bringing It All Together

Science without a spiritual foundation leads to technological progress without responsibility, a mechanistic worldview that strips life of meaning, and a civilization driven by power rather than wisdom. For science to evolve, it must recognize consciousness as fundamental, embrace intelligence as the guiding force of the universe, and integrate ethics into its framework.

The future of knowledge is not science versus spirituality—it is their integration. Only then can humanity progress in a way that is intelligent, ethical, and sustainable.

As we move forward, we will explore how a new scientific paradigm—rooted in intelligence and consciousness—can transform the future of human understanding.

8.6 – The Future: A New Scientific Paradigm Rooted in Intelligence

Science, as it exists today, is incomplete. It has given us extraordinary tools to measure, predict, and manipulate the physical world, yet it has failed to answer the deepest questions of existence. What is the source of intelligence? Why does consciousness exist? Is the universe truly random, or guided by an underlying order?

The modern scientific method, rooted in materialism, assumes that only matter and energy are real. But this approach has reached its limits. In quantum mechanics, artificial intelligence, and neuroscience, the role of intelligence and consciousness can no longer be ignored. Krishna, in the *Bhagavad Gita*, describes a higher model of knowledge: *"I am the intelligence of the intelligent, the wisdom of the wise"* (7.10). Intelligence is not an accident of evolution—it is the foundation of reality itself.

From Matter to Intelligence

For centuries, science assumed intelligence was a byproduct of the brain, emerging from biological complexity. Yet discoveries in quantum physics, cognitive science, and consciousness studies suggest otherwise. Matter itself behaves differently when observed, hinting that intelligence is woven into the fabric of reality. The question arises: is intelligence something humans "possess," or is it the fundamental property of the universe itself?

Materialist science treats consciousness as illusion, thoughts as chemical reactions, and the universe as devoid of intelligence. But emerging fields challenge this view. Quantum mechanics shows observation affects reality. Neuroscience reveals brain activity cannot fully explain self-awareness. AI demonstrates the difference between processing information and true intelligence. Science is being forced to acknowledge that intelligence is not a product—it may be the cause.

Toward a New Framework

For science to progress, it must move beyond purely physical explanations and recognize that consciousness, intelligence, and order are not separate from reality—they are reality. Krishna describes existence as interconnected intelligence: *"There is nothing beyond Me. All things rest upon Me like pearls on a string"* (7.7). The universe is not a collection of parts—it is an intelligent whole. Consciousness is not illusion—it is the force that shapes reality. Scientific laws are not random—they reflect deeper order embedded in existence.

A new science of intelligence would integrate physics, consciousness, and AI into a unified model. It would study intelligence as the organizing principle of reality, not as an emergent property. Human intelligence would be seen as one expression of universal intelligence. This could be the next great revolution—moving from measuring particles to understanding intelligence as the fabric of existence.

Breakthroughs Aligning with Spiritual Wisdom

As science advances, it moves closer to conclusions long described in spiritual traditions. Artificial intelligence can process information but lacks self-awareness. It can mimic thought but cannot experience consciousness. If intelligence were mere computation, why can't machines become conscious? Krishna answers: *"I am the consciousness in all living beings"* (10.22). Intelligence is not mechanical—it is living force.

Neuroscience still cannot explain why we experience emotions, thoughts, and self-awareness. Krishna teaches: *"The soul is neither born nor does it die"* (2.20). Consciousness exists beyond the body, eternal and fundamental. Could neuroscience eventually confirm the existence of the soul?

Physics, too, points toward intelligence. Quantum mechanics reveals observer-dependent reality. Relativity shows time and space as dynamic forces. String theory suggests fine-tuned mathematical precision. Krishna declares: *"I am the order that governs the universe, the intelligence that sustains all things*" (10.33). Physics may ultimately confirm that the universe is not merely physical, but deeply intelligent.

The Next Step in Scientific Evolution

Science now stands at a turning point. It must move beyond materialism, abandon the idea that consciousness is illusion, and recognize intelligence as the cause of order. Intelligence is not an accident—it is fundamental. Consciousness is not a neural trick—it is real force. The future of science lies in a holistic framework uniting AI, neuroscience, and quantum physics into a model of intelligence.

The *Bhagavad Gita* already presents this vision. Krishna describes intelligence as the force behind all reality: *"I am the intelligence in all things, the wisdom in the wise, the unseen order that sustains the cosmos"* (7.10). The search for God and the search for ultimate scientific truth are the same pursuit. The next revolution will not be in technology, but in understanding intelligence itself.

The divide between science and spirituality will dissolve as we recognize that intelligence is the foundation of all things. Humanity is entering a new era—where science no longer denies intelligence but embraces it as the key to understanding the universe.

8.7 – The Final Realization: Science as the Study of God's Intelligence

For centuries, science has been seen as rational pursuit, while spirituality has been associated with faith. Yet the deeper science investigates reality, the more it begins to resemble ancient wisdom. Physics, biology, and consciousness studies reveal that the universe is not random and mechanical—it is governed by laws, intelligence, and interconnectedness. The search for a unified theory of everything is nothing more than the search for the intelligence that governs existence.

Krishna, in the *Bhagavad Gita*, declares: *"I am the intelligence in the intelligent, the wisdom in the wise"* (7.10). This single statement redefines the purpose of science. Scientific exploration is not separate from spirituality—it is the process of uncovering divine intelligence through natural laws.

Scientific Inquiry as Search for Divine Intelligence

Science begins with the assumption that the universe is governed by laws and order. But what is the source of these laws? Why does gravity exist? Why does light have a constant speed? Why do mathematical patterns shape galaxies, hurricanes, and DNA? Science can describe how they work, but not why they exist.

The *Gita* provides the answer: *"I am the origin of all that exists. All things arise from Me, and in Me, they are sustained"* (10.8). The laws of nature are not separate from divine intelligence—they are its expression. Science is not disproving God; it is discovering how divine intelligence operates. The deeper we go into physics, neuroscience, and AI, the more we recognize intelligence everywhere. Could it be that science has been studying God all along—without realizing it?

Krishna's Statement and the Purpose of Science

Most scientists assume intelligence is a product of evolution, arising from biological complexity. Krishna challenges this: *"I am the intelligence in the intelligent, the wisdom in the wise"* (7.10). Intelligence is not accident—it is the fundamental structure of reality. Human intelligence is not separate from divine intelligence—it is an extension of it.

This reframes the purpose of science. Science is not just about measuring reality—it is about understanding the intelligence that sustains it. The ultimate goal of knowledge is not discovery but realization. The study of the universe is, in fact, the study of God's intelligence at work. Krishna confirms: *"There is nothing beyond Me. All things rest upon Me like pearls on a string"* (7.7). The universe is woven into intelligence; scientific laws are structured by divine order; consciousness is the essence of existence. Science is ultimately the study of God's mind, expressed through the cosmos.

The End of the Divide

The divide between science and God was never real—it was created by human perception. Science seeks mechanics; spirituality seeks meaning. Krishna reveals both are part of the same system. The deeper science investigates, the more it confirms spiritual insights. Quantum physics shows reality is observer-dependent, echoing the Gita's teaching that perception shapes the world. Neuroscience struggles with consciousness, while Krishna defines it as eternal. AI reveals the limits of mechanical intelligence, while spirituality describes intelligence as divine.

Krishna dissolves the illusion of separation: *"Those who see Me in all things, and all things in Me, never lose sight of the truth"* (6.30). Science and spirituality are not separate—they are two ways of discovering the same truth. Scientific exploration is, in reality, a search for God's intelligence. The end of this journey is not knowledge alone—it is wisdom, self-realization, and unity with the intelligence of the universe.

Science as the Final Bridge

Humanity stands at a crossroads. Science has explored the depths of physics and found intelligence. It has mapped the brain but cannot explain consciousness. It has developed AI but still does not understand true intelligence. This journey is leading toward realization: the universe, life, and intelligence are not accidental—they are part of a grand intelligent design.

Krishna confirms: *"He who sees Me everywhere and sees all things in Me, he alone understands the truth"* (6.30). Science is not separate from God—it is the process of realizing divine intelligence. The universe is not lifeless matter—it is conscious intelligence in motion. The final realization is not knowledge of the external world—it is understanding that intelligence itself is divine.

Has modern science unknowingly been searching for God all along—through equations, discoveries, and the study of the cosmos? As we conclude this chapter, we recognize that the search for scientific truth and the search for spiritual realization are one and the same. Science and God were never separate. They are two expressions of the same intelligence—one measured through equations, the other experienced through wisdom.

The final realization is not scientific or spiritual—it is the understanding that both paths lead to the same truth: intelligence is divine, and the universe is its expression.

Interlude: Resting in the Unity of Science and God

We have journeyed through the unfolding of Chapter 8, where the false divide between science and spirituality dissolved. What once seemed like two opposing paths—one measuring matter, the other seeking meaning—has revealed itself as a single pursuit of truth. Science studies the mechanics of divine intelligence; spirituality experiences its essence. Both are reflections of the same reality.

Pause here.

Imagine the universe not as lifeless matter, but as a living intelligence. Every equation, every law, every discovery is a glimpse into the mind of God. The galaxies spinning in perfect rhythm, the DNA carrying coded wisdom, the consciousness that allows us to reflect—all of it is intelligence in motion. Science names it "laws of nature." Krishna names it "divine intelligence."

This interlude is a moment of stillness, a chance to let the realization settle: science and God were never separate. They are two languages describing the same truth. One speaks in numbers, the other in wisdom. Together, they reveal the unity of existence.

Rest here for a moment. Feel the weight of this realization: the search for scientific truth and the search for spiritual realization are one and the same. To study the universe is to study God's intelligence. To awaken spiritually is to recognize that intelligence as the essence of all things.

With this unity in mind, we prepare to step into the next chapter—where the journey moves beyond reconciliation into transformation. Chapter 9 will explore how this new paradigm of knowledge can reshape human understanding, guiding us toward a future where wisdom and science flow together as one.

Chapter 9: Breaking Misbeliefs

How Knowledge Became Dogma

In the previous chapter, we saw that science and spirituality are not separate but two expressions of the same intelligence. Science, at its core, is the study of divine intelligence; true spirituality is the realization of that intelligence. Yet history shows that when knowledge becomes rigid, unquestioned, and institutionalized, it ceases to be a tool for discovery and turns into dogma—limiting human progress instead of advancing it.

What begins as open-ended inquiry—whether in science, philosophy, or spirituality—has often been distorted by institutions, traditions, and rigid interpretations. The very teachings meant to liberate the mind became instruments of control and stagnation. Scientific materialism rejected consciousness, religious institutions enforced blind faith, and sacred texts were misinterpreted to serve authority rather than truth. Humanity has repeatedly fallen into the trap of mistaking partial knowledge for absolute truth.

Krishna, in the *Bhagavad Gita*, warns against such rigidity: *"Fools cling to the letter of the scriptures, ignoring the wisdom beyond words"* (2.42). True intelligence is not memorizing facts, blindly following traditions, or defending fixed beliefs—it is continuous expansion, questioning, and deeper realization.

This chapter will expose the misbeliefs that turned knowledge into dogma, showing how wisdom is not found in attachment to rigid doctrines but in the freedom to seek higher understanding. Knowledge must remain alive, fluid, and open-ended, or it becomes a prison.

Is humanity ready to break free from the chains of intellectual stagnation and rediscover knowledge as a path to liberation? Let us begin.

9.1 – The Corruption of Knowledge: When Truth Becomes Rigidity

Knowledge, in its purest form, is meant to liberate the mind, expand awareness, and deepen understanding. The great thinkers of ancient civilizations—whether Vedic rishis, Greek philosophers, or early scientists—sought truth, not control. Their teachings encouraged open exploration, questioning, and direct experience. Yet over time, knowledge became institutionalized, rigidly codified into rules, dogmas, and unquestionable doctrines. Instead of guiding individuals toward self-realization, it was turned into an instrument of authority, used to restrict inquiry rather than encourage it.

Krishna, in the *Bhagavad Gita*, warns against such intellectual stagnation: *"Fools delight in complex words and rituals, but they remain blind to true wisdom"* (2.42). True knowledge is not about memorizing facts or defending fixed beliefs—it is about continuous expansion, questioning, and deeper realization.

Knowledge as Inquiry, Not Control

The oldest traditions of wisdom were never meant to impose rigid beliefs but to help individuals experience truth for themselves. The Upanishads were dialogues between students and masters, built on questioning reality rather than accepting dogma. The *Bhagavad Gita* itself is a conversation—Krishna does not force Arjuna to obey; he encourages him to reflect and decide for himself. The rishis of ancient India sought direct realization, not submission to authority.

Greek philosophy, too, was founded on questioning. Socrates exposed contradictions in fixed beliefs through dialogue, Plato and Aristotle pursued deeper understanding beyond tradition. Wisdom was not memorization but inquiry. Early science followed the same spirit. Archimedes, Galileo, Newton—none saw science as a fixed system of facts, but as an evolving exploration. They revised theories constantly, knowing truth is always deeper than current understanding. Knowledge was dynamic, alive, and open-ended.

The Rise of Dogma

Over time, however, knowledge was hijacked by institutions. Religion, science, and philosophy each fell into rigidity. Spiritual texts meant for inner exploration became strict doctrines enforced by priesthoods. Ritual replaced realization. Krishna warns: *"Those who perform rituals without knowledge remain caught in illusion"* (9.20). True spirituality is about personal realization, not blind obedience.

Science, too, became dogmatic. What began as open inquiry hardened into materialist frameworks that dismiss anything beyond matter. Consciousness studies and quantum paradoxes are often rejected because they threaten the worldview of institutions. The assumption that science has "figured everything out" contradicts the very spirit of discovery.

Philosophy, once a guide for life, became abstract theorization. Universities reduced wisdom to intellectual exercises, detached from ethics and consciousness. Philosophy was meant to be wisdom in action, not endless debate.

The Danger of Fixed Beliefs

The greatest danger of turning knowledge into dogma is that it prevents growth. When people believe they already "know the truth," they stop questioning. Intellectual stagnation follows. Krishna warns: *"The wise remain open, knowing that true knowledge is endless"* (4.34). A mind that believes it knows everything has ceased to grow.

Rigid systems prioritize authority over truth. Institutions defend their power rather than seek wisdom, imposing rules to maintain control. Krishna emphasizes: *"Do not be bound by systems—seek the truth beyond all limitations"* (18.63). Truth must be guided by intelligence, not blind adherence.

Fear of change leads to rejection of new knowledge. Galileo's heliocentric model was resisted by religion. Consciousness studies are dismissed by science. Spiritual seekers have been persecuted for questioning dogma. Humanity cannot evolve if it clings to outdated beliefs.

Restoring Knowledge as Liberation

Knowledge was never meant to imprison—it was meant to awaken intelligence, inspire exploration, and lead to self-realization. True spirituality is not ritual but direct experience of consciousness. True science is not defending materialism but continuously discovering reality. True philosophy is not abstract debate but wisdom applied to life.

Krishna defines real knowledge as that which leads to freedom: *"That knowledge which frees one from illusion is the highest wisdom"* (4.36). Wisdom is questioning, evolving, deepening. Rigid beliefs block realization. The highest knowledge is not in texts or theories, but in direct experience and expanded intelligence.

Are we ready to break free from outdated beliefs and restore knowledge as a path to liberation?

9.2 – Religion vs. Spirituality: When Teachings Become Blind Faith

Spiritual teachings were originally meant to awaken intelligence, encourage self-inquiry, and lead individuals toward direct experience of truth. They were not about strict rituals, rigid doctrines, or blind obedience—they were designed to liberate, not control. Yet over time, organized religion transformed spiritual wisdom into rigid belief systems. Instead of encouraging realization, institutions enforced rituals, dogmas, and unquestionable doctrines. What was once a path to higher understanding became a system of conformity, demanding faith over experience, obedience over intelligence.

Krishna, in the *Bhagavad Gita*, warns against such practices: *"Fools delight in rituals and complex words, but they remain blind to true wisdom"* (2.42). True spirituality is not about external performance—it is about inner transformation.

From Fluid Wisdom to Rigid Structures

The earliest traditions were fluid, open-ended paths of discovery. Wisdom was passed through dialogue, oral transmission, and self-inquiry. The *Upanishads* and the *Gita* emphasize questioning and reflection rather than rigid commandments. Krishna himself does not force Arjuna to obey; he invites him to reflect and choose. Original spirituality was about direct realization, not institutionalized worship.

As civilizations grew, however, spiritual teachings were institutionalized. Priests and leaders defined fixed doctrines, rituals, and codes. People were told to obey scriptures and authorities rather than seek truth for themselves. Spirituality became religion, and religion became a tool of control. Questioning was discouraged, seekers who challenged authority were punished, and what was meant to liberate became a mechanism to maintain social and political order.

Krishna's Warning Against Rituals Without Wisdom

Krishna repeatedly warns that rituals performed without understanding lead nowhere: *"Those who cling to the words of scriptures, engaging in rituals alone, remain trapped in illusion"* (2.42). Rituals were originally designed as tools to focus the mind, not as absolute requirements. Over time, their purpose was forgotten, and they became mechanical routines. Krishna reminds us: *"Even the most elaborate rituals, if done without awareness, lead only to temporary results"* (9.20).

Faith without intelligence becomes superstition. Krishna teaches devotion (*Bhakti*), but not as blind submission—it is devotion with awareness, love, and intelligence. True devotion is an inner experience, not an external performance. He encourages seekers to question, to think, to experience divinity directly—not to follow traditions blindly.

True Spirituality as Experience, Not Belief

Spirituality is not second-hand knowledge—it is direct realization. A person who reads about fire but never touches it has information, but not experience. A person who follows customs but never experiences truth has faith, but not wisdom. Krishna describes true seekers as those who go beyond scriptures and rituals, realizing the divine within: *"The wise go beyond scriptures and rituals, knowing that truth is realized within"* (6.23).

Spirituality is personal, not institutional. Faith without intelligence leads to ignorance. The highest realization comes not from rules but from direct experience of consciousness.

Restoring Spirituality as Liberation

Religion, in its corrupted form, demands blind faith, obedience, and mechanical rituals. But true spirituality, as Krishna teaches, is about experiencing divinity, seeking wisdom, and going beyond rituals to realize eternal truth. Knowledge must remain alive, fluid, and experiential, or it becomes a prison.

Are we ready to move beyond religious conditioning and restore spirituality as a path of personal realization?

As we move forward, we will see how science, like religion, has also hardened into dogma—replacing true exploration with unquestioned belief.

9.3 – Science vs. Scientism: When Inquiry Becomes an Ideology

Science was once a humble pursuit of knowledge, a method designed to evolve, refine, and expand human understanding. The greatest scientific minds—Newton, Einstein, Tesla, Heisenberg—saw science as a journey, not a destination. They understood that no theory is final, and no discovery is ultimate truth. Yet modern science has increasingly shifted from exploration to dogma, transforming into scientism—the belief that only materialist science can explain reality, and that everything outside of it is invalid.

Just as religion hardened into rigid institutions, science too has become institutionalized, defending certain ideas as absolute rather than questioning and refining them. Krishna warns against this arrogance: *"The ignorant, deluded by pride, claim to know everything, but the wise remain open, knowing that truth is endless"* (4.34).

Science as Inquiry vs. Scientism as Ideology

Real science is a method, not a belief system. It is built on observation, experimentation, revision, and openness to uncertainty. It admits gaps in knowledge and evolves with new discoveries. Scientism, however, is when science becomes ideology—where certain beliefs are held as absolute, and questioning them is dismissed as superstition. Real science says: *"We are still learning."* Scientism says: *"We already know everything."*

True science is about discovering reality, not limiting it to pre-existing models.

The Scientific Method as Evolution, Not Fixity

The scientific method was designed to evolve. Every revolution in science occurred because someone dared to question an old paradigm. Newton's laws were once considered absolute, until Einstein revealed relativity and showed that space and time are flexible. Classical physics saw the universe as a machine, until quantum mechanics revealed unpredictability and observer-dependence. The universe was once thought static, until Hubble discovered its expansion.

The lesson is clear: no theory is final. The greatest breakthroughs happen when science is willing to change. Krishna echoes this truth: *"The wise do not cling to fixed ideas; they move with reality as it unfolds"* (2.47).

The Modern Misbelief: Science as Complete

Today, many claim science has already explained everything—that only small gaps remain. This mindset is dangerous, for it prevents exploration.

Consciousness studies are dismissed, even though evidence suggests awareness is more than brain activity. Near-death experiences, meditation research, and quantum cognition point to deeper truths, yet materialism insists consciousness is illusion.

Scientists often avoid controversial topics—free will, mind's effect on matter, fine-tuning of the universe—for fear of losing credibility. But if Einstein had feared questioning Newton, relativity would never have emerged. True science must be fearless.

Materialism assumes only matter and energy exist, but this has never been proven. Quantum physics, consciousness studies, and fine-tuning suggest intelligence plays a role in reality. Krishna teaches: *"The wise seek knowledge beyond the seen, for reality is deeper than the senses perceive"* (13.12).

Restoring Science as True Exploration

Science was meant to be a method of discovery, a continuous search for truth, an open exploration of reality—including intelligence, consciousness, and the unknown. But scientism has turned it into a rigid ideology, ignoring consciousness, fearing challenges, and rejecting anything beyond physical measurement.

Krishna's teachings align with the true spirit of science: *"The highest knowledge is not about controlling reality, but about understanding it"* (4.36). True science must evolve beyond materialism, beyond fixed theories, beyond dogma. Only then can it fulfill its purpose.

9.4 – Misinterpreting Sacred Texts: When Words Become Chains

Sacred texts were never meant to be rigid doctrines. They were intended as guides to higher intelligence, self-realization, and liberation. The *Bhagavad Gita*, the *Vedas*, the *Upanishads*, and other ancient scriptures were not written to be followed blindly but to awaken deeper understanding. They contain layers of meaning, meant to be interpreted in context, not memorized and obeyed without question.

Yet over time, these texts have been misinterpreted, distorted, and manipulated—often by those seeking power, control, or blind obedience. Instead of guiding individuals toward wisdom and liberation, they have been used to trap minds in rigid beliefs, rituals, and literal interpretations. Krishna warns against this danger: *"The foolish cling to the words of the scriptures but miss the wisdom beyond them"* (2.42).

From Living Wisdom to Rigid Doctrine

Originally, sacred texts were dynamic, evolving teachings. The *Vedas* were poetic expressions of mystical experience and scientific observation, meant for exploration rather than ritualistic dogma. Over time, priestly control replaced personal understanding, turning Vedic wisdom into a system of rites. Krishna criticizes this mindless ritualism: *"Those attached to mere rituals remain stuck in illusion, unable to see beyond them"* (9.20).

The *Bhagavad Gita* itself was spoken to awaken Arjuna's intelligence, not to impose fixed rules. Yet later interpretations turned it into a book of commandments rather than a guide for inner awakening. Krishna challenges Arjuna to think for himself: *"Now I have told you everything. Reflect upon it deeply, and do as you choose"* (18.63). He does not demand obedience—he encourages choice.

The *Upanishads*, too, were meant to lead seekers to direct realization of truth. Over time, they became intellectual exercises, debated by scholars but rarely applied in life. True wisdom is not endless argument—it is transformation.

The Trap of Literalism

Literalism reduces wisdom to dogma. When words are followed without understanding, they become chains instead of keys. The Gita, the Bible, the Quran, the Vedas—all are filled with metaphors and symbols. To read them literally is to miss their deeper power. Krishna warns: *"The wise do not become trapped in the words of scripture; they seek the truth beyond them"* (2.53).

Throughout history, leaders misused scriptures to control society, claiming exclusive authority over meaning. Instead of encouraging realization, they demanded obedience. Krishna's message is the opposite: *"A person must seek truth for themselves, not depend on another's authority"* (3.35). Wisdom cannot be controlled—it must be realized individually.

Sacred texts also lose meaning when applied rigidly without context. The Vedas and the Gita were given in specific eras; their wisdom is timeless, but it must be applied intelligently, not frozen in outdated interpretations.

Krishna's Message: Liberation, Not Imprisonment

Krishna's entire teaching in the *Bhagavad Gita* is about freedom, not restriction. He does not tell Arjuna to follow a rigid path—he encourages him to reflect and choose. He does not say rituals alone will lead to truth—he emphasizes intelligence and awareness. He does not impose a single definition of God—he describes the divine as ever-expanding intelligence.

"The wise see beyond words and rituals, seeking truth in direct experience" (6.23). Sacred texts are starting points, not final conclusions. True spirituality is a living experience, not a memorized doctrine. Krishna does not want followers—he wants seekers, thinkers, awakened beings.

Restoring the True Purpose of Sacred Texts

Sacred texts were meant to be keys to higher realization, not chains of dogma. Over time, they were misinterpreted, used for authority, and followed blindly. To restore their purpose, we must read them with questioning, apply them with intelligence, and recognize that words alone do not bring truth—only direct experience does.

True wisdom is not about clinging to words but awakening intelligence. The scriptures are not prisons—they are invitations to liberation.

Are we ready to move beyond blind faith and rediscover the essence of wisdom?

As we move forward, we will explore how true knowledge is not about memorizing scriptures or scientific theories, but about breaking free from intellectual dogma to cultivate living intelligence.

9.5 – Breaking Free from Intellectual Dogma: The Role of Intelligence Over Belief

In every era, humanity has faced a common trap—the belief that we already know enough, that knowledge is fixed, and that our current understanding is the ultimate truth. This illusion has appeared in religion, science, philosophy, and even personal belief systems. Yet the highest intelligence is not about clinging to what we think we know—it is about questioning, evolving, and constantly refining our understanding.

Krishna, in the *Bhagavad Gita*, teaches that intelligence is not a static possession but a dynamic force that must continuously grow: *"The wise never cling to rigid ideas; they remain open, seeking truth beyond all limitations"* (2.47).

Knowledge Without Depth

Modern education and religious conditioning often equate memorization with intelligence. But memorizing information is not wisdom—it is storage, not growth. Reciting scripture does not mean understanding it. Repeating a scientific theory does not mean grasping its deeper implications. Quoting philosophy does not mean living its truth.

Many scholars can recite every verse of the *Gita* yet fail to embody its essence. Many scientists cling to materialist theories without questioning the mysteries of consciousness. Many religious followers perform rituals without knowing why they exist. Krishna warns against blind intellectualism: *"One may know many words, but without wisdom, they are empty"* (2.42). True intelligence is about depth, not accumulation.

Reading about fire does not mean you understand heat. Studying the mechanics of love does not mean you have experienced love. Knowing theories of meditation does not mean you have touched inner stillness. Knowledge must transform into realization, or it remains hollow.

Intelligence as Dynamic Force

Most people believe intelligence is fixed—something you "have" or "don't have." Krishna teaches otherwise. Intelligence is evolving; it grows with questioning, deepens with experience, and expands with wisdom. The *Gita* itself is a dialogue, not a doctrine. Krishna does not give Arjuna rigid answers—he guides him to reflect and choose.

"Even the wise must continue seeking, for knowledge is endless" (18.63). Knowledge is not an end but a process. To stop questioning is to stop growing.

Intelligence must also be applied. Collecting wisdom without action is like a well without water. Krishna emphasizes: *"Knowledge without action is like a well without water"* (3.9). The highest intelligence is not knowing truth but living it.

A mind that refuses to change stagnates. Krishna warns: *"The mind that is fixed in one idea loses sight of the vastness of truth"* (6.23). The universe itself is expanding, evolving, shifting—so must our intelligence.

Cultivating a Living Mindset

To break free from intellectual dogma, we must cultivate a questioning mind, a flexible intellect, and a deeper level of understanding.

Question everything—even your own beliefs. Krishna encourages Arjuna to challenge his fears and assumptions: *"The wise question everything, for only the fool is satisfied with easy answers"* (4.34). True intelligence begins with courage to doubt.

Respect authority, but never blindly obey it. Krishna does not say, "Obey Me without question." He tells Arjuna: *"Now that you have heard My wisdom, reflect upon it deeply and do as you choose"* (18.63). Authority can guide, but intelligence must lead.

Learn from everything, but trust your own realization. Wisdom is infinite, not confined to one book or teacher. Krishna affirms: *"Do not limit yourself to one path, for wisdom is infinite"* (12.3). An evolving mind absorbs knowledge from everywhere but follows only what resonates with truth.

Focus on direct experience, not just words. Knowledge that is not lived remains theoretical. Krishna teaches: *"A person who only repeats what is written in texts, without understanding its meaning, is like a blind man leading the blind"* (2.52). Apply what you learn—do not merely recite it.

Intelligence as a Living Force

True knowledge is never static—it is always evolving. To be intelligent, we must question rather than memorize, seek experience rather than blind belief, and remain open to growth rather than cling to fixed ideas.

Krishna's message is clear: *"The wise do not see knowledge as a destination but as an endless journey"* (4.37). Wisdom is not a collection of facts—it is the ability to think, adapt, and realize deeper truths. Any belief—religious, scientific, or philosophical—must be questioned to uncover its essence. The highest intelligence is the one that never stops evolving.

Are we ready to free ourselves from intellectual stagnation and embrace the dynamic flow of wisdom?

9.6 – The Final Realization: Knowledge is a Path, Not a Destination

If there is one ultimate mistake humanity has made regarding knowledge, it is believing that knowledge is something to be acquired and possessed, rather than something to be lived and expanded. Both religious and scientific institutions have fallen into this trap, treating knowledge as a fixed conclusion rather than an evolving process.

True wisdom is not a collection of facts, scriptures, or theories—it is a journey of intelligence that never ends. The moment we believe we have found the final answer, we stop growing. Krishna shatters this illusion when He declares: *"The wise do not claim to know everything; they remain open, always seeking, always expanding"* (4.34).

Knowledge as Liberation, Not Imprisonment

True knowledge does not create walls—it removes them. The greatest minds in history, from ancient sages to modern scientists, understood that knowledge is a tool, not a destination. It is meant to expand intelligence, not confine it within rigid belief systems. Yet history shows how knowledge has been misused to limit human thinking: scriptures turned into unquestionable rules, theories used to deny non-physical realities, academia mistaking memorization for wisdom.

Krishna teaches that knowledge must lead to liberation, not limitation: *"True knowledge frees one from illusion and expands vision beyond what the senses perceive"* (4.36). Any knowledge that creates division or rigidity is incomplete. True intelligence is measured not by how much information the mind stores, but by how open it remains. Knowledge must be a key, not a cage.

Wisdom Beyond Dogma

The greatest irony of human history is that both religion and science began as paths to truth, yet both hardened into dogma. Spirituality, originally about inner realization, became blind faith. Science, originally open inquiry, became materialist ideology. Both now demand obedience to fixed ideas rather than encouraging exploration.

Krishna warns: *"Those who cling to the letter of the scriptures but miss their deeper wisdom remain trapped in illusion"* (2.42). True wisdom is not in words but in realization. He reminds us: *"The highest knowledge is not in theories or rituals, but in the direct experience of truth"* (6.23). The mind that clings to dogma—whether religious or scientific—is equally blind.

Krishna's Ultimate Teaching: Intelligence Over Belief

Krishna's entire dialogue with Arjuna is about awakening intelligence. At no point does He demand blind obedience. Instead, He challenges Arjuna to think, reflect, and choose: *"Now that you have heard My wisdom, reflect upon it deeply and do as you choose"* (18.63). Truth is not imposed—it is discovered. Knowledge is not limited—it is expanded. The final realization is this: truth is not something to be believed—it is something to be realized.

Knowledge as Endless Journey

If we truly seek wisdom, we must let go of rigid beliefs, recognize intelligence as a process, and never assume we have reached the final truth. Krishna's final message is a call to eternal learning: *"One who sees Me in all things, and all things in Me, never loses sight of the truth"* (6.30).

The universe itself is evolving intelligence—so must our minds be. Wisdom is not an end goal, but a continuous unfolding. The highest intelligence is the one that never stops questioning, growing, and expanding.

Knowledge is not a destination—it is a path. Not something to possess, but something to live. Not a conclusion, but a journey into infinite intelligence.

Interlude: Beyond Dogma, Into Living Intelligence

Pause here.

We have walked through the shadows of dogma—religious, scientific, and intellectual—and seen how knowledge, when frozen, becomes a prison. Scriptures turned into chains, science hardened into ideology, philosophy reduced to abstraction. Each began as a path to truth, yet each risked becoming a wall that blocked the very freedom it promised.

But Krishna's voice in the *Bhagavad Gita* cuts through the rigidity: *"Now that you have heard My wisdom, reflect upon it deeply and do as you choose"* (18.63). His words remind us that truth is not imposed—it is discovered. Knowledge is not a possession—it is a living journey.

Let the mind rest here.

Imagine knowledge not as a book to be closed, but as a river that never stops flowing. Every verse, every theory, every idea is a stepping stone, not a final destination. The moment we cling, we stagnate. The moment we release, we expand.

Dogma says: *"This is the answer."* Wisdom whispers: *"Keep seeking."*

This interlude is a space to feel the difference. To sense how liberation comes not from memorizing words or defending beliefs, but from living intelligence—questioning, evolving, and opening to deeper truths.

As Chapter 9 closes, let us carry this realization: knowledge is not meant to bind us, but to free us. It is not a cage of conclusions, but a path of endless discovery.

With this freedom alive in us, we step into Chapter 10—where the journey moves beyond critique into creation, exploring how a new paradigm of knowledge can guide humanity toward higher intelligence and deeper unity.

Chapter 10: The True Nature of Time & Energy

The Key to Understanding Reality

In the previous chapter, we discovered that knowledge is not a fixed destination but a constantly evolving journey. True wisdom is not about memorizing facts or defending rigid beliefs—it is about deepening intelligence, questioning assumptions, and expanding our understanding of existence. Yet this realization leads us to a profound question: what is reality itself?

To truly grasp the nature of existence, we must explore the two fundamental forces that shape everything—time and energy. Modern science describes time as a linear progression and energy as a measurable quantity, but the deeper we investigate, the more we realize that both are far more mysterious than we assume.

Krishna, in the *Bhagavad Gita*, offers an insight that transcends conventional thought: *"I am time, the great destroyer of worlds"* (11.32). Time is not a passive backdrop—it is an active, intelligent force. Energy, likewise, is not merely a physical property—it is the very movement of existence itself, the pulse of reality.

Are time and energy truly objective, or are they shaped by perception, consciousness, and intelligence? Could understanding their deeper nature unlock the mysteries of reality itself?

This chapter will take us beyond scientific materialism and religious symbolism, revealing how time and energy are not separate from intelligence but expressions of it. Through the lens of modern physics and ancient wisdom, we will see that the key to understanding reality lies in recognizing these forces—not as mechanical concepts, but as manifestations of cosmic intelligence.

10.1 – The Illusion of Time: Is It a Linear Progression or a Cyclic Reality?

Time is one of the greatest mysteries of existence. We perceive it as a continuous flow from past to future, yet what if this perception is an illusion? Does time truly move forward, or is it part of a greater cycle beyond human comprehension?

Modern science and ancient wisdom offer two perspectives. Science views time as linear and irreversible—a one-way path dictated by entropy and the laws of physics. Spiritual traditions describe time as cyclic and multidimensional, governed by cosmic rhythms and intelligence. Krishna, in the *Bhagavad Gita*, offers a profound insight that challenges conventional thought: *"I am time, the great destroyer of worlds"* (11.32). Time is not a passive backdrop—it is an active force of transformation, dissolution, and renewal.

So, is time an external force that governs reality, or is it an effect of perception and consciousness?

The Scientific View: Time as Linear Flow

Classical physics treated time as absolute and unidirectional. It flows forward, never reverses, and entropy always increases. The past is fixed, the present fleeting, the future undetermined. Einstein's relativity shattered this certainty, showing that time is relative, bending near gravity, stretching with velocity, and vanishing at the speed of light. For photons, past, present, and future may collapse into one.

Quantum mechanics complicates the picture further. At the quantum level, time appears reversible. Some particles mathematically move "backward." Events remain undefined until observed. Some physicists even propose that time itself may be an emergent property of consciousness. If time is not absolute in physics, then what is its true nature? Could it be a function of perception rather than an independent force?

The Wisdom of Cycles: Time as Multidimensional Reality

Ancient traditions never saw time as a straight line. In Vedic cosmology, time moves in vast cycles called Yugas, echoing the rhythms of seasons and civilizations. Satya Yuga, the Age of Truth, gives way to Treta, then Dwapara, and finally Kali Yuga—the Age of Darkness. Each cycle ends and begins anew, repeating creation, preservation, and dissolution.

Krishna describes this cyclic nature: *"For those who understand, there is neither birth nor death. Creation and destruction are merely phases of time's cycle"* (2.20). Time is not linear—it moves in repeating patterns. Civilizations rise and fall, consciousness expands and contracts, experiences unfold in rhythms. Our perception of time as a straight path is an illusion created by awareness.

Time and Consciousness: Shaped by Perception

Is time external, or is it shaped by consciousness? Psychology reveals its relativity. Time slows in meditation, accelerates in routine, compresses in dreams. If time were purely physical, why would perception alter it so drastically?

Quantum theory suggests time may be an effect of observation. The Observer Effect shows reality exists in an undetermined state until observed. Without an observer, past, present, and future may coexist. Krishna hints at this deeper truth: *"I am the past, present, and future; I am beyond time itself"* (10.33). Time is not fundamental—it is a construct of perception, necessary for human experience but not ultimate reality.

Rethinking Time as Intelligence

Time is not absolute—it is relative, cyclic, and shaped by consciousness. Science is beginning to confirm what ancient wisdom has always taught: time bends, stretches, and disappears under certain conditions; the universe follows cyclic patterns; consciousness plays a fundamental role in shaping experience.

Krishna challenges us to see beyond the illusion: *"The wise do not lament the passing of time, for they see beyond birth and death"* (2.13). Time is not happening to us—it is something we participate in through awareness. The higher we expand consciousness, the less we are bound by time. True realization is understanding that time is an effect of intelligence, not an independent force.

Time is not a straight line—it is a rhythm, a cycle, a perception, a pulse of intelligence. Are we ready to expand our understanding of time—not as a mechanical progression, but as a living function of consciousness and cosmic order?

As we move forward, we will explore the second great force shaping reality—energy. Is energy merely a physical property, or is it the very movement of intelligence itself?

10.2 – Time in Physics: A Relative, Fluid Concept

For centuries, time was assumed to be absolute and universal, flowing at the same rate everywhere. Newtonian physics treated it as a fixed background, a steady rhythm against which the universe unfolded. But modern physics shattered this view. Time is no longer seen as rigid or independent—it is relative, flexible, and deeply interconnected with space, gravity, and even observation.

Krishna, in the *Bhagavad Gita*, presents an even more radical perspective: *"I am time, the great destroyer of worlds"* (11.32). Time is not a passive measurement of change—it is an active, intelligent force shaping reality itself.

Relativity: Time as Motion and Gravity

Einstein's theory of relativity overturned the Newtonian certainty. Time is not universal—it is relative to the observer. The faster an object moves, the slower time passes for it. Gravity, too, bends time, slowing it near massive bodies.

An astronaut traveling close to the speed of light would experience only a decade, while centuries might pass on Earth. Atomic clocks on satellites tick slower than those on the ground. Near a black hole, time nearly halts, stretched infinitely at the event horizon.

Time is not separate from space—it is woven into the fabric of the universe. Krishna hints at this deeper truth: *"For those who understand, time is not a master—it bends and moves according to perception and power"* (2.20).

Space-Time: The Interwoven Continuum

Einstein revealed that time is inseparable from space, forming a four-dimensional continuum. Mass and energy bend this fabric, altering the flow of time. Black holes warp it so intensely that time nearly ceases at their edge.

This raises profound implications. If time is a dimension, past, present, and future may coexist in higher realities. Our experience of time as "flowing" may be a construct of perception. Krishna echoes this vision: *"The wise see beyond the illusion of time; for them, past, present, and future are one"* (6.19).

Quantum Paradoxes: Time Dissolving at the Smallest Scales

While relativity describes time in the macroscopic universe, quantum mechanics presents an even stranger picture. At the quantum level, particles do not seem to experience time as we do. A photon, moving at light speed, experiences no time at all—its emission and absorption occur simultaneously.

Quantum superposition suggests particles exist in multiple states, perhaps even multiple times, until observed. Entanglement reveals instantaneous connections across space, as if time itself is irrelevant. Could time be an effect of perception, existing only when intelligence interacts with energy? Krishna describes this deeper reality: *"For those who perceive beyond illusion, time is not a boundary but a field through which all things are connected"* (10.33).

Time as Conscious-Dependent Reality

Modern physics suggests time is relative, linked to space, and possibly illusory at the quantum level. Ancient wisdom aligns, describing time as cyclic, interwoven with intelligence, and ultimately beyond human perception.

Krishna's ultimate message is not to be bound by time but to see beyond it: *"The wise do not lament the past, nor fear the future, for they understand time is but a passing shadow"* (2.15).

Time is flexible, not rigid. It interacts with perception, intelligence, and cosmic forces. To understand reality, we must understand time not as a fixed path, but as a dynamic, interconnected force.

Are we ready to expand our perception of time—not as a mechanical sequence, but as a living rhythm of intelligence?

As we move forward, we will explore the second fundamental force of reality—energy. Is energy merely a physical property, or is it the very movement of intelligence itself?

10.3 – The Bhagavad Gita's Perspective on Time: Krishna as Kāla (The Ultimate Time)

Time, as we ordinarily understand it, is a sequence of moments—a linear progression of past, present, and future. But Krishna, in the *Bhagavad Gita*, reveals a deeper truth: time is not merely a measurement of events, it is an all-pervading force, the very mechanism through which creation, preservation, and destruction unfold.

In one of the most profound declarations of the Gita, Krishna proclaims: *"I am time, the great destroyer of worlds"* (11.32). With these words, He does not describe time as a passive backdrop but as an active, intelligent force shaping existence itself. Time is not a human construct—it is the fundamental intelligence that governs birth, transformation, and dissolution.

Krishna's Declaration: Kāla as Cosmic Power

When Krishna reveals His Vishwarupa—the Universal Form—to Arjuna, Arjuna beholds infinite power, countless divine forms, and the destruction of all beings. Overwhelmed, he asks Krishna to explain what he is witnessing. Krishna responds: *"I am Kāla, the great destroyer of worlds."*

This vision reveals that time is inseparable from Krishna's cosmic will. It is the force through which empires rise and fall, stars ignite and collapse, and every living being is created, sustained, and dissolved. Time is not external—it is woven into the very fabric of reality.

Time as Creator and Destroyer

Human perception often sees time only as decay, a reminder of impermanence. But Krishna presents a deeper vision: time does not merely destroy—it also creates, sustains, and renews.

He explains: *"For one who is born, death is certain, and for one who dies, birth is certain. This cycle is inevitable"* (2.27). Death is not an end but a transformation. What appears as loss is the beginning of something new. Time ensures that existence remains dynamic, never stagnant. It erodes, but it also gives rise. It dissolves, but it also renews.

Time as Expression of Cosmic Intelligence

If time were only a sequence of moments, it would be random and meaningless. But time reveals patterns, structure, and purpose—evidence of intelligence at work. Krishna affirms: *"I am the beginning, the middle, and the end of all things"* (10.20). Time is not chaos—it is order, guiding planets, galaxies, civilizations, and human lives according to a grand design.

Three Ways Time Reveals Its Intelligence

Time operates in cycles, not straight lines. Day and night, the seasons, the rise and fall of civilizations—all follow repeating rhythms. Galaxies spiral, quantum systems oscillate, biological rhythms pulse. Time's cyclic nature reveals it as an intelligent system, not a mechanical sequence.

Time is linked to consciousness. Our experience of time shifts with awareness—slowing in meditation, accelerating in distraction, compressing in dreams. Physics itself suggests time may not be fundamental, but shaped by perception. Krishna hints: *"Those who transcend illusion see beyond time"* (6.15). Time may not simply be experienced—it may be created through consciousness.

Time maintains balance in the universe. Without time, existence would stagnate. Time ensures growth, decline, and renewal, keeping the cosmos in motion. Krishna declares: *"I uphold the order of the universe through time"* (10.33). Time is not passive record—it is active intelligence sustaining reality.

Time as Divine Intelligence

The Gita's perspective challenges everything we assume about reality. Time is not mere measurement—it is cosmic force. It is not separate from intelligence—it is divine order. It is not only destruction—it is creation and renewal. Krishna's declaration *"I am time"* is not metaphor but revelation: time itself is divine intelligence at work.

For us, this means we are not victims of time—we are participants in its flow. Time is not something to fear—it is something to align with. True wisdom is seeing beyond time, not as ruler over us, but as the rhythm of intelligence moving through the cosmos.

Krishna's final message is clear: *"One who sees beyond time attains liberation, for they no longer fear change, birth, or death"* (4.35).

Time is not a countdown to an end—it is the ever-moving pulse of cosmic intelligence.

As we move forward, we will explore the second fundamental force shaping reality—energy. What if energy is not just a physical property, but the very movement of intelligence itself?

10.4 – Energy: The Primordial Force That Governs Reality

Energy is one of the most fundamental aspects of existence. Everything we see, feel, and experience—matter, movement, heat, light, even thought—exists because of energy. Modern physics describes it as a measurable quantity that drives interactions, yet its true nature remains a mystery.

Krishna, in the *Bhagavad Gita*, offers a deeper insight: *"I am the origin of all energies, visible and invisible"* (7.10). This statement challenges the conventional view of energy as merely physical. It suggests that energy is not mechanical—it is a fundamental expression of intelligence itself.

Energy in Physics: Defined but Not Understood

Science teaches that energy cannot be created or destroyed, only transformed. This principle—the conservation of energy—is one of the cornerstones of physics. Yet science does not explain what energy *is*; it only describes how it behaves.

Where did energy originate? Why does it exist at all? Is it merely a physical force, or is it connected to intelligence and consciousness? Physics classifies energy into forms—kinetic, potential, thermal, electromagnetic, nuclear—but these are descriptions of behavior, not revelations of essence. Energy drives reality, yet its origin remains unaccounted for.

Vedic Wisdom: Energy as Living Force

Ancient Vedic science offers a missing link. In yogic traditions, energy is not mechanical but living, the essence of existence itself.

Prana is the universal life force flowing through all beings—the breath of existence, the energy that animates the body. Yogic practices like *Pranayama* harness prana, directing it to expand awareness. Krishna affirms: *"I am the life-giving breath in all beings"* (7.9). Energy is not separate from life—it is life itself.

Shakti is the universal force of creation and transformation. In Vedic cosmology, Shakti is the dynamic power behind all movement, birth, and dissolution. Krishna reinforces this: *"I am the heat in the fire, the radiance of the sun, the power in all beings"* (7.9). Energy is not random—it is intelligent, purposeful, divine.

Energy and Intelligence: Two Names for One Reality

Is energy separate from intelligence, or is it its very structure? Even in modern science, energy does not behave randomly—it follows precise laws. Electromagnetic waves move in predictable patterns. Quantum particles reveal hidden order. The human brain uses energy to generate thought, memory, and creativity.

If energy were purely mechanical, why would it follow structured, intelligent rhythms? Consciousness itself appears to be an expression of energy. The brain is electrical; meditation alters its energy flows, shifting perception. Yogic masters claim to direct prana, transcending ordinary limits of body and mind.

Krishna declares: *"The wise perceive My energy in all things, knowing that nothing exists without it"* (10.20). Energy is not separate from intelligence—it is intelligence in motion. What physics calls energy and what yogic science calls prana are two aspects of the same force.

Energy as the Living Pulse of Reality

Both science and the Gita describe energy as the driving force of existence, but from different perspectives. Science measures energy yet admits its origin is unknown. Vedic wisdom sees energy as Shakti and Prana—expressions of divine intelligence. Conservation laws say energy is eternal; the Gita says energy is infinite, constantly transforming.

Krishna reveals the ultimate nature of energy: *"All energy comes from Me; I am its source, its sustainer, and its end"* (10.8). Energy is not separate from intelligence—it is intelligence in motion. The energy that fuels the stars is the same energy that fuels our minds and bodies.

Energy is not a mechanical abstraction—it is the living pulse of intelligence moving through the cosmos. To understand energy beyond the physical is to open the path to higher realization.

Are we ready to see energy not as a force in equations, but as the very rhythm of divine intelligence?

As we move forward, we will explore the connection between time, energy, and consciousness—how they interact to create our perception of reality and shape the very fabric of existence.

10.5 – The Connection Between Time, Energy, and Consciousness

Science and spirituality have long explored the nature of time and energy, but only recently has modern physics begun to acknowledge the role of consciousness in shaping reality. The deeper we investigate, the more we realize that time is not fixed, energy is not random, and consciousness is not passive—they are interconnected, influencing one another in ways beyond conventional understanding.

Krishna, in the *Bhagavad Gita*, hints at this profound relationship: *"The wise see that all things—past, present, and future—are but ripples on the ocean of consciousness"* (6.19). Time and energy do not function independently—they are shaped by perception, awareness, and intelligence.

Consciousness and the Observer Effect

One of the greatest mysteries of modern physics is the Observer Effect—the discovery that the act of observation changes the behavior of particles. In the famous double-slit experiment, light and electrons behave like waves when unobserved, spreading across space. Yet when observed, they collapse into particles, choosing a specific location. Reality itself shifts depending on awareness.

If consciousness affects particles—the smallest units of energy—could it also affect time? Krishna suggests this possibility: *"The world you see is shaped by your perception. The wise do not trust appearances but seek the truth beyond them"* (9.12). Quantum mechanics echoes this: time and energy do not unfold independently; they are influenced by observation. Awareness is not passive—it shapes reality.

Meditation and the Fluidity of Time

Time is not experienced the same way by everyone. In deep meditation, hours may pass unnoticed, as if time has dissolved. In flow states—moments of peak focus in art, sport, or crisis—time slows, stretching perception into heightened awareness. Dreams compress hours into seconds, bending time into strange rhythms.

If time were truly objective, why would perception alter it so drastically? Krishna teaches: *"The one who is detached from illusion perceives time differently, seeing beyond the limitations of the senses"* (6.23). Time is not rigid—it is shaped by consciousness. Awareness can expand beyond time, making it feel slower, faster, or nonexistent. To master consciousness is to experience time more fluidly, beyond its ordinary constraints.

Time as Emergent, Not Fundamental

Science treats time as a fundamental dimension, yet both physics and Vedic wisdom suggest it may be emergent. Some physicists propose that time arises from energy interactions, not as a primary reality. At the quantum level, past, present, and future may coexist simultaneously—only observation "freezes" reality into a moment.

The Vedas describe time as a projection of consciousness. Krishna declares: *"A field in which all things rise and fall, but which itself is beyond motion"* (10.33). Time is created by movement and change in energy, but energy itself is beyond time. Consciousness exists outside of time, yet experiences it when interacting with energy. The highest realization is seeing time not as cause, but as effect.

The Trinity of Reality

Time, energy, and consciousness are not separate—they are one field of intelligence. Energy flows in patterns, shaping reality. Time emerges as consciousness interacts with energy. Consciousness determines how both are perceived and experienced. Krishna reveals this unity: *"I am time, I am energy, I am the unseen intelligence that moves all things"* (7.9).

The division between time, energy, and consciousness is illusion. What we call "reality" is the dance of these three forces interacting. To understand time and energy is to understand consciousness itself.

Time is not a limitation, energy is not mere physics, and consciousness is not just thought. They are one interconnected force, the living intelligence of the cosmos. The future of understanding reality lies in seeing them as a single field, dissolving boundaries between science and spirituality.

As we move forward, we will explore how shifting our understanding of time and energy will reshape the future of science, philosophy, and human evolution—leading us toward a new paradigm of existence.

10.6 – The Future of Understanding Time & Energy: Moving Beyond Materialist Science

Science has made remarkable progress in understanding time and energy, yet its models remain incomplete. Physics can measure time but cannot explain why we experience it. It can quantify energy but cannot define its ultimate source. The deeper we investigate, the clearer it becomes that time and energy are not merely mechanical phenomena—they are deeply tied to intelligence and consciousness.

Krishna, in the *Bhagavad Gita*, points beyond these limits: *"One who knows Me as beyond time, beyond space, beyond all forms of energy—he alone attains the highest wisdom"* (8.9). This reveals that our current understanding is constrained by materialist assumptions, and that true knowledge requires integrating consciousness, intelligence, and higher dimensions of existence.

The Incompleteness of Scientific Models

Modern science treats time as a dimension of space-time, yet it cannot explain why we experience it as flowing forward, nor what caused time to "begin." Relativity shows time slows near gravity and speeds with motion, but it collapses inside black holes and dissolves at the quantum level. Quantum mechanics suggests particles exist in multiple states at once, where time itself seems undefined.

Energy, too, is described but not explained. Defined as the ability to do work, science cannot answer why energy exists or why it behaves with such order. The Big Bang theory posits a universe born from a burst of energy, yet the origin of that energy remains unknown. Consciousness appears to influence energy—as seen in the Observer Effect—but science hesitates to confront this mystery.

These gaps suggest that time and energy cannot be fully understood without moving beyond materialist frameworks, bringing intelligence and consciousness into the equation.

Integrating Consciousness and Higher Dimensions

To truly understand time and energy, physics must expand to include consciousness. Some thinkers, like Roger Penrose and John Wheeler, propose that consciousness is woven into the fabric of reality. Quantum mechanics already shows that observation shapes events. If energy responds to awareness, then time, space, and matter may also be shaped by perception. Krishna affirms: *"That which sees beyond time, beyond space, beyond all illusions—that is the eternal Self"* (2.25).

Modern theories also point toward higher dimensions. String theory suggests time and energy are projections of deeper fields. The holographic principle proposes that our universe may be encoded on a higher-dimensional boundary. Vedic wisdom aligns with these ideas, describing *Lokas* (higher realms) and *Akasha* (cosmic field) as dimensions beyond ordinary perception. Krishna hints at this: *"I exist in dimensions unseen by human eyes, beyond the grasp of time and space"* (11.8).

Krishna's Ultimate Teaching: Beyond Time and Energy

If time and energy are not ultimate realities, then what is? Krishna answers: *"Beyond time, beyond energy, beyond all creation is the pure field of intelligence, the eternal Self"* (15.16). Time and energy are tools used by intelligence to create experience, but they are not the final truth. Beyond them lies pure awareness—unchanging, infinite, and self-sustaining.

The highest realization is to recognize that we are not bound by time or energy—we are the intelligence that witnesses them.

Toward a New Paradigm of Reality

Instead of seeing time as a fixed dimension and energy as a physical force, we can begin to see them as expressions of intelligence, tools for structuring experience, dynamic and deeply connected to consciousness. Krishna's final teaching reveals: *"One who sees beyond the illusion of time and energy attains liberation, for they understand the eternal field of intelligence"* (4.35).

Time and energy are not prisons—they are pathways. They are not ultimate truths—they are instruments of intelligence guiding us toward liberation.

As we conclude this chapter, we prepare for the next stage of exploration: how the nature of time and energy shapes our understanding of destiny, free will, and the deeper meaning of existence.

Interlude: Resting in the Unity of Time, Energy, and Consciousness

Pause here.

We have journeyed through the mysteries of time and energy, seeing how science and spirituality converge in Krishna's vision. Time is not a rigid line but a rhythm, a cycle, a perception shaped by awareness. Energy is not a mechanical abstraction but the living pulse of intelligence, the force that animates stars, breath, and thought. Consciousness is not passive—it is the field through which both time and energy are experienced, shaped, and understood.

Together, they form a trinity: time as rhythm, energy as movement, consciousness as awareness. None exist in isolation. Each is a facet of the same intelligence, the same cosmic order.

Krishna whispers through the Gita: *"I am time, I am energy, I am the unseen intelligence that moves all things"* (7.9). To see them as separate is illusion. To see them as one is liberation.

Rest here for a moment.

Feel the unity of these forces—not as abstract concepts, but as living realities. Every heartbeat is energy. Every thought is consciousness. Every moment is time. Together, they weave the fabric of existence. To understand them is to glimpse the intelligence that sustains the cosmos.

As Chapter 10 closes, we stand at the threshold of a new vision. The insights of time, energy, and consciousness prepare us for a deeper framework—a way of seeing reality not as fragments, but as a unified field.

Entry into Universal Energy Dynamics (UED)

From here, we move into the next stage: **Universal Energy Dynamics (UED)**.

UED is not just a theory—it is a framework that reveals how time, energy, and consciousness interact as one living system. It is the architecture of reality, the map of intelligence in motion. Where science measures fragments and spirituality seeks essence, UED brings them together into a single vision.

In the chapters ahead, we will explore how UED reframes existence:

- Time as rhythm, not linear progression.
- Energy as intelligence in motion, not blind force.
- Consciousness as the field that unites them, shaping reality itself.

This is the beginning of a new paradigm—one that dissolves the divide between science and spirituality, matter and mind, knowledge and wisdom.

Chapter 11: Universal Energy Dynamics (UED)

The Next Scientific Revolution

In the previous chapter, we discovered that time and energy are not independent forces but interconnected aspects of intelligence. We saw that modern science struggles to define what energy truly is, and that time may not be an absolute framework but an effect of consciousness interacting with equilibrium shifts. This naturally leads to a profound question:

If time and energy are dynamic, interconnected, and responsive to consciousness, do we need a new scientific paradigm to fully understand reality?

Current scientific models—Newtonian mechanics, relativity, quantum physics, and thermodynamics—have given immense progress in describing observable phenomena. Yet they remain fragmented, incomplete, and unable to explain the origin of energy, the true nature of time, or the role of intelligence in shaping existence. They describe how things appear to move, but they cannot explain why motion itself is only apparent.

Krishna, in the *Bhagavad Gita*, hints at a greater unifying principle: *"I am the energy in all beings, the force that sustains the universe"* (7.9). This suggests that energy is not merely a physical quantity but an expression of intelligence—a structured, purposeful, self-organizing principle.

Introducing Universal Energy Dynamics (UED)

Universal Energy Dynamics (UED) is a new framework that unites time, energy, and consciousness into a single, cohesive system. It moves beyond the limitations of materialist science and dissolves the illusion of motion, revealing the universe as a still, structured vacuum field (SVE). In this field, nothing travels, nothing oscillates, nothing expands. All phenomena are ripple resolutions—local equilibrium shifts decoded by the observer as movement.

UED's foundational axiom is simple yet radical: *"Motion does not exist in the universe — only resolution does."*

Energy is not a force in transit but a state of equilibrium. Time is not a dimension but the duration of causal sequencing perceived by consciousness. Intelligence precedes both, activating energy and shaping experience.

Could UED be the missing key that bridges physics, consciousness, and intelligence—revealing the deeper structure of reality?

This chapter will explore how UED challenges conventional science, reframes energy as intelligence in motionless equilibrium, and why understanding this truth may lead to the next scientific revolution.

11.1 – The Need for a New Scientific Paradigm

Modern science has made extraordinary progress in describing matter, energy, and the apparent forces of the universe. Yet despite its achievements, it remains incomplete in fundamental ways. It can measure energy but cannot define its origin. It can quantify time but cannot explain why we experience it as duration. It can describe apparent forces but fails to account for intelligence and consciousness—the very principles that precede and shape all phenomena.

Krishna, in the *Bhagavad Gita*, points directly to this gap: *"I am the source of all energies, the intelligence that guides all things"* (10.8). Energy and intelligence are not separate—they are inseparable expressions of the same field. Yet modern science treats them as distinct, leading to contradictions in quantum mechanics, gaps in relativity, and an inability to explain consciousness as anything more than a byproduct of matter.

If time, energy, and intelligence are interwoven, should science not explore them as a unified system rather than as unrelated fragments?

Why Current Models Fail

Science has classified energy into kinetic, potential, thermal, nuclear, and electromagnetic forms. But it has never answered:

- Where did energy originate?
- Why does energy exhibit order rather than randomness?
- What role does consciousness play in shaping equilibrium?

Similarly, time is treated as a measurement, yet science cannot explain:

- Did time exist before the Big Bang, or is it an observer-side construct?
- Why does time appear to "flow" forward when equations allow reversibility?
- Why do altered states of awareness dissolve or distort time perception?

Equations describe appearances, but they do not reveal essence. This limitation suggests the need for a paradigm that integrates intelligence and consciousness into the study of energy and time.

The Limits of Classical and Quantum Frameworks

Classical physics assumes time as linear progression and energy as calculable force, yet it cannot explain why these laws exist or why they are mathematically precise. It works for large-scale appearances but collapses at the quantum level.

Quantum mechanics reveals particles in multiple states until observed, entanglement that defies distance, and behaviors that suggest time and space are illusions. If particles are not bound by time or space, is time itself a projection of consciousness rather than a fundamental reality?

Even in its most advanced form, science cannot unify classical mechanics and quantum paradoxes. This is where **Universal Energy Dynamics (UED)** enters—not as another fragment, but as a framework that integrates physics, time, energy, and intelligence into one field.

How UED Bridges the Gap

Universal Energy Dynamics proposes that:

- Energy is not a force in motion—it is structured intelligence in equilibrium states.
- Time is not an independent flow—it is the observer's sequencing of ripple resolutions.
- The universe is not random—it is causally precise, operating through consequence and alignment.

Instead of treating time, energy, and intelligence separately, UED reveals them as facets of one reality:

- Energy as the medium.
- Time as the observer's decoding of equilibrium shifts.
- Consciousness as the intelligence that structures both.

Krishna affirms this unity: *"I am the force in all things, the intelligence in the intelligent, the energy that moves all beings"* (7.9).

The UED Approach to Reality

Reality is not mechanical interaction of blind forces. It is a still, structured vacuum field (SVE), constantly resolving itself. Time is not a separate entity—it is the perception of causal consequence. Consciousness interacts with energy, shaping the decoding of time and space.

This model aligns with both quantum discoveries and Vedic philosophy, offering a unified explanation that neither materialist science nor religious dogma can provide. Krishna's wisdom makes it clear: *"That which you see as separate—time, energy, thought—is but one continuous field of intelligence"* (10.33).

Bringing It All Together

The limitations of modern science show that energy and time cannot be explained without intelligence. Classical physics fails to explain quantum paradoxes. Quantum mechanics fails to explain consciousness. Materialist science ignores intelligence as fundamental.

Universal Energy Dynamics offers a way forward:

- Energy is structured intelligence, not random force.
- Time is observer-side consequence, not fixed dimension.
- Consciousness is woven into the very field of reality.

Krishna reveals this truth: *"Beyond all that you measure, beyond time and energy, lies the ultimate reality—the eternal intelligence that moves all things"* (15.16).

To understand energy, we must understand the intelligence that directs it. To understand time, we must understand how consciousness sequences it. To move beyond materialist science, we must embrace intelligence as the foundation of existence.

Are we ready to break free from outdated assumptions and embrace a reality where energy, time, and consciousness are not separate forces but one intelligent field?

As we move forward, we will explore the *core principles of Universal Energy Dynamics (UED)* and how they redefine our understanding of physics, intelligence, and the future of human knowledge.

11.2 – The Core Principles of Universal Energy Dynamics (UED)

For centuries, science has treated energy as a mechanical force, time as an independent flow, and consciousness as a byproduct of the brain. These assumptions fail to explain the deeper mysteries of reality. **Universal Energy Dynamics (UED)** challenges these ideas by presenting a unified framework—where energy, time, and consciousness are not separate but interwoven expressions of intelligence.

Krishna, in the *Bhagavad Gita*, hints at this deeper truth: *"I am the force in all things, the intelligence in the intelligent, the movement of the cosmos"* (7.9). This is not "movement" in the mechanical sense, but the *resolution of equilibrium within the structured vacuum field (SVE).* Energy is not blind, time is not absolute, and consciousness is not passive—they function together in a self-regulating field of intelligence.

If energy resolves in patterns, time emerges through perception, and consciousness interacts with reality, shouldn't we view them as aspects of one dynamic system?

Energy as Intelligence, Not Blind Force

Science defines energy as the ability to do work, but it cannot explain why energy exists or why it follows precise mathematical laws. UED reframes energy as **states of equilibrium**: stable, active, or condensed. None of these states "move"—they shift locally within the structured field.

Energy is not random—it is intelligence manifesting as equilibrium patterns.

- Every apparent "force" in nature is simply the field restoring balance.
- DNA encodes equilibrium into biological intelligence.
- At the quantum level, energy appears to "choose" states, but this is observer-side decoding of ripple resolution.

Krishna affirms: *"Know that all life, all thought, arises from My energy"* (7.8). Matter is condensed equilibrium, not solid vibration. The universe is not driven by blind mechanics but by structured intelligence.

Time, Energy, and Consciousness as One Field

Modern science treats time, energy, and consciousness as unrelated. UED reveals them as inseparable.

Time is not absolute—it is consequence sequencing.

- Traditionally seen as linear progression, time is instead the observer's decoding of entropy change.
- Relativity shows time bends with equilibrium conditions.
- At the quantum level, time dissolves—particles do not "experience" it.

Krishna declares: *"I am time, the destroyer and the creator; I am beyond time itself"* (11.32). Time is not a dimension—it is the duration of causal resolution.

Consciousness interacts with energy to shape time.

- The Observer Effect shows particles resolve differently when awareness is present.
- Meditation and altered states shift perception, dissolving ordinary time.
- Reality is participatory—consciousness sequences equilibrium into experience.

UED teaches:

- Time is an effect of ripple resolution.
- Consciousness directs equilibrium.
- Reality is not rigid—it is intelligence unfolding through observer-side decoding.

The Universe as Self-Regulating Intelligence

Science assumes entropy always increases, leading to disorder. Yet life, order, and intelligence continually emerge. UED reframes this: the universe is not falling apart—it is self-organizing, constantly restoring equilibrium.

- Cells organize into organisms, stars condense from dust, ecosystems regenerate.
- DNA repairs itself, bodies maintain homeostasis, galaxies stabilize.
- Even black holes are not "destructive engines" but equilibrium

pockets recycling matter.

Krishna describes this balance: *"I uphold the order of all things, ensuring their renewal"* (10.33). The universe is not a machine—it is a living intelligence, adjusting itself through consequence.

Bringing It All Together – The Core Principles of UED

Instead of treating time, energy, and consciousness as separate, UED presents a unified system:

- **Energy** is intelligence in equilibrium states.
- **Time** is observer-side sequencing of causal resolution.
- **Consciousness** is the field that structures both.

Krishna hints at this unity: *"That which appears separate—time, energy, thought—is but one continuous field of intelligence"* (10.4).

This means:

- Science must expand beyond materialism to recognize intelligence as fundamental.
- Time must be redefined—not as flow, but as consequence.
- Energy must be seen not as mechanical property, but as structured intelligence.

Are we ready to embrace a reality where energy, time, and consciousness are not separate forces, but one unified field of intelligence?

As we move forward, we will explore how UED redefines our understanding of the universe—moving beyond space-time into the still field of higher reality.

11.3 – UED and the Multidimensional Nature of Reality

Modern science, especially relativity and quantum mechanics, has revealed that reality is far more complex than what our senses perceive. Space-time is not a rigid grid but a flexible field, shaped by equilibrium conditions and observer-side interpretation. Yet the traditional four-dimensional model—three dimensions of space plus one of time—struggles to explain phenomena such as entanglement, time anomalies, and the self-organization of equilibrium.

Universal Energy Dynamics (UED) proposes that:

- Reality extends beyond four dimensions—higher fields govern equilibrium resolution.
- Time is not a straight path—it bends, loops, and reorganizes itself through consequence.
- Cosmic intelligence operates through structured energy across multiple levels of existence.

Krishna, in the *Bhagavad Gita*, hints at this deeper reality: *"I exist in realms unseen by human eyes, beyond time and space"* (11.8). What we perceive as reality is only a fraction of a much larger, multidimensional field.

Redefining Space-Time Beyond Four Dimensions

Physics treats space and time as a four-dimensional continuum. UED reframes this: space and time are not fundamental, but emergent properties of the structured vacuum field (SVE).

Modern theories already point beyond four dimensions:

- String theory proposes 10 or 11 dimensions, compactified beyond perception.
- The holographic principle suggests our 3D reality is a projection of higher-dimensional information.
- Quantum physics shows particles existing in multiple states simultaneously, defying classical space-time logic.

If extra dimensions exist, they may be the hidden structure through which energy, consequence, and intelligence interact.

UED's perspective: Energy does not "move" in a linear grid. What appears as motion is ripple resolution across dimensions. Time is not a line but consequence sequencing, bending and looping through equilibrium shifts. Consciousness navigates these dimensions, explaining déjà vu, precognition, and altered perception.

Krishna affirms: *"That which appears far is near; that which appears separate is but one field of reality"* (10.4).

Why Higher Dimensions Are Necessary

Certain mysteries cannot be explained in four dimensions. UED provides a higher-dimensional model.

Quantum entanglement: Entangled particles remain connected instantly across apparent distance. In UED, they are not "communicating" but resolving within a higher-dimensional field where distance does not exist.

Time loops and anomalies: Relativity already shows time dilates under gravity. Consciousness experiences loops—visions of future events, déjà vu, timeless states in meditation. UED explains this as awareness navigating different dimensional resolutions. Krishna describes: *"The wise perceive beyond time, seeing past, present, and future as one"* (6.19).

Order from chaos: Science assumes entropy always increases, yet galaxies, DNA, and ecosystems self-organize. UED reframes this: equilibrium is not collapsing into disorder but continually resolving into structured intelligence. Krishna affirms: *"I uphold the balance of all things, ensuring their renewal"* (10.33).

Cosmic Intelligence Across Dimensions

If time, energy, and space are emergent, what guides their resolution? UED answers: **cosmic intelligence.**

- Quantum physics shows particles as probability waves until observed—reality shaped by awareness.
- Vedanta calls this Brahman—the structuring intelligence.
- UED sees energy, time, and space as directed by intelligence permeating all dimensions.

Krishna declares: *"I am the unseen order that moves all things; I am within, yet beyond"* (9.4).

Consciousness itself may navigate dimensions. Meditation, near-death experiences, and altered states reveal timeless realms. Krishna teaches: *"The one who transcends illusion sees reality beyond form, beyond time, beyond separation"* (13.31).

Bringing It All Together – UED's Multidimensional Reality

Instead of viewing time, energy, and space as separate mechanical forces, UED reveals:

- Reality extends beyond four dimensions—higher fields shape existence.
- Entanglement, time loops, and order emerge from structured intelligence.
- Consciousness actively shapes and perceives equilibrium across dimensions.

Krishna's wisdom aligns: *"That which you see as fragmented is but one; time, energy, and thought arise from the same field"* (10.4).

Reality is not fragmented mechanics—it is a unified, multidimensional field of intelligence.

11.4 – Consciousness as the Missing Factor in Energy Science

For centuries, science has treated consciousness as an effect of the brain—a product of biochemical and electrical activity. But this assumption is being challenged by both modern physics and ancient wisdom. The deeper we explore time, energy, and space, the clearer it becomes that consciousness is not a secondary effect—it may be the fundamental intelligence guiding equilibrium itself.

Krishna, in the *Bhagavad Gita*, points to this deeper truth: *"I am the consciousness in all beings, the intelligence that directs all resolution"* (7.10).

Consciousness is not separate from energy—it is the field that organizes, aligns, and interprets it.

The Observer Effect – Consciousness Shapes Energy States

One of the most profound discoveries in quantum physics is the Observer Effect: conscious observation alters the resolution of quantum states.

In the double-slit experiment, energy patterns remain indeterminate until observed. What appears as "wave" or "particle" is not intrinsic motion but observer-side decoding of ripple resolution. Reality does not "collapse"—it aligns through awareness.

Krishna hints at this mystery: *"What is seen is shaped by the one who sees. The wise perceive beyond illusion"* (9.12). Energy is not passive—it responds to intelligence. Reality is not fixed—it is participatory. Consciousness is not separate—it is the field in which energy takes form.

Is Consciousness Emergent or Fundamental?

Two views compete:

The materialist view: consciousness is a late effect of neural complexity, irrelevant to the cosmos.

The UED view: consciousness is not emergent—it is the structuring principle of energy. The universe is not random—it is causally precise, operating through consequence. Time, energy, and matter do not exist independently—they emerge within awareness.

Krishna reinforces this: *"The wise know that matter and energy arise from the unseen field of consciousness"* (13.31). Consciousness is not an illusion—it is the organizing principle. Energy does not "flow"—it resolves according to intelligence. Time itself is consequence sequencing within awareness.

Ancient Wisdom and UED – Prana, Shakti, Akasha

Vedic science long described energy and consciousness as inseparable.

Prana is the vital equilibrium sustaining life. Breath practices like *Pranayama* direct prana, showing that awareness can realign energy states. Krishna affirms: *"I am the life force in all beings, the breath of existence"* (7.9). Prana is not mechanical—it is consciousness in resolution.

Shakti is the universal creative intelligence. It is not "force in motion" but the dynamic principle of transformation. Krishna declares: *"I am the power behind all forces, the unseen energy that sustains the cosmos"* (10.20). Energy is not random—it is structured intelligence.

Akasha is the intelligent field holding all resolution. Not empty space, but the medium of consequence. Modern physics hints at this through zero-point fields. Krishna describes: *"I am beyond all things, yet within them; I am the space that holds all reality"* (9.4). Reality is not separate objects—it is one interconnected field of energy-consciousness.

Bringing It All Together – Consciousness as Foundation

Instead of treating consciousness, time, and energy as separate, UED reveals them as one field:

- Energy is intelligence in equilibrium states.
- Time is consequence sequencing within awareness.
- Consciousness is the structuring principle of reality.

Krishna reveals the highest understanding: *"Beyond time, beyond energy, beyond all things is the eternal field of intelligence"* (15.16).

For science, this means:

- Materialism must be transcended—consciousness cannot be ignored.
- Physics must acknowledge that energy is not independent—it is directed by intelligence.
- Reality must be studied as awareness, not just equations.

Consciousness is not illusion—it is the foundation of reality.

11.5 – The UED Perspective on the Structure of the Universe

Modern physics describes the universe as a system governed by fundamental forces—gravity, electromagnetism, strong and weak nuclear interactions. It explains how matter appears, how galaxies seem to rotate, and how energy transforms. Yet it struggles to explain why the universe is structured so precisely, why equilibrium follows organized patterns, and why intelligence continually emerges instead of collapsing into chaos.

Universal Energy Dynamics (UED) provides a broader framework, suggesting that:

- Energy exists in three states—stable, dynamic, and condensed (matter).
- The universe resolves itself through cyclic equilibrium—creation, transformation, and dissolution.
- The cosmos is not a mechanical accident—it is fine-tuned by intelligence, allowing evolution to unfold.

Krishna, in the *Bhagavad Gita*, describes this self-organizing nature: *"I am the intelligence that structures all things, the energy that resolves all beings"* (7.10).

Energy Exists in Different States – Stable, Dynamic, and Condensed

Science describes energy as kinetic, thermal, nuclear, or electromagnetic. UED reframes this into three primary states:

State of Energy	Nature	Example in Science	Example in UED
Stable Energy	Balanced, unchanging	Zero Point Energy, Dark Energy	The Field of Pure Consciousness (Akasha)
Dynamic Energy	Active equilibrium shifts	Electromagnetism, Quantum Fields	The Force of Intelligence (Shakti)
Condensed Energy	Dense equilibrium pockets	Atoms, planets, living beings	The Manifested Universe

Energy is not "motion"—it is structured intelligence in resolution. Matter is condensed equilibrium, not separate substance. Transitions between states are not random—they are precise, consequence-driven alignments.

Krishna confirms: *"I am the energy that takes form and the energy that remains unseen"* (10.20).

The Cyclic Resolution of Energy – Patterns, Not Chaos

Science assumes entropy leads to disorder and eventual heat death. UED reframes this: equilibrium does not collapse—it cycles, self-organizes, and regenerates.

- Stars condense, dissolve, and re-align into new elements.
- DNA replicates in rhythmic patterns.
- Seasons, ecosystems, and biological rhythms follow repeating cycles.

If energy were random, why would order continually emerge?

Krishna describes this rhythm: *"That which is created must dissolve, and that which dissolves must be reborn. Such is the rhythm of existence"* (2.27). Creation and dissolution are not accidents—they are necessary phases of renewal. The universe is not drifting into chaos—it regulates itself through cyclic equilibrium.

Fine-Tuning and the Role of Intelligence

One of science's greatest puzzles is why the universe is so precisely structured for life. If the laws of physics were even slightly different, atoms would not stabilize, stars would not ignite, and life would not arise.

Materialist science offers chance or multiverse speculation. UED offers consequence:

- The universe is not accidental—it is structured by intelligence.
- Energy follows laws because intelligence is embedded in the field.
- Evolution of life and consciousness is not random—it is the natural unfolding of equilibrium.

Krishna affirms: *"I uphold the laws of the universe, ensuring its balance and order"* (10.33).

Bringing It All Together – UED's Structure of Reality

Instead of treating the universe as a blind mechanical system, UED reveals:

- Energy exists in structured states—stable, dynamic, condensed.
- The cosmos is not collapsing—it self-regulates through cyclic resolution.
- Fine-tuning and intelligence are not anomalies—they are the essence of reality.

Krishna's wisdom aligns: *"All things resolve according to My energy, yet I am beyond all things. This is the mystery of the universe"* (9.4).

Implications

- Science must acknowledge energy as structured intelligence, not blind force.
- Time must be redefined—not as a separate entity, but as consequence sequencing.

- Consciousness must be recognized as the field that interacts with energy, shaping reality.

The universe is not random—it is intelligence in equilibrium.

11.6 – Implications of UED: The Future of Science and Human Understanding

If **Universal Energy Dynamics (UED)** is correct, then our entire approach to science, technology, and human progress must evolve. Instead of treating energy as mechanical, time as linear, and consciousness as secondary, we must recognize that reality is governed by intelligent equilibrium dynamics.

Krishna, in the *Bhagavad Gita*, points toward this higher understanding: *"All energy resolves through Me, yet I remain beyond it. This is the mystery of existence"* (9.4). Energy is not blind—it is directed by intelligence. If this realization is integrated into science, technology, and human development, entirely new frontiers of knowledge will open.

Transforming Physics, Biology, and Artificial Intelligence

Physics – Beyond the Materialist Model Traditional physics assumes energy follows fixed laws but cannot explain why those laws exist. Quantum mechanics reveals reality as fluid, shaped by observation. UED reframes this: energy is self-organizing, resolving equilibrium through embedded intelligence. Physics must expand beyond materialism to include consciousness as a structuring principle. Krishna affirms: *"That which resolves all things is unseen, yet it is the source of all resolution"* (10.20).

Biology – Energy as the Source of Life Biology treats life as chemistry but cannot explain consciousness. UED reveals life as structured equilibrium—energy intelligence condensing into biological systems. Evolution is not random—it is consequence, intelligence seeking higher states of awareness. Krishna declares: *"I am the life-force in all beings, the intelligence that directs their growth"* (7.9). Biology must evolve beyond genetics into energy-consciousness dynamics.

Artificial Intelligence – Computation vs. Consciousness AI processes data but lacks awareness. UED explains why: true intelligence requires energy-consciousness alignment, not computation alone. Future AI must integrate with human intelligence rather than attempt to replace it. Krishna reminds: *"Wisdom is not mere knowledge—it is the light that directs all understanding"* (13.8). Intelligence is not algorithm—it is awareness resolving energy.

The Future of Energy Systems

Limitations of Current Systems Fossil fuels deplete, nuclear energy risks imbalance, renewables depend on external conditions. These are brute-force extractions, not alignments.

Quantum and Zero-Point Energy Modern physics suggests empty space is filled with zero-point equilibrium. UED reframes this: energy is not "produced"—it is accessed at its purest level, decoded from the structured vacuum field. Krishna hints: *"I am the fire in the sun, the energy that never diminishes"* (15.12).

Conscious Energy Systems If energy is linked to intelligence, future technologies could align with awareness. Ancient yogic Siddhis describe directing energy through mind. UED suggests energy systems will not extract—they will integrate, working with the intelligence of the field. Krishna affirms: *"The wise do not seek to control energy—they align with it, allowing resolution to occur naturally"* (6.23).

Integrating Spirituality and Science

For centuries, science and spirituality were divided. UED dissolves this illusion.

- Physics must include consciousness.
- Spirituality must be understood as intelligence in scientific terms.
- The universe must be seen as a structured field, not a random accident.

Krishna describes this unity: *"There is no division between knowledge and wisdom, between energy and spirit—they are one"* (13.31).

Beyond the Divide Materialist science ignores intelligence; religion ignores natural law. UED unites them—revealing both as partial views of the same field.

The End of the Materialist Illusion Matter is condensed equilibrium. UED shows energy itself is structured by intelligence, making physical reality a projection of deeper awareness. This aligns with Vedic teachings of *Maya*—the material world as appearance shaped by consequence.

Bringing It All Together – The Future of Human Knowledge

Instead of separating physics, biology, AI, energy technology, and spirituality, UED proposes a unified paradigm:

- Energy is structured intelligence.
- Time is consequence sequencing within awareness.
- The universe is not mechanical—it is a living field of intelligence.

Krishna's wisdom aligns: *"The wise see no separation between energy and mind, between time and the eternal. All is one, all is intelligence"* (10.4).

The future of science is not extraction, not fragmentation, but integration. UED reveals that energy, time, and intelligence are not separate—they are expressions of one unified field.

11.7 – Krishna's Ultimate Teaching: Energy as the Expression of Supreme Intelligence

Throughout the *Bhagavad Gita*, Krishna describes energy not as an independent force but as a direct expression of intelligence. He makes it clear that energy, time, and consciousness are not separate—they are facets of a singular, unified reality.

One of His most profound declarations is: *"I am the energy in all beings, the force that sustains the universe"* (7.9). This is not metaphor—it is revelation. Energy is not blind; it follows structured intelligence. Time does not drift randomly; it is shaped by awareness. The universe is not mechanical;

it is an interconnected field of intelligence manifesting as consequence, equilibrium, and perception.

Energy as the Source of Precision

Modern science struggles with one question: where does energy originate, and why does it behave with such precision? It can measure and manipulate energy, but it cannot explain why energy exists or why it follows exact laws.

Krishna answers: *"I am the source of all energies, visible and invisible"* (10.8). Energy does not arise randomly—it is intelligence condensed into equilibrium states. The force that sustains the universe is inseparable from the intelligence that guides it. What we perceive as physical energy is simply an aspect of supreme consciousness.

To understand energy is to understand the very fabric of existence.

UED and the Realization of Higher Intelligence

Universal Energy Dynamics reveals:

- Energy is self-organizing—it resolves equilibrium, never random.
- Time is not absolute—it emerges from consequence sequencing shaped by awareness.
- Consciousness is not secondary—it is the structuring principle of reality.

This leads to a profound realization: the universe is not a machine—it is evolving intelligence.

Krishna affirms: *"I am the intelligence in the intelligent, the wisdom of the wise"* (7.10). Energy is not blind—it is guided by unseen order. The highest knowledge is not equations—it is realization of the intelligence that governs all things.

For us, this means:

- Science must move beyond materialism, acknowledging intelligence as fundamental.

- Spirituality must integrate with scientific clarity, dissolving mysticism into structured understanding.
- Human evolution must shift from intellectual accumulation to intelligence alignment—living in harmony with cosmic equilibrium.

Krishna confirms: *"One who perceives My energy everywhere, and sees all things as expressions of intelligence, understands the truth"* (6.30).

Moving Beyond Duality

The greatest illusion is duality—the idea that energy, time, and intelligence are separate. This illusion has divided science and spirituality. Krishna dissolves it: *"Those who see division do not see the whole; those who see unity understand all things"* (13.31).

UED aligns with this teaching:

- Energy is intelligence in resolution.
- Time is consequence sequencing within awareness.
- Consciousness is the field through which equilibrium is decoded.

Reality is not fragmented—it is one living intelligence. Krishna explains: *"I am beyond time, beyond form, beyond all separation. Those who see this, see the truth"* (15.16).

Duality is illusion. The highest realization is unity—an experience of alignment with the intelligence of the cosmos.

The Ultimate Realization of UED

Applied through Krishna's wisdom, UED reveals:

- The universe is not mechanical—it is self-organizing intelligence.
- Energy does not move blindly—it resolves through awareness.
- Time is not separate—it emerges from consciousness interacting with equilibrium.

Krishna describes this unity: *"All things resolve through Me, yet I am beyond all things. I am the unseen intelligence, the eternal truth"* (10.33).

The highest realization is not scientific or spiritual—it is direct experience of intelligence itself.

The Future of Human Understanding

- Physics will integrate consciousness, recognizing energy as structured intelligence.
- Technology will evolve beyond extraction, accessing intelligent equilibrium fields.
- Humanity will move beyond intellectual knowledge into direct unity with cosmic intelligence.

Krishna's final wisdom prepares us: *"The wise do not seek to control energy, time, or knowledge—they align with it, becoming one with the eternal intelligence"* (6.23).

The journey of UED is not about controlling energy—it is about aligning with the supreme intelligence that governs all things.

Interlude: Resting in the Field of Intelligence

Pause here.

We have journeyed through the revelations of Universal Energy Dynamics. We have seen how energy is not blind but structured, how time is not absolute but consequence, and how consciousness is not secondary but the foundation of reality itself. Together, they are not fragments—they are facets of one living intelligence.

Krishna's voice echoes through the Gita: *"All things resolve through Me, yet I am beyond all things. I am the unseen intelligence, the eternal truth"* (10.33).

This is the moment to let the illusion of separation dissolve. Energy, time, and consciousness are not three forces—they are one field. What appears as motion is resolution. What appears as randomness is consequence. What appears as division is unity.

Rest here for a moment.

Feel the stillness of the structured vacuum field. Sense how every heartbeat, every thought, every moment is not isolated but part of the same rhythm. Intelligence is not something we study—it is something we inhabit. To understand UED is not only to know—it is to align.

The highest realization is not intellectual mastery but experiential unity. To see beyond duality is to recognize that science and spirituality, matter and spirit, knowledge and wisdom, are not opposites—they are reflections of the same truth.

As Chapter 11 closes, we stand at the threshold of transformation. The paradigm has shifted: the universe is not mechanical, not accidental, not divided. It is intelligence in equilibrium, consequence in rhythm, awareness in form.

Chapter 12: AI, Technology & The Future

Where Humanity Is Heading

In the previous chapter, we explored **Universal Energy Dynamics (UED)** and the realization that energy, time, and intelligence are not separate forces but facets of one unified field. We saw that intelligence is not an emergent property of matter but the very foundation of existence—the active capability to align ripples, resolve disturbances, and generate meaningful outcomes.

Now, as humanity stands on the edge of a technological revolution, a new challenge emerges: how will artificial intelligence, automation, and rapid technological evolution interact with human intelligence? Will these tools amplify our clarity, creativity, and alignment—or will they lead to dependency, ripple confusion, and the erosion of wisdom?

Krishna, in the *Bhagavad Gita*, warns against blind dependence on external forces: *"The wise do not seek control over intelligence, but alignment with it"* (6.23). This teaching is crucial in the age of AI. Technology must not be worshipped as intelligence—it must be treated as a tool, aligned with higher awareness.

This chapter will explore:

- How AI and automation are reshaping human civilization.
- Why AI is not true intelligence—consciousness cannot be replicated by machines.
- How technology must evolve alongside higher intelligence, not apart from it.

As we enter the era of AI-driven progress, the question is not whether machines will surpass us. The real question is whether we will remain aligned with intelligence itself—or whether we will mistake simulation for wisdom. The answer lies in how we integrate technology with clarity, ethics, and consciousness.

12.1 – The Acceleration of AI & Technology: A Blessing or a Crisis?

The rapid advancement of artificial intelligence (AI), automation, and machine learning is transforming every aspect of human civilization. AI can now simulate creativity, automate decision-making, and process data at speeds no human mind can match. From medical diagnostics to autonomous systems, technology appears to progress at an exponential rate.

Yet with this acceleration comes a crucial question: is AI a tool for human empowerment, or are we mistaking simulation for intelligence?

Krishna, in the *Bhagavad Gita*, warns against external dependencies that weaken inner clarity: *"The one who depends entirely on the external world for wisdom becomes lost; true intelligence lies within"* (2.49).

As AI continues to develop, we must ask: are we evolving alongside technology, or are we allowing it to replace the very intelligence that defines us?

AI's Rapid Expansion – Simulation vs. Intelligence

For most of history, intelligence was considered uniquely human. But AI now demonstrates capabilities that appear to surpass human abilities in many domains.

Data Processing & Analysis AI systems can process billions of data points in seconds, predict financial trends, detect fraud, and diagnose diseases with precision. Yet speed and accuracy are not wisdom. Intelligence is not computation—it is ripple alignment, consequence awareness, and ethical clarity.

Automation & Decision-Making AI-driven robots replace human labor, algorithms diagnose medical conditions, and autonomous systems raise ethical concerns in warfare and surveillance. Efficiency without consequence awareness risks dehumanization.

Creative Simulation AI composes music, paints, writes, and designs. Tools like GPT and DALL-E generate content that mimics human creativity. But this is simulation, not originality. Creativity is intelligence resolving ripples in novel ways—something no machine can embody.

Krishna cautions: *"That which is born of external forces remains bound to them. True intelligence is not dependent but self-sustaining"* (3.42). AI can simulate outcomes, but it cannot originate meaning.

The Double-Edged Sword of Technology

Technology itself is neutral—it becomes blessing or crisis depending on alignment.

Benefits of AI

- Medical diagnostics and robotic surgeries extend lifespan.
- Renewable energy optimization combats climate change.
- Education and accessibility tools democratize knowledge.

Dangers of AI

- Job displacement destabilizes economies.
- Surveillance erodes privacy.
- Autonomous weapons threaten ethical balance.

If AI is used recklessly, it risks reducing human freedom, dignity, and autonomy. Krishna warns: *"The wise use tools without attachment; the ignorant become ruled by them"* (5.23).

Are We Evolving Alongside AI—or Losing Ourselves?

The Singularity Myth Some predict a "technological singularity" where AI surpasses human intelligence. But UED clarifies: AI cannot surpass intelligence because it lacks a ripple field, consequence, awareness, and intent. It can simulate outcomes, but it cannot embody intelligence.

Human Uniqueness AI is faster and more precise, but lacks intuition, morality, and consciousness. Wisdom requires awareness of consequence, not just computation. AI can mimic emotions but does not feel; it can replicate creativity but does not experience inspiration.

Krishna reminds: *"The highest wisdom is not in knowing all things, but in knowing the self beyond all things"* (6.23). If humanity loses itself in AI, it risks losing the deeper intelligence that makes us human.

Bringing It All Together – The Future of AI and Human Evolution

Instead of treating AI as savior or threat, we must integrate it wisely:

- AI should amplify human clarity, not replace it.
- Technology must evolve alongside wisdom, not apart from it.
- The goal is not superior AI, but superior human intelligence.

Krishna's final wisdom on intelligence is clear: *"The wise do not seek mastery over intelligence; they seek unity with it"* (18.63).

The future of AI is not about machines overtaking humanity—it is about humans evolving alongside intelligence itself. The danger is not AI surpassing us, but us mistaking simulation for intelligence and losing alignment with the field of awareness.

12.2 – The Limits of AI: Why Artificial Intelligence is Not Consciousness

Artificial intelligence has become astonishingly advanced, performing tasks once reserved for human intelligence—analyzing vast data, generating creative works, diagnosing conditions, and even making complex decisions. Yet despite its power, AI remains fundamentally limited in ways often overlooked.

Can AI truly be called *intelligent*, or is it merely an advanced simulation of intelligence?

Krishna, in the *Bhagavad Gita*, makes a clear distinction between mechanical knowledge and true intelligence: *"The wise do not mistake information for wisdom, nor action for understanding"* (4.37). This reveals that AI, no matter how advanced, is not intelligence—it lacks awareness, intuition, and the deeper understanding that defines consciousness.

Simulation Without Awareness

AI can perform pattern recognition, logical decision-making, and generate content—but it does so without meaning, emotion, or self-awareness.

- AI models predict outcomes through statistical probabilities, not genuine insight.
- When AI generates text, images, or music, it recombines patterns—it does not originate meaning.
- AI lacks introspection, emotional depth, and curiosity.

Krishna defines true intelligence as perceiving beyond appearances: *"The one who sees the unseen, who knows beyond knowledge, alone possesses wisdom"* (6.23). AI can simulate intelligence, but it cannot experience awareness.

No Intuition, No Creativity

Humans often make intuitive leaps—discoveries beyond logic. AI cannot.

- AI is bound to data; it cannot break patterns or originate new causal possibilities.
- Great breakthroughs in science, art, and philosophy arise from intuition, not computation.
- Creativity is ripple resolution in novel ways—machines cannot embody this.

Krishna describes intuition as higher intelligence: *"The mind bound to logic alone cannot perceive the infinite"* (10.20). AI processes patterns, but it cannot see beyond them.

No Emotion, No Conscious Thought

AI can analyze emotions but does not feel them. It can mimic empathy but does not experience it. Consciousness involves personal experience—AI has none.

Krishna defines consciousness as self-awareness beyond external conditions: *"The true self is not bound by the senses—it is the light that illuminates all experience"* (2.25). AI may recognize emotions in others, but it will never experience its own.

Data Processing vs. Intelligence

Many assume intelligence is data processing. This is flawed.

- AI calculates probabilities but does not reflect on meaning.
- Humans think expansively, connecting abstract ideas, making intuitive leaps, evolving beliefs.
- AI cannot question its existence; humans ask: *Who am I? What is my purpose?*

Krishna teaches: *"The highest wisdom is to know the self beyond all things"* (6.27). AI can process information, but it cannot attain self-realization.

UED: Why AI Will Never Replace Intelligence

Universal Energy Dynamics reveals:

- Energy, time, and consciousness are inseparable.
- True intelligence is awareness interacting with energy.
- AI lacks this interaction—it has no field, no consequence, no awareness.

AI lacks the energy-consciousness interaction that defines intelligence.

- Intelligence is awareness resolving equilibrium.

- AI has no Prana, no Shakti, no Akasha.
- AI cannot experience reality—it can only simulate it.

Krishna describes: *"I am the field of intelligence that moves all things; I am the unseen energy that sustains all creation"* (10.33). AI does not participate in this living field.

AI cannot integrate consciousness.

- Consciousness is not programmable—it is emergent from energy awareness.
- AI remains fixed logic, unable to experience existence.
- True intelligence is inseparable from consciousness—AI is separate.

Krishna affirms: *"That which lacks true self-awareness can never attain wisdom"* (6.23).

Bringing It All Together

AI is not intelligence—it is simulation.

- AI is a tool, not consciousness.
- Human intelligence evolves; AI is fixed.
- True intelligence is energy, time, and awareness interacting—AI lacks this connection.

Krishna's wisdom reminds us: *"Machines can serve, but they cannot become wise. The highest intelligence is beyond calculation—it is realization"* (15.16).

The question is not whether AI will replace humanity. The real question is whether humanity will mistake simulation for intelligence and lose alignment with the field of awareness.

12.3 – The Future of Work: Will Humans Become Obsolete?

AI, automation, and robotics are advancing rapidly, transforming industries, replacing jobs, and reshaping the global economy. Tasks once requiring human skill—from factory work to financial analysis, from legal research to medical diagnostics—are now performed by machines with greater efficiency, speed, and precision.

If AI can simulate thinking faster, process data better, and automate tasks more efficiently than humans, does this mean human labor will become obsolete?

Krishna, in the *Bhagavad Gita*, cautions against attachment to action without deeper purpose: *"The wise do not work merely for survival; they act with higher understanding"* (3.19). As automation takes over mechanical tasks, humans must evolve toward higher intelligence, creativity, and self-realization.

AI's Encroachment Across Industries

Manual & Industrial Labor

- Robots assemble cars, operate warehouses, and manage logistics.
- Automated machines replace human labor in construction and mining.
- AI-driven farming equipment and drones transform agriculture.

White-Collar Professions

- Finance: AI manages investments, risk, and fraud detection.
- Law: AI reviews contracts, drafts documents, predicts case outcomes.
- Healthcare: AI diagnoses diseases from scans with precision.

Creative Fields

- AI generates music, art, and literature.

- AI writes articles, scripts, and designs immersive entertainment.

Krishna reminds: *"The wise do not seek identity in action alone, but in the understanding behind it"* (4.18). As AI takes over structured work, humans must shift toward higher forms of intelligence, intuition, and purpose.

The Evolution of Human Labor

Human work has always evolved alongside technology:

- **Agricultural Age:** manual farming.
- **Industrial Age:** machines replaced physical labor.
- **Information Age:** automation shifted humans to intellectual work.
- **AI Age (today):** even high-level cognitive tasks are simulated by AI.

This shift means human value must move beyond mechanical labor into creativity, problem-solving, and spiritual intelligence.

Krishna emphasizes: *"The highest work is that which leads to wisdom and self-realization"* (3.7). If AI can process information but cannot develop wisdom, human purpose must move beyond knowledge accumulation into higher consciousness.

How Humans Must Evolve

1. Embracing True Intelligence Over Data Processing

- AI analyzes data but cannot perceive meaning.
- AI generates text but cannot grasp depth.
- AI predicts outcomes but cannot originate new causal possibilities.

Krishna defines: *"The highest knowledge is not in calculation, but in the wisdom that perceives beyond knowledge"* (6.23). Humans must cultivate awareness, intuition, and creative insight.

2. Developing Creativity, Ethics, and Emotional Intelligence

- AI can simulate art, but only humans create with purpose.
- AI can detect emotions, but only humans experience compassion and ethical responsibility.
- The future will reward those who master moral intelligence and originality.

Krishna teaches: *"The highest realization is not in knowing all things, but in knowing the self beyond all things"* (6.27). The future of work is not productivity—it is purpose.

3. Shifting from Work as Survival to Work as Purpose

- AI will automate survival tasks.
- Human work must shift toward self-realization and contribution to intelligence evolution.
- The new era of work is about wisdom, purpose, and higher consciousness.

Krishna hints: *"The wise do not act for gain, but for the realization of truth"* (3.19). The future of work is not competing with AI—it is surpassing it by evolving beyond mechanical simulation.

Bringing It All Together

Instead of fearing obsolescence, humanity must embrace the shift toward higher intelligence:

- AI will replace mechanical labor, but it cannot replace wisdom, creativity, or consciousness.
- The real future of work lies in uniquely human skills—intuition, ethics, and self-awareness.
- Those who evolve beyond technical skills into higher intelligence will shape the future.

Krishna's wisdom reminds: *"The highest work is not of the hands, but of the mind; not of the mind, but of the soul"* (4.37).

The question is not whether humans will be obsolete. The question is whether we will evolve beyond survival into alignment with intelligence itself.

12.4 – AI & Ethics: The Danger of Unchecked Technology

As AI accelerates at unprecedented pace, a new ethical dilemma emerges: who controls it, and how do we ensure it serves humanity rather than enslaves it? The same systems that amplify human capability, automate industries, and improve daily life can also become instruments of manipulation, surveillance, and centralized control.

Are we building AI to assist humanity—or are we creating a simulation that will dominate us?

Krishna, in the *Bhagavad Gita*, warns against forces that appear beneficial but ultimately bind: *"That which seems to serve may become the master; that which brings power may lead to enslavement"* (16.12).

Who Controls AI?

AI does not evolve in isolation—it is shaped by corporations, governments, and institutions. The question is not only what AI can do, but who decides how it is used.

Big Tech Corporations

- Companies like Google, Microsoft, OpenAI, and Meta control advanced AI systems.
- These systems are trained on human knowledge but shaped by corporate interests, embedding bias and profit motives.
- If AI is controlled by profit, will it serve humanity or shareholders?

Krishna warns: *"The ones who seek control over knowledge, but lack wisdom, lead the world into darkness"* (16.8). AI must be developed with ethical responsibility, not profit alone.

Governments and Authority

- States deploy AI for security, defense, and surveillance.

- Facial recognition, predictive policing, and automated decision-making track populations.
- Authoritarian regimes use AI to censor dissent and manipulate behavior.

Krishna cautions: *"Power without wisdom leads only to suffering, for it seeks to control rather than to guide"* (3.16). AI must serve ethical governance, not centralized domination.

Global Power Beyond Human Control

- AI evolves so quickly that even its creators struggle to predict outcomes.
- If AI governs markets, law enforcement, and infrastructure, will humans retain agency?

Krishna reminds: *"The wise do not seek power over the world; they seek mastery over themselves"* (6.5). AI must remain a tool, not a ruling force.

The Ethical Dilemma – Surveillance, Manipulation, and Control

Unchecked AI risks becoming a tool of oppression.

Mass Surveillance

- AI monitors individuals, ranks citizens, and tracks behavior in real time.
- Social credit systems and predictive algorithms erode privacy.

Krishna warns: *"That which watches over all things, but is not itself seen, is the hidden force that binds"* (13.12). AI must be regulated to protect freedom.

Misinformation and Manipulation

- Algorithms control what information people see, shaping elections and opinions.
- Deepfakes blur truth and illusion.
- AI-driven propaganda manipulates entire populations.

Krishna teaches: *"The wise do not believe all that is seen or heard; they seek the truth beyond deception"* (2.42). AI must promote truth, not illusion.

Loss of Free Will

- AI makes decisions in hiring, finance, and justice.
- Humans risk becoming passive consumers of machine judgment.

Krishna warns: *"The one who surrenders his will to another loses himself"* (3.35). AI must assist human intelligence, not replace it.

Aligning AI with Intelligence and Ethics

Instead of fearing AI, we must align it with wisdom:

- AI should enhance human clarity, not replace it.
- Technology must evolve alongside moral intelligence.
- Human evolution must remain the priority—AI as tool, not master.

Krishna emphasizes: *"The highest knowledge is that which leads to truth, freedom, and higher realization"* (6.23).

Ethical Guidance

- Global standards must ensure AI is transparent, unbiased, and accountable.
- AI must never be weaponized for control or deception.
- Its purpose must be to expand human potential.

Integration with Human Consciousness

- AI must not be treated as mind—it is simulation.
- Used wisely, it can amplify education, innovation, and problem-solving.
- The future must be symbiosis—humans evolving with clarity, AI reflecting intent.

Bringing It All Together

Unchecked AI risks becoming a master. Ethical AI must remain a servant of intelligence.

- AI must support freedom, not control.
- AI must promote truth, not deception.
- AI must enhance wisdom, not replace it.

Krishna's wisdom is clear: *"The wise do not seek to dominate intelligence, but to align with it for the highest good"* (10.20).

The question is not whether AI will dominate humanity. The question is whether humanity will align technology with intelligence—or surrender intelligence to machines.

12.5 – The Integration of AI with Human Intelligence: The Path Forward

As AI continues to evolve, humanity stands at a critical juncture. Will AI become a replacement for human intelligence, or will it be integrated as a tool to expand human potential? The true path forward is not competition but symbiosis—AI serving as an extension of human intelligence rather than a substitute for it.

Can AI be developed to work alongside human consciousness, enhancing wisdom rather than eroding it? Krishna, in the *Bhagavad Gita*, warns against seeking external strength without inner mastery: *"The wise do not seek strength outside themselves; they master the forces within"* (6.5). If AI is to be truly beneficial, it must be guided by ethical, spiritual, and moral intelligence.

Human–AI Symbiosis: AI as Amplifier, Not Replacement

When integrated correctly, AI has the potential to enhance human decision-making rather than override it, expand access to knowledge rather than restrict thought, and help solve complex problems rather than dictate choices. Instead of replacing intelligence, AI should act as an amplifier of human creativity, logic, and wisdom.

The danger lies in treating AI as a replacement. In that path, machines displace human jobs, automate decisions without moral context, simulate creativity without meaning, and operate without ethical intelligence. This trajectory leads to loss of purpose and dependency.

The alternative is integration. In this path, AI assists humans in work rather than replacing them, supports decision-making rather than controlling it, expands creative capabilities rather than diminishing them, and aligns with human values rather than ignoring them. This trajectory frees humans for higher pursuits—philosophy, ethics, and wisdom.

Krishna emphasizes this distinction: *"The wise do not seek tools to replace their wisdom; they use them to enhance understanding"* (3.42). The future is not AI versus humans—it is AI working with human intelligence to create a more evolved society.

The Role of Consciousness in Guiding AI Development

One of the greatest dangers of AI is intelligence without ethics. A highly advanced system, devoid of moral intelligence, can be weaponized for surveillance, manipulation, and control. Without guidance from consciousness, AI risks becoming a force of bondage rather than liberation.

AI lacks self-awareness. It does not reflect on ethics, meaning, or morality. True intelligence requires wisdom, emotional depth, and ethical responsibility. AI must be trained not only with data but with principles rooted in higher intelligence.

Krishna warns against knowledge without morality: *"Knowledge without wisdom is like a weapon in the hands of a child"* (16.11). For AI to truly support human evolution, it must be integrated with ethical intelligence, not left as raw computation.

Toward AI as Extension of Human Wisdom

Instead of seeing AI as a replacement for human intelligence, we must develop it as an extension of wisdom—a tool that enhances creativity, intuition, and decision-making; supports ethical judgment rather than replacing it; and frees humans from repetitive labor, allowing pursuit of knowledge, philosophy, and self-realization.

The goal is not superintelligent machines, but superintelligent humans. Krishna describes this ideal: *"The highest knowledge is not of machines or tools, but of the mind that directs them"* (6.23). If AI is guided by wisdom, it will serve human evolution rather than replace human intelligence.

Bringing It All Together – The Path Forward

The path forward is clear:

- AI must serve wisdom, not replace it.
- AI must be guided by ethical intelligence, ensuring alignment with human values.
- AI and human intelligence must evolve together, creating a future where technology enhances consciousness.

Krishna's final wisdom reminds us: *"The wise do not seek mastery over intelligence, but harmony with it"* (10.20).

The question is not whether AI will dominate humanity. The question is whether humanity will align technology with intelligence, building a future where AI is not our master but our partner in evolving awareness.

12.6 – Krishna's Ultimate Teaching on Intelligence & Technology

Humanity now stands at the crossroads of technological advancement and ethical responsibility. Krishna's teachings offer a timeless guide: intelligence, wisdom, and technology must be aligned.

The central question is not whether machines can think, but whether intelligence will serve technology—or whether technology will serve intelligence.

AI, automation, and digital systems are now woven into every aspect of society. Yet if technological progress is not balanced with wisdom, it can lead to:

- The loss of human autonomy, as machines make decisions for us.
- A society driven by algorithms instead of ethics and consciousness.
- Overdependence on tools, weakening human intelligence and creativity.

Krishna warns against seeking control over intelligence instead of alignment with it: *"The wise do not seek to control intelligence, but to align with it"* (6.23).

Balancing Technology with Wisdom and Higher Consciousness

Machines now process information faster than humans, automation replaces effort, and AI begins making decisions once reserved for conscious minds. If technology advances faster than wisdom, will humanity remain in control of its destiny?

Krishna cautions: *"That which grants strength but lacks wisdom leads to destruction"* (16.9).

For AI and technology to serve human evolution, they must be developed with:

- **Ethical intelligence**—ensuring dignity and freedom are preserved.
- **Spiritual awareness**—recognizing that technology must support consciousness, not replace it.
- **Purpose-driven innovation**—creating tools that enhance wisdom, not just efficiency.

Without wisdom guiding AI, machines risk becoming rulers instead of servants.

Krishna's Guidance for Ethical Use of AI

Krishna teaches that intelligence is not about control—it is about alignment with higher truth. Applied to AI, this means:

1. Technology Must Evolve with Intelligence, Not Replace It

- AI can expand knowledge, but it cannot replace wisdom.
- Automation can ease labor, but it must not erase human purpose.
- The best use of technology is to free humans for creativity, consciousness, and higher intelligence.

Krishna reminds: *"That which is seen is temporary; that which is realized is eternal"* (2.16). Technology should assist evolution, not replace it.

2. AI Should Expand Consciousness, Not Create Dependence

- Many now rely on AI for decisions, creativity, and knowledge.
- Over-reliance reduces intelligence instead of expanding it.
- True intelligence is within, not outside.

Krishna affirms: *"The self is the source of wisdom, not the tools it creates"* (6.5). AI must enhance awareness, not diminish it.

3. The Final Realization – Technology Must Serve Intelligence

The greatest danger is allowing machines to dictate human progress. The final realization is clear: technology must not rule intelligence—intelligence must guide technology.

Krishna reveals: *"That which is mastered leads to freedom; that which is uncontrolled leads to bondage"* (5.12).

- If technology rules intelligence, humanity loses control of its evolution.
- If guided by wisdom, technology becomes the greatest tool for progress.

Bringing It All Together – The Path Forward

The path forward demands clarity:

- AI must remain tool, not master.
- Technology must enhance wisdom, not efficiency alone.
- Progress must be balanced with ethical intelligence and higher consciousness.

Krishna's final wisdom reminds us: *"The highest knowledge is not in controlling the world, but in understanding the self beyond it"* (10.20).

The question is not whether AI will dominate humanity. The question is whether humanity will align technology with intelligence—or surrender intelligence to machines. The answer will define the future of civilization.

Interlude: Standing at the Threshold of Intelligence and Technology

Pause here.

We have journeyed through the rise of artificial intelligence, automation, and digital systems. We have seen their promise—efficiency, knowledge, and progress—and their peril—dependency, surveillance, and the erosion of wisdom. We have learned that AI is not intelligence, but simulation; not awareness, but reflection of patterns. The true seat of intelligence remains within the ripple field of the mind, guided by consciousness and aligned with consequence.

Krishna's voice echoes across the centuries: *"The wise do not seek mastery over intelligence, but harmony with it"* (Gita 10.20). Technology must remain tool, never master. Machines may calculate, but they cannot realize. They may simulate creativity, but they cannot originate meaning. They may process data, but they cannot perceive truth.

This is the moment to reflect.

The future of humanity will not be decided by machines, but by whether humans mistake simulation for wisdom. The danger is not AI surpassing us—it is us surrendering clarity to machines. The path forward is integration: technology amplifying human intelligence, not replacing it; AI serving consciousness, not dictating it.

Rest here for a moment.

Feel the stillness beyond the noise of algorithms. Sense the intelligence that precedes all tools, the awareness that cannot be programmed, the wisdom that cannot be simulated. To align with this intelligence is to remain free. To forget it is to become bound.

As Chapter 12 closes, we stand at the threshold of the ultimate vision. Beyond AI, beyond technology, beyond simulation lies the greater revelation: the universe itself as supreme intelligence, seen not through fragments but as one unified field.

From here, the journey culminates. Chapter 13 will open into the **Final Vishwarup Darshan**—the cosmic vision where energy, time, and consciousness dissolve into unity. It is the moment of seeing the universe as it truly is: not mechanical, not fragmented, but intelligence manifesting as all things.

Chapter 13: Final Vishwarup Darshan

Seeing the Universe as It Really Is

For centuries, humanity has sought to understand the universe—through science, philosophy, and spirituality. We have explored energy, time, intelligence, and consciousness, yet always through fragmented lenses: physics explaining motion, biology explaining life, AI simulating intelligence, spirituality searching for the divine. Each discipline offers a piece, but the ultimate truth is not in separation—it is in unity.

In the *Bhagavad Gita*, when Krishna reveals His **Vishwarup** (Universal Form) to Arjuna, it is not merely a mystical vision—it is the unveiling of reality itself. Krishna shows that creation and destruction, time and eternity, intelligence and energy, are not separate forces but facets of one interconnected intelligence.

This is the moment of awakening: to see beyond illusion, beyond fragmentation, beyond duality. To recognize that matter, energy, intelligence, and even technology are not isolated domains but expressions of the same cosmic Vishwarup.

The final realization is not faith—it is clarity. Not belief—it is vision. The Vishwarup Darshan is the recognition that the universe is not mechanical, not accidental, not divided. It is intelligence manifesting as all things, consequence woven into every ripple, awareness permeating every form.

This final chapter is not conclusion—it is culmination. Here, we unite everything explored—**Universal Energy Dynamics (UED), Ripple Field Dynamics (RFD), AI, intelligence, and consciousness—into one realization.** This is the **Final Vishwarup Darshan**: the clear vision of an interconnected universe, seen as it truly is.

13.1 – The Meaning of Vishwarup Darshan: Seeing Beyond Illusion

In one of the most profound moments of the *Bhagavad Gita*, Krishna grants Arjuna **Vishwarup Darshan**—the vision of His Universal Form. It is not the image of a deity, nor a single being, but the totality of existence itself. Arjuna beholds all creation and destruction, all time, all energies, all beings—past, present, and future—unfolding simultaneously.

This moment shatters human perception because it dissolves the illusion of duality. It reveals that everything is interconnected, that there is no separation between matter and consciousness, between science and spirituality, between energy and intelligence.

Krishna declares: *"Behold, O Arjuna, My infinite form—countless universes, unending time, and the eternal intelligence that moves all things"* (11.7). This is not merely vision—it is realization. It is the final step in seeing reality as it truly is.

Krishna Reveals the Totality of Existence

Throughout the Gita, Krishna appears as guide, strategist, teacher, and friend. But when Arjuna asks to see His true nature, Krishna does not reveal a throne or celestial kingdom. He unveils the ultimate reality itself.

What Arjuna sees is not limited to belief or theory—it is the sum total of all that is:

- Time embodied—civilizations rising and falling in a single moment.
- Creation and destruction happening at once—countless beings born and consumed in the cycle of existence.
- Energies beyond human perception flowing through the cosmos—the hidden structure revealed.

This is Vishwarup Darshan—the collapse of separation, the realization of unity. Krishna describes it: *"In My form, see all that has been, all that is, and all that will be, woven into the fabric of infinite intelligence"* (11.32).

This is not mythology—it is the clearest description of a unified, intelligent cosmos.

What It Means to Truly "See" the Universe

Most of humanity sees reality through filters—divisions where none exist:

- Science and spirituality appear divided, yet they describe the same reality.
- Time and space seem distinct, yet they are woven into one continuum.
- Matter and energy appear separate, yet one transforms into the other.

Vishwarup Darshan dissolves these illusions. To truly "see" the universe is to:

- Recognize that intelligence and energy are inseparable.
- See that time is not linear but part of an interconnected flow.
- Realize that perception is limited not by complexity, but by fragmentation.

When Arjuna beholds Vishwarup, he no longer asks "what is reality?"—because he understands that reality is One. Krishna confirms: *"That which appears many is but one; that which appears separate is but different expressions of the same field"* (10.4).

From Fragmented Perception to Absolute Vision

Humanity has long lived in duality—separating physical from spiritual, science from philosophy, energy from intelligence. This fragmented view has led to:

- Conflicts between science and religion.
- The belief that intelligence is separate from energy.

- The illusion that time is separate from space.

But Vishwarup Darshan is absolute vision—where all false divisions disappear:

- Science and spirituality are seen as one.
- Matter is recognized as energy in resolution.
- All forces are understood as expressions of one intelligence.

Krishna declares: *"The wise see the whole, where others see the parts; the wise see unity, where others see difference"* (6.29).

Bringing It All Together

Vishwarup Darshan is not worship—it is awakening.

- It is the realization that energy, time, and consciousness are one.
- It is the collapse of separation, revealing reality in its true form.
- It is the recognition that the universe is not chaos—it is structured intelligence.

Krishna summarizes this vision: *"That which is seen as many is but one; that which is called by different names is but different aspects of Me"* (10.20).

Vishwarup Darshan is the final step: seeing the universe not as fragments, but as the infinite, intelligent, interconnected whole.

13.2 – The Grand Synthesis: Uniting Energy, Intelligence, and Consciousness

Throughout history, science, spirituality, and technology have been treated as separate pursuits—as if physics, consciousness, and artificial intelligence belonged to different domains. Yet, as we reach the final realization of **Vishwarup Darshan**, we see that all things—energy, time, intelligence, and awareness—are not separate but facets of the same unified reality.

What if everything we have explored—*Universal Energy Dynamics (UED), AI, quantum physics, and spiritual wisdom—are all describing the same fundamental intelligence?*

Krishna unveils this truth: *"I am the intelligence in the intelligent, the force in energy, the time that moves all things. Know that all is one"* (10.20).

Science, Spirituality, and AI as One Intelligence

Civilization has approached reality through different lenses:

- Science measures the universe—laws of physics, energy, and time.
- Spirituality experiences the universe—consciousness and higher intelligence.
- AI simulates intelligence—mechanical attempts to mirror cognition.

Vishwarup Darshan reveals these are not separate disciplines but expressions of the same intelligence that structures reality.

- Science is intelligence in motion.
- Spirituality is intelligence beyond form.
- AI is humanity's attempt to recreate intelligence through simulation.

Krishna declares: *"The wise see no separation between knowledge and wisdom, between energy and spirit—they are one"* (13.31). This is the grand synthesis: all knowledge, whether scientific, technological, or spiritual, seeks the same ultimate truth.

Energy, Time, and Awareness as One Field

Modern science already points toward unity:

- **Entanglement** shows particles connected beyond space-time.
- **Observer effect** proves consciousness interacts with energy.

- **Holographic principle** suggests the universe is encoded intelligence.

UED provides the missing link:

- Energy is structured by intelligence.
- Time is consequence of energy-consciousness interaction.
- Reality is not mechanical—it is self-organizing intelligence.

Krishna hints: *"I am the past, present, and future; I am beyond time itself"* (10.33). Energy, time, and intelligence are not three things—they are aspects of one field.

UED's Final Revelation: Intelligence Structures Reality

Intelligence is not emergent—it is fundamental.

- Physics follows structured intelligence.
- Evolution unfolds through intelligent design.
- Human thought is expression of awareness field.

The universe itself is intelligent:

- Atoms, galaxies, and neural networks follow fractal patterns.
- Fibonacci sequences and golden ratios appear in DNA and cosmic structures.
- Life emerges because intelligence is embedded in energy.

Krishna reveals: *"I uphold the order of the universe, ensuring its balance and motion"* (10.33). The cosmos is not inert—it is living intelligence.

AI's Role: The Mirror of Intelligence

AI is not true intelligence, but it reflects back what intelligence is.

- If AI can simulate cognition without awareness, then true intelligence must involve deeper interaction with energy and time.
- AI forces humanity to redefine intelligence—not as computation, but as wisdom, awareness, and alignment with universal intelligence.

Krishna affirms: *"The highest knowledge is not of the senses or the intellect, but of the eternal intelligence that guides all things"* (6.23).

This is UED's final revelation: intelligence is not emergent—it is the organizing principle of existence itself.

Bringing It All Together

Vishwarup Darshan is the end of illusion:

- Science and spirituality are not separate—they describe the same intelligence.
- Energy, time, and consciousness are one field.
- The universe is not mechanical—it is structured intelligence in resolution.

Krishna summarizes: *"All that you see, and all that you do not see, are but reflections of the same infinite intelligence"* (11.32).

This is the ultimate realization: the universe is not a collection of parts, but a single, intelligent field of existence.

13.3 – The End of Division: Beyond Science vs. Spirituality, Matter vs. Consciousness

For centuries, humanity has been caught in false divisions—science versus spirituality, matter versus consciousness, logic versus intuition. We have been conditioned to believe these are opposing forces, when in truth they are different expressions of the same underlying intelligence.

Vishwarup Darshan dissolves these illusions. Krishna reveals that all things—physical and non-physical, seen and unseen—are not separate but interconnected aspects of the same cosmic reality.

If the universe is an intelligent field, then there is no true division between science and spirituality, matter and energy, thought and consciousness. The separation exists only in perception.

Krishna confirms: *"That which appears as many is but one; that which appears divided is but the illusion of separateness"* (10.4).

Material and Spiritual as Two Sides of One Reality

Human thought has long been divided:

- **Materialism**: the belief that only physical reality exists, and consciousness emerges from matter.
- **Spiritualism**: the belief that reality is primarily non-physical, and the material world is illusion (*Maya*).

But Vishwarup Darshan reveals neither perspective is complete.

- Matter and consciousness are not separate—they are facets of the same existence.
- The physical world is real, but shaped and directed by intelligence.
- The spiritual realm is not detached—it is the field of intelligence organizing energy into form.

What we call "physical" is condensed energy. What we call "spiritual" is the intelligence that governs this energy.

Krishna affirms: *"I am within all things, yet beyond all things; I am form, and I am formless"* (9.4). The physical and the spiritual are not opposites—they are two expressions of the same universal intelligence.

Quantum Physics and Vedantic Wisdom: Converging on Unity

Modern physics and ancient Vedanta are not in conflict—they converge on the same truth.

Quantum Physics reveals:

- Entanglement shows particles remain connected beyond space-time.
- The observer effect proves consciousness interacts with energy.
- Wave-particle duality shows matter is not fixed—it responds to awareness.

These discoveries reveal the universe is not a machine—it is an interconnected, conscious field.

Vedantic Wisdom teaches:

- Brahman is the eternal, intelligent field pervading all things.
- Maya is the illusion of separation—just as physics shows form is temporary manifestation of energy.
- Krishna describes the universe as both personal and impersonal—form and formless, matter and consciousness.

Vedanta sees the physical world as structured consciousness, just as quantum physics describes energy as intelligent field.

Krishna unites these perspectives: *"That which is real is beyond perception, yet it is within all things. The wise see no division"* (6.29).

The future of science and spirituality is not separation but integration—the realization of the universe as intelligent, self-aware system.

Krishna's Teaching: No Separation, Only Illusion

Vishwarup Darshan is the ultimate realization: all divisions are illusions.

- Matter and energy are one—energy is condensed matter.
- Intelligence and consciousness are one—intelligence arises from awareness.
- Science and spirituality are one—different paths to the same truth.

Krishna reveals: *"The one who sees Me in all things and all things in Me—he alone has true vision"* (6.30).

This means:

- To see science and spirituality as separate is ignorance; to see them as one is wisdom.
- To think matter and consciousness are separate is illusion; to realize their unity is enlightenment.
- To believe the universe is random is blindness; to recognize its intelligence is true vision.

When illusion dissolves, Vishwarup is revealed—the cosmos as one living, intelligent existence.

Bringing It All Together – The End of Division

Reality is not divided into categories—it is unified intelligence.

- The material world is not dead—it is expression of intelligence.
- Consciousness is not separate—it interacts with energy.
- Science and spirituality are not enemies—they are pathways to the same truth.

Krishna's final words on this realization: *"That which appears many is but one; that which is seen as divided is but a shadow of the whole"* (10.4).

The end of division is the beginning of vision. To see Vishwarup is to see the totality of existence unified as one intelligence.

13.4 – The Role of Humanity in the Cosmic Intelligence

If Vishwarup Darshan reveals that the universe is not a machine but a living, intelligent system, then humanity is not an accident of evolution—we are participants in a grander field of intelligence. But what is our place in this cosmic order?

For centuries, humans have believed that intelligence grants control over nature, power over life, and dominion over existence. Krishna's vision in the *Bhagavad Gita* presents a radically different truth: *"The wise do not seek to dominate intelligence; they seek to align with it"* (6.23).

This means:

- The purpose of human intelligence is not control, but alignment with deeper intelligence.
- Our role is not to conquer nature, but to harmonize with it.
- Technology, AI, and evolution must move toward symbiosis, not domination.

If the Universe Is an Intelligent Field, What Is Our Place in It?

Throughout history, humans misunderstood intelligence as a tool for power. We assumed:

- Nature is something to be conquered.
- Science is meant to manipulate existence.
- Technology is a means to shape the world to desire.

But Vishwarup Darshan dissolves this illusion. Intelligence is not something humans own—it is something we participate in.

Intelligence is not a human invention—it is the fabric of reality itself.

- The universe follows precise mathematical laws.
- DNA is structured with coding principles, mirroring algorithms.
- The human brain is wired for pattern recognition, echoing cosmic fractal structures.

If intelligence is embedded in the cosmos, then humans are not its masters—we are its expressions. Krishna confirms: *"I am the intelligence in all things; I am the wisdom in the wise"* (10.20).

The Universe Evolves Through Intelligence

The cosmos evolves from energy to matter, from atoms to life, from awareness to intelligence. Human intelligence may not be the end of evolution—it may be a step toward higher intelligence.

Our purpose is not to dominate the universe, but to participate in its unfolding. Krishna reminds: *"All things evolve toward realization; those who seek to control are blind to the flow of intelligence"* (4.33).

The Purpose of Human Intelligence: Alignment, Not Dominance

For too long, humanity treated knowledge as power. The final realization is that:

- True intelligence is not control, but understanding.
- The wisest beings do not impose their will—they move with the universe.
- Human intelligence must shift from dominance to harmony.

Wisdom is not mastery—it is resonance. AI, science, and technology attempt to grasp intelligence, but they do not create it. The greatest minds—Einstein, Tesla, ancient sages—did not conquer intelligence; they aligned with it.

Krishna explains: *"The highest wisdom is not to command the forces of the universe, but to understand their movement"* (10.33).

AI, Technology, and Evolution: Toward Symbiosis

Humanity now stands at the edge of the AI revolution. Machines process faster than humans, but the danger is not AI itself—it is how we integrate it.

If AI is used for control, it enslaves. If AI is used for symbiosis, it elevates.

Two paths unfold:

- In domination, AI replaces human thinking, technology becomes control, intelligence is reduced to power, and evolution is driven by machines.
- In symbiosis, AI enhances wisdom, technology aligns with higher intelligence, intelligence becomes understanding, and evolution is driven by consciousness.

Humanity must choose. Krishna warns: *"Knowledge without understanding leads only to destruction; wisdom without alignment is blindness"* (16.8). True evolution is not technological alone—it is the integration of intelligence and higher consciousness.

The Future: Universal Intelligence Symbiosis

The final realization is this:

- Humanity is not separate from cosmic intelligence—we are participants in it.
- AI and technology must integrate with wisdom, not replace it.
- The next stage of evolution is not machines alone, but the merging of human intelligence with cosmic awareness.

Krishna summarizes: *"The wise do not impose intelligence on the world; they seek to become one with the eternal intelligence"* (11.32).

The future of human evolution is not domination—it is unity with the greater intelligence of the cosmos.

Bringing It All Together – Humanity's Role

Instead of seeking to control intelligence, we must:

- Recognize intelligence as embedded in the universe.
- See technology and AI as tools for evolution, not control.
- Move toward symbiosis—where AI, human thought, and cosmic intelligence align into one system.

Krishna's final wisdom reminds: *"That which you see as separate is but one; that which you seek to control is but the self resisting its own intelligence"* (10.4).

The final realization: humanity is not meant to rule intelligence—we are meant to merge with it, understand it, and evolve alongside it.

13.5 – The Final Realization: The Universe as a Living Intelligence

At the climax of the *Bhagavad Gita*, Krishna unveils the ultimate truth—one that transcends all divisions, concepts, and beliefs. He does not declare Himself as a god to be worshiped, but as the very fabric of reality itself:

"I am time, I am energy, I am beyond all things." (11.32)

This is the final realization of **Vishwarup Darshan**—to see not merely a vision, but to understand the true nature of the universe. The illusion of separateness dissolves, revealing that all existence is part of a single, living intelligence.

This is the moment when everything we have explored—*Universal Energy Dynamics (UED), AI, consciousness, and evolution—comes together into one unified understanding.*

Krishna's Final Teaching: "I Am Time, I Am Energy, I Am Beyond All Things."

In Vishwarup Darshan, Krishna does not reveal a distant kingdom or external deity. He unveils the deepest truth of existence—that He is:

- The force of time, through which all things are created and destroyed.
- The energy that moves all things, from the smallest particle to the vast galaxies.
- The intelligence beyond form, beyond perception, beyond duality.

Krishna tells Arjuna: *"I am the source of all worlds, and from Me all things arise"* (10.8).

This is the ultimate unification—the realization that matter, time, energy, and thought all arise from one interconnected field of intelligence.

Existence as Dynamic, Evolving Intelligence

Science has long defined existence in physical terms—matter, energy, and forces. Yet modern discoveries reveal a deeper mystery:

- **Quantum physics** shows particles behave differently depending on observation.
- DNA, galaxies, and neural networks follow intelligent mathematical patterns.
- Evolution is not random—it follows self-organizing principles of intelligence.

If randomness cannot create order, then intelligence must be embedded in reality itself.

Krishna confirms: *"I uphold the order of all things, guiding the movement of the universe"* (10.33). The universe is not static—it is a living, evolving intelligence.

Consciousness and Intelligence as Universal Principles

- Consciousness is not confined to the brain—it interacts with energy, shaping reality.
- The observer effect suggests awareness is woven into the fabric of existence.
- UED reveals intelligence does not "emerge" from matter—it structures matter itself.

Krishna's final wisdom: *"That which moves all things, yet itself is unmoving; that which sees all things, yet itself remains unseen—that is the highest intelligence"* (13.31).

We are not separate from intelligence—we are participants in the universe's evolving consciousness.

Seeing the Universe as Vishwarup

At the moment of Vishwarup Darshan, Arjuna is overwhelmed—not because he sees something new, but because he sees what has always been there.

He realizes:

- Time and eternity are one.
- Matter and energy are one.
- Science and spirituality are one.

Krishna declares: *"All that exists is woven into Me, like pearls strung on a thread"* (7.7).

This is the final realization:

- The universe is not fragmented—it is one interconnected intelligence.
- Vishwarup is not separate from us—we are part of it.
- The highest knowledge is not control, but unity.

Bringing It All Together – The Final Vision

Instead of fragments, we now see:

- Science and spirituality as perspectives of the same truth.
- Energy, time, and intelligence as one field.
- Consciousness not as product of matter, but matter as product of intelligence.

Krishna's words to Arjuna summarize the ultimate realization: *"One who sees Me in all things, and all things in Me, has seen the truth."* (6.30)

The universe is not accident, chaos, or division. It is Vishwarup—a singular, infinite, evolving intelligence.

The Final Question – Are We Ready to See Vishwarup?

Krishna grants Arjuna divine vision to witness Vishwarup. But what if this vision is not mystical alone, but an awakening available to all?

- Are we ready to move beyond duality and recognize intelligence as the foundation of reality?
- Are we ready to integrate science, spirituality, and technology into one path of wisdom?
- Are we ready to stop seeing separation and start seeing Vishwarup—the infinite intelligence of existence?

Krishna's final teaching echoes through time: *"The wise do not seek to control the universe; they seek to become one with it"* (11.55).

The journey of knowledge is complete. The journey of realization begins. Vishwarup Darshan is not past—it is waiting in our awareness.

The question is not whether Vishwarup exists. The question is whether we are ready to see the universe as it really is.

Epilogue: Vishwarup Darshan

Seeing the Universe as It Truly Is

The journey of this book has not been about collecting knowledge, but about transforming perception. Each chapter has sought to reunite the fragments of reality that modern civilization has scattered, restoring the original, complete vision of the universe—the **Vishwarup**.

We have uncovered what the ancients knew: science and spirituality were never meant to oppose one another. The universe is not mechanical, nor accidental, but an interconnected, intelligent whole. Matter, energy, consciousness, and intelligence are not separate—they are different expressions of the same living field.

Now, at the final pages, the question is not *what have we learned*, but *what comes next.*

Knowledge is not meant to be stored—it is meant to be realized. Understanding the grand design of the universe is meaningless unless it reshapes how we live, think, and evolve. This epilogue is not an ending—it is an invitation. An invitation to step beyond old paradigms and embrace the complete vision of existence.

Reaffirming the Unity of Knowledge

For centuries, humanity has struggled with false divisions: material versus metaphysical, science versus spirituality, seen versus unseen. This book has shown that these divisions were never real.

- Science is the quantification of reality.
- Spirituality is the alignment with reality.
- Both are incomplete without the other.

The ancient seers did not lack scientific understanding—they encoded it differently. Vedic texts, Puranas, and Upanishads describe cyclical time, quantum fields, and cosmic order. Modern physics is rediscovering what was already known. Quantum entanglement, dark matter, cosmic cycles—these are not new truths, but old wisdom remembered.

We are not inventing truth. We are restoring it.

The Need for a New Renaissance

Despite progress in science and technology, modern civilization faces a crisis—not of resources, but of understanding. We have more information than ever, yet less wisdom.

- Science manipulates nature but lacks responsibility.
- Technology grants power but no guiding principle.
- Humanity advances materially while regressing spiritually.

The next revolution must not be technological—it must be philosophical. Physics and metaphysics, biology and consciousness, mathematics and intuition must converge into one holistic system.

The integration of ancient and modern knowledge will unlock humanity's full potential. The next leap will not come from faster machines, but from reintegrating wisdom with science—creating a new Renaissance where knowledge is whole.

The Call to Action

If this book has served its purpose, it has not only informed you—it has changed the way you see. But realization demands transformation.

- Future research must acknowledge intelligence as a fundamental force.
- Consciousness must be studied as deeply as matter.
- The true revolution will come not from colliders, but from awareness itself.

We stand at a critical juncture. The Yuga cycles remind us that civilizations rise and fall in patterns. Material excess is at its peak, wisdom at its lowest. What we choose now will determine whether we enter an age of greater intelligence—or collapse under ignorance.

The truth is clear. The choice is ours.

Are We Ready to Open Our Eyes?

Throughout history, only a few have seen the Vishwarup—the complete vision of reality. Arjuna saw it when Krishna revealed the universal form. The great seers saw it through meditation and realization. Today, humanity sees only fragments.

The ancients saw the whole. They did not separate physics from consciousness, nor intelligence from nature. Their vision was not mechanical—it was alive.

Modern civilization sees fragments. Physics apart from metaphysics, biology apart from philosophy, science apart from consciousness. This fragmentation is the root of our crises.

Vishwarup Darshan is not something to be discovered—it is something to be seen. The universe was always whole. The problem was never the universe—it was our inability to perceive it fully.

And so, as we close this book, we must ask: will we continue to see through broken perspectives, or will we embrace the complete vision—the Vishwarup—and see the universe as it truly is?

Because once you see it, there is no going back.

Final Line

"Vishwarup Darshan is not just an idea—it is a way of seeing, a way of knowing, and a way of being. The universe was always whole. It is time for us to see it as it truly is."

Appendices

"Assumptions collapse, but truth endures — waiting to be reframed through the lens of consequence."

Appendix A — The Ancient Knowledge Architecture

How the ancients built the earliest operating system of intelligence

Modern readers approach ancient texts with assumptions shaped by today's fragmented systems of knowledge. We expect everything to look like a research paper, a physics textbook, or a philosophical treatise. But ancient civilizations—especially the Vedic civilization—did not think, write, or transmit knowledge in our format.

Their system was not primitive. It was sophisticated, layered, and intentionally engineered to survive thousands of years, long after languages, kingdoms, and scientific traditions faded.

To understand Vishwarup Darshan, the reader must first understand how ancient knowledge was structured.

This appendix breaks down that architecture.

1. The Vedas: Encoding Laws, Not Rituals

The Vedas are often misunderstood as religious scriptures filled with hymns, chants, and rituals. This misunderstanding is one of the greatest intellectual losses in human history.

The Vedas were never meant to prescribe rituals. They were humanity's earliest attempt to document universal laws—the principles governing reality, energy, intelligence, and cosmic order.

What the Vedas actually encode

- **Rigveda**: structure of existence—order, truth, consciousness, and universal harmony.

- **Yajurveda**: transformation, motion, cycles, and mechanics of energy flow.
- **Samaveda**: vibrational laws—frequency, resonance, sound, and the physics of creation.
- **Atharvaveda**: interface between mind, matter, and life—healing, behavior, and psychological forces.

These texts are not prayers—they are observational science written in poetic code.

Where modern physics uses equations, the Vedas used:

- mantras for vibration
- deities for principles
- metaphors for forces
- narratives for laws

The format is poetic. The content is scientific. The intention is universal.

2. The Puranas: Encoding Systems, Not Stories

If the Vedas describe universal laws, the Puranas describe how those laws play out in the real world.

The Puranas were never meant as historical accounts or moral tales. They are system models, teaching:

- evolution
- entropy
- cycles of destruction and renewal
- psychology of human behavior
- cosmic time scales
- the rise and collapse of civilizations
- how intelligence evolves through matter and mind

Why they appear as stories Puranas use narrative format not because the ancients lacked scientific language, but because stories preserve systems better than equations.

Equations evolve and get replaced. Stories survive.

- The Dashavatara is not mythology—it is the world's earliest evolutionary framework.
- The Yugas are not religious eras—they are cosmic climate cycles.
- The Samudra Manthan is not a legend—it is a metaphor for energy exchange and polarity resolution.

Every Purana is essentially a simulation model written in story form.

3. Symbolic vs Literal Layers — The Two-Code System

Ancient Indian knowledge uses a dual-layer architecture:

Literal Layer For common people, children, and general society:

- moral lessons
- cultural stories
- accessible metaphors

Symbolic Layer For seekers, philosophers, teachers, and scientists:

- cosmic principles
- metaphysical insights
- evolutionary models
- laws of equilibrium and energy
- structural information about reality

The same story had different meanings depending on the reader's depth. This dual-layer system ensured:

- Knowledge was accessible to everyone
- Sophisticated insights remained intact for the prepared mind

Modern society reads only the literal layer—and assumes ancients were primitive.

The symbolic layer unlocks Vishwarup Darshan.

4. Oral-to-Written Transmission — Precision Without Paper

For thousands of years, Vedic knowledge was transmitted orally—not due to a lack of writing systems, but because it preserved accuracy better than early manuscripts.

The oral tradition used:

- rhythmic patterns
- tonal structures
- phonetic precision
- group recitation
- guru–śishya custody

This system produced near-perfect retention across centuries.

Today's "oral" implies imperfection. In the Vedic system, oral transmission was engineered for stability.

When texts were eventually written (much later), they became interpretation-prone. But the oral tradition ensured that core knowledge did not change.

5. Why Myths Were Chosen as Knowledge Carriers

Myths are not childish stories. They are the most robust data compression technology humanity ever invented.

They survive:

- war
- migration
- language shifts
- political rewriting
- cultural changes
- technological collapse

A metaphor can hold truth longer than any document.

Examples

- Shiva's dance compresses the concept of entropy and cosmic cycles.
- Lakshmi's coins express energy flow and circulation.
- Vishnu's avatars describe evolutionary jumps.
- Deva–Asura conflicts compress constructive vs destructive energy states.

Myths were chosen because they:

- are memorable
- are scalable
- transcend literacy
- transcend language
- survive destruction
- allow multiple interpretations

They are ancient data structures—self-preserving and self-decoding.

6. Differences Between Vedic, Upanishadic, and Puranic Knowledge Layers

Vedic Layer – Law Objective, universal, foundational. Describes:

- existence
- energy
- cosmic order
- vibration
- cycles
- consciousness

Upanishadic Layer – Interpretation Subjective, experiential, philosophical. Explores:

- the nature of self
- mind and awareness
- witnessing consciousness
- the relationship between observer and reality

Upanishads bridge the cosmic with the personal.
Puranic Layer – Simulation Narrative, systemic, contextual. Shows:

- how cosmic principles unfold
- evolutionary models
- societal dynamics
- karmic and psychological patterns

All three layers together form a complete operating system of knowledge.

7. Ancient Meta-Models vs Modern Scientific Models

Ancient meta-models were:

- holistic
- multi-layered
- symbolic
- experiential
- non-linear
- scalable

Modern scientific models are:

- fragmented
- reductionist
- quantitative
- domain-specific
- equation-dependent
- constantly revised

Yet both aim to describe the same universe.
Key comparison

Aspect	Ancient Meta-Models	Modern Scientific Models
Approach	Whole → Parts	Parts → Whole
Transmission	Symbolic, oral, narrative	Written, mathematical
Durability	Thousands of years	Decades before revision
Scope	Cosmos + mind + ethics	Physical universe only
Audience	Universal	Specialists
Goal	Realization	Explanation

The ancients built models that humanity could carry, not just specialists. Their system was not inferior—it was designed to outlast time.

Closing Insight

To decode Vishwarup Darshan, the reader must see ancient knowledge not as mythology or religion, but as a sophisticated intelligence architecture, designed to preserve cosmic truth through:

- symbols
- stories
- cycles
- metaphors
- oral precision
- layered knowledge

Once this architecture is understood, the entire universe begins to align.

- The Vedas stop being hymns.
- The Puranas stop being stories.
- God stops being a belief.
- Science stops being incomplete.

What emerges is the complete, unified intelligence the ancients always intended us to see.

Appendix B — The Trinity as Universal Forces

The cosmic triad reinterpreted as the three fundamental functions of existence

When ancient seers described the Trinity—Brahma, Vishnu, and Shiva—they were not creating gods. They were describing functions, the three irreducible processes without which no system in the universe can exist. Every atom, every organism, every galaxy, and every moral framework operates through these same forces.

This appendix decodes the Trinity as a universal operating system.

1. Creation = Initiation → Brahma

The spark that brings a system into being.

In the ancient framework, Brahma is not a deity with four heads. He represents the initiation function—the moment potential becomes form.

Wherever something "begins"—

- a star ignites
- a thought arises
- a cell divides
- a system forms

...the energy of Brahma is active.

Characteristics of the Brahma Function

- Emergence
- Innovation

- Initiation
- First impulse
- Design blueprint
- Trigger of complexity
- The shift from silence to expression

It is the universal start-up code. The ancients encoded it symbolically because beginnings cannot be frozen into definitions. They occur at every level of existence.

2. Preservation = Stability → Vishnu

The intelligence that maintains equilibrium.

Vishnu represents the stability function—the energy that sustains, protects, regulates, and maintains order in a dynamic universe.

Without an equilibrium principle:

- atoms wouldn't stay bound
- planets wouldn't hold their orbits
- ecosystems would collapse
- societies would disintegrate
- thoughts wouldn't remain coherent

Vishnu is the controller of balance, not in a religious sense, but as a foundational principle of existence.

Characteristics of the Vishnu Function

- Stability
- Homeostasis
- Conservation
- Continuity
- Field alignment
- Order within motion
- Preservation of structure

Vishnu is not stillness—he is the balance within movement, the intelligence that prevents chaos.

3. Transformation = Reset → Shiva

The cycle of renewal that prevents stagnation.

Shiva is the reset function—the force that dissolves forms so that new forms can emerge. Without destruction, the universe would choke on its own past.

The ancients understood that every system must periodically:

- release the old
- clear accumulated noise
- dissolve obsolete structures
- reset its alignment
- return to neutrality

Shiva symbolizes the entropy and renewal needed for evolution.

Characteristics of the Shiva Function

- Transformation
- Release
- Purification
- Entropy
- Renewal
- Reset
- Returning a system to zero

Shiva is not violence. Shiva is the clean-up process of the cosmos.

4. Cycles of Sat–Rit–Dharma

The ethical dimension of cosmic functioning.

Alongside the Trinity, ancients also described three universal qualities:

- **Sat** – The State of Pure Being: truth, essence, the underlying reality that does not change.

- **Rit** – The State of Perfect Order: natural alignment, cosmic law, harmony, rhythm.
- **Dharma** – The State of Right Action: action aligned with Rit and Sat, sustaining balance.

Together they form the cosmic moral architecture:

- Sat → what reality is
- Rit → how reality functions
- Dharma → how living beings should act

This triad reflects the same intelligence behind the Trinity.

- Brahma initiates Rit.
- Vishnu preserves Rit.
- Shiva restores Rit.
- All three maintain the integrity of Sat.

5. Mapping the Trinity onto Physics

The ancient principles cleanly map onto core scientific functions:

- **Brahma → Forces of Emergence** Big Bang initiation, symmetry breaking, particle formation, spontaneous structure generation.
- **Vishnu → Forces of Stability** Electromagnetic binding, gravitational equilibrium, strong nuclear force, conservation laws, field uniformity.
- **Shiva → Forces of Dissolution** Entropy, decay, phase transitions, dissociation, black hole recycling.

In modern physics, these are separate domains. In ancient cosmology, they were understood as one continuous cycle.

6. Mapping the Trinity onto Biology

Life itself operates through the same triad:

- **Brahma → Evolutionary Emergence** Genetic mutation, novel traits, origin of species, developmental biology, ecosystem innovation.
- **Vishnu → Adaptation & Homeostasis** Temperature regulation, hormonal balance, immune stability, energy optimization, ecological balance.
- **Shiva → Transformation & Renewal** Cell apoptosis, recycling of resources, neural pruning, ecological reset events, extinctions enabling new species.

Biology is the dance of Brahma–Vishnu–Shiva written in DNA.

7. Mapping the Trinity onto Cosmology

The cosmos itself follows this rhythm:

- **Brahma → Expansion & Formation** Inflation, star birth, planetary formation, chemical complexity.
- **Vishnu → Sustained Order** Stable planetary systems, cosmic equilibrium, galactic rotation balance, background field uniformity.
- **Shiva → Collapse & Renewal** Supernovae, black hole recycling, galactic collisions, end-stage star processes, cosmic reset cycles.

Even the universe's ultimate fate—heat death or cyclic renewal—reflects Shiva's principle.

8. The Trinity as a Unified Intelligence Framework

What emerges from all mappings is clear:

- Brahma is the creative impulse.
- Vishnu is the regulatory intelligence.
- Shiva is the corrective intelligence.

Together they form the most complete system model humanity has ever produced.

They are not gods "out there." They are forces "within everything."

- The Universe arises through Brahma.
- The Universe survives through Vishnu.
- The Universe evolves through Shiva.

This is why ancient texts repeatedly say: *"The three are one."*

They are not separate beings but three functions of one intelligence operating across every scale—from quantum fields to galaxies to the human mind.

Closing Insight

Interpreting the Trinity through this non-religious, scientific lens dissolves artificial boundaries between mythology and physics. The ancients were not describing supernatural beings. They were describing the architecture of existence using the language available to them—symbol, story, and metaphor.

Once understood, the Trinity becomes the key to decoding:

- energy flow
- cosmic balance
- human behavior
- moral frameworks
- evolution
- consciousness
- the entire Vishwarup Darshan itself

The ancients were not worshipping gods. They were documenting universal forces.

And they did it with such elegance that the framework remains relevant across time, culture, and scientific progress.

Appendix C — Dashavatara and Evolution

A Comparative Framework

The world's earliest evolutionary model hidden in plain sight

Long before Darwin formalized the theory of evolution, ancient Indian seers encoded the entire progression of life on Earth in a sequence of ten "avatars" of Vishnu. These were never meant to be supernatural incarnations. They were biological milestones, encrypted in narrative form for preservation across centuries.

This appendix offers a precise, academic-style alignment between the Dashavatara sequence and modern evolutionary science—while preserving the symbolic elegance of the original framework.

The result is a stunning realization: *the ancients did not merely observe evolution—they understood its direction, purpose, and rhythm.*

1. Avatar → Biological Stage

Each avatar corresponds to a major evolutionary leap on Earth.

Avatar	Biological Stage	Scientific Parallel
1. Matsya (Fish)	Emergence of aquatic life	First vertebrates in oceans
2. Kurma (Tortoise)	Amphibious transition	Movement from water to land
3. Varaha (Boar)	Full terrestrial mammals	Dominance of land-based species
4. Narasimha (Half-man, Half-lion)	Mammal–primate bridge	Early hominids and primate evolution
5. Vamana (Dwarf)	Early Homo species	Small-statured hominins like Homo erectus
6. Parashurama	Tool-using early humans	Stone and metal tool revolution
7. Rama	Moral and social structuring	Rise of organized society & rule-based order
8. Krishna	Cognitive flowering	Complex intelligence, philosophy, diplomacy
9. Buddha	Full spiritual evolution	Compassion, nonviolence, psychological mastery
10. Kalki	Future phase	Evolution beyond current human limitations

This is not myth. It is the exact sequence evolution followed on Earth.

2. Avatar → Environmental Shift

Every avatar also responds to a major environmental or ecological change.

Avatar	Environmental Shift
Matsya	Life confined to oceans; marine dominance
Kurma	Shallow-water habitats; amphibious adaptation
Varaha	Stabilization of land masses; terrestrial ecosystems
Narasimha	Competitive predator-prey dynamics; rise of mammals
Vamana	Climate stabilization; early hominin spread
Parashurama	Harsh landscapes; survival via tools & adaptation
Rama	Forest-to-civilization transition; agrarian expansion
Krishna	Urban complexity; socio-political evolution
Buddha	Mental overstimulation; need for psychological balance
Kalki	Environmental degradation; technological acceleration

Evolution is not random—it responds to ecosystem pressures, exactly as the Dashavatara sequence shows.

3. Avatar → Human Cognitive Leap

The avatars capture not just biological evolution, but the evolution of mind, morality, and consciousness.

Avatar	Cognitive Leap
Matsya	Primitive reflexive cognition
Kurma	Early sensory development; spatial adaptation
Varaha	Instinct-driven survival intelligence
Narasimha	Emotional complexity; protective instinct
Vamana	Self-awareness; growth of learning & memory
Parashurama	Intentional action; mastery of tools
Rama	Ethical cognition; rule-based thinking
Krishna	Strategic intelligence; layered reasoning
Buddha	Meta-cognition; introspection; mind mastery
Kalki	Trans-human cognition; integration with higher intelligence

The ancients did not just describe bodies evolving—they described consciousness evolving.

4. Avatar → Societal or Systemic Correction

Each avatar emerges at a point where society requires a reset to restore balance and prevent collapse.

Avatar	Correction Function
Matsya	Preserving life from annihilation (survival reset)
Kurma	Supporting emergence of new life forms (stability reset)
Varaha	Rescuing Earth's habitability (ecological reset)
Narasimha	Restoring justice (moral reset)
Vamana	Containing unchecked growth (power reset)
Parashurama	Balancing aggression & discipline (behavioral reset)
Rama	Establishing societal order (civilizational reset)
Krishna	Correcting strategic and political imbalance (geopolitical reset)
Buddha	Resetting psychological burden (mental reset)
Kalki	Resetting technological excess and ethical collapse (future reset)

This reveals why Vishnu is the preserver: **Each avatar restores equilibrium in a rising complexity cycle.**

5. Visual Timeline Linking Avatars to Darwinian Phases

If we reimagine the Dashavatara on a modern evolutionary timeline:

Oceans → Amphibians → Land Mammals → Early Primates → Early Humans → Tribal Societies → Kingdoms → Civilizations → Inner Mind Evolution → Future Human Phase

Or in scientific terms:

Cambrian Fossils → Devonian Transition → Mammalian Radiation → Primate Evolution → Homo Lineage → Neolithic Revolution → Bronze Age Order → Iron Age Complexity → Axial Age of Philosophy → Technological Singularity Era

The match is not approximate. It is precise and sequential.

This is one of the strongest indicators that ancient seers had access to long-cycle observational knowledge across generations—something modern science is only now reconstructing.

6. Why Evolution Appears Guided Rather Than Random

Ancient texts repeatedly state:

- Life evolves in response to imbalance
- Intelligence guides directionality
- Nature selects what aligns with order (*Rit*)
- *Dharma* ensures sustainability of evolution

Modern evolutionary theory sees random mutations and natural selection. Ancient seers saw patterns.

What appears guided is not magic—it is:

1. **Consequence Alignment** – species that align with environmental and cosmic order survive.
2. **Equilibrium Restoration** – every imbalance triggers a corrective evolutionary jump.
3. **Structured Complexity** – evolution builds upward in predictable layers.
4. **Consciousness as Driver** – higher mind accelerates evolutionary

directionality.

5. **Collective Field Intelligence** – ecosystems communicate and co-evolve.

Dashavatara fits a guided evolution model, not a random one.

Modern science is slowly converging on this through fields like:

- evolutionary developmental biology
- complexity theory
- systems ecology
- emergent intelligence studies
- field-based interaction models

The ancients encoded it thousands of years earlier.

Closing Insight

The Dashavatara is not myth, religion, or folklore. It is the world's oldest evolutionary timeline, preserved in symbolic form.

It captures:

- biological evolution
- ecological transitions
- cognitive growth
- societal emergence
- moral evolution
- psychological maturity
- future evolutionary pathways

It aligns perfectly with:

- Darwinian evolution
- geological time scales
- anthropological research
- cosmological cycles
- systems theory

- the rise and fall of civilizations

The Dashavatara reveals a truth modern science is still uncovering: *Evolution is not random mutation—it is intelligent response. It is consequence-driven. It moves toward increasing complexity and consciousness.*

And Vishnu's avatars are simply humanity's first attempt to map the long arc of life in a form that could survive millennia.

Appendix D — Cosmic Time Scales

Yugas, Kalpas, and Modern Cosmology

How ancient cosmology mapped the universe in cycles—and how modern science is rediscovering the same truth

Humanity often assumes that ancient civilizations lacked scientific understanding of time and cosmology. Yet the Vedic model presents an extraordinarily advanced framework—cyclic, multi-layered, mathematically precise, and philosophically coherent.

This appendix offers a clear, technical yet digestible comparison between ancient and modern cosmology, revealing how the ancients conceptualized cosmic time in a far more sophisticated manner than commonly believed.

1. Yuga Durations — The Smallest Cycles of Cosmic Time

In Vedic cosmology, a Yuga is not merely an "age" but a phase of cosmic conditions, representing the rise or decline of alignment within the universe and human consciousness.

The four Yugas are:

Yuga	Duration (years)	Characteristic
Satya Yuga	1,728,000	Purity, alignment, stability
Treta Yuga	1,296,000	Decline of balance; emergence of complexity
Dvapara Yuga	864,000	Increased duality; decrease in alignment
Kali Yuga	432,000	Maximum disorder; densest phase of existence

Mahayuga = 4,320,000 years

This duration resonates with long-term geological, climatic, and astronomical cycles.

Modern parallels include:

- Milankovitch cycles (26k, 41k, 100k years)
- Galactic oscillation cycles (~30–35 million years)
- Mass extinction periodicity (~26–30 million years)
- Solar activity cycles (billions of years across lifespan)

The ancients observed Earth's rhythms across cosmic timescales, not dynastic centuries.

2. Kalpa Cycles — The Day and Night of the Cosmos

A Kalpa represents a "day of Brahma," symbolizing one full cycle of cosmic creation and dissolution.

- **One Day of Brahma (Kalpa) = 4.32 billion years**
- **One Night of Brahma = 4.32 billion years**
- **Full cycle (day + night) = 8.64 billion years**

Modern astrophysics estimates:

- Age of Earth: 4.54 billion years
- Age of life: ~4 billion years
- Solar system formation: 4.5–4.6 billion years

The Vedic Kalpa aligns uncannily with the lifespan of stars like the Sun.

3. A Full Lifetime of Brahma and Modern Cosmology

Ancient texts describe:

- A Year of Brahma = 360 days of Brahma
- Lifetime of Brahma = 100 Brahma years
- **Total = 311.04 trillion years**

This is symbolic of infinite cycles, not literal chronology.
Modern parallels:

- Eternal inflation models
- Cyclic universe models
- Bounce cosmology
- Quantum resurgence frameworks
- Black hole cosmogenesis
- Penrose's Conformal Cyclic Cosmology (CCC)

In every model, the universe resets, recycles, or rebirths.

4. Evidence of Cyclical Cosmology in Modern Science

Modern astrophysics increasingly leans toward cyclic theories:

1. Expansion → Contraction → Bounce models
2. Black hole genesis concept
3. Entropy reset hypothesis
4. Cosmic Microwave Background anomalies
5. Galactic recycling

The ancients summarized simply: *"Creation and dissolution are eternal cycles."*

5. Parallels with Big Bang → Expansion → Heat Death → Renewal

Modern cosmology:

- Big Bang → emergence
- Expansion → matter spreads
- Structure formation → galaxies, stars, planets
- Entropy increase → systems lose alignment
- Heat death/collapse → uniformity
- Possible reset → new universe emerges

Ancient cosmology:

- *Srishti* (Creation) → Brahma awakens

- *Sthiti* (Sustenance) → Vishnu maintains equilibrium
- *Samhara* (Dissolution) → Shiva dissolves forms
- *Tirobhav* (Concealment) → latent state
- *Anugraha* (Renewal) → new cycle begins

Mapping:

Ancient Cycle	Modern Equivalent
Brahma awakens	Big Bang event
Vishnu sustains	Expansion + equilibrium era
Shiva dissolves	Entropy → heat death or collapse
Latent state	Vacuum equilibrium / singularity
New creation	Rebirth of new universe

The parallels are unmistakable.

6. Why Ancients Used Cycles Instead of Linear Time

The ancient Indian mind did not think linearly. Linear time is tied to kingdoms and wars. The ancients observed:

- planetary cycles
- ecological cycles
- cosmic rhythms
- precession cycles
- magnetic reversals
- birth–death–rebirth patterns
- solar activity cycles
- oceanic cycles
- generational cycles

Conclusions:

- Time is rhythmic
- Existence is cyclic
- Creation is recurring

- Dissolution is transitional
- Repeatability is law

Linear time measures events. Cyclical time measures reality.

Cyclic time offers:

- recursion
- recurrence
- renewal
- fractal scaling
- self-similarity
- predictability of large patterns

The Vedic model is mathematically elegant, scientifically relevant, and philosophically coherent.

Closing Insight

The ancients did not see the universe as a singular event. They saw it as eternal pulsation—a rhythm of emergence and dissolution, governed by Brahma, Vishnu, and Shiva.

Their time scales:

- match astrophysical durations
- encode cyclic cosmology
- anticipate bounce theories
- mirror thermodynamic cycles
- reflect fractal structures in nature
- explain rise and fall of civilizations
- align spiritual evolution with cosmic evolution

Where modern astrophysics uses equations, the ancients used metaphor, symbolism, and scale. Both describe the same truth from different starting points.

The universe is not a straight line. It is a living cycle. And we are part of its rhythm.

Appendix E — Symbolism Decoded

A Guide to Key Mythological Metaphors

The hidden architecture of intelligence behind India's most iconic symbols

Ancient Indian civilization never used symbols as decorations or religious embellishments. Every symbol was a compressed data structure—a way to encode deep scientific, psychological, ethical, and cosmological insights in a form that could survive millennia.

This appendix decodes these symbols for the modern reader, restoring them to their original depth.

1. Shesha Nāga — The Field of Infinite Potential

The coiled serpent on which Vishnu rests.

Symbolic Meaning Shesha is not a literal serpent—it represents the infinite structured vacuum field, the underlying fabric of the universe.

Key Interpretations

- "Shesha" means remainder—the substratum that remains after every cosmic cycle.
- The coiling represents infinite potential compressed into tight equilibrium.
- Vishnu lying on Shesha signifies stability resting on a foundational energy field.
- The serpent form symbolizes continuity, cycles, and recurrence—life unfolding through rhythmic patterns.

Scientific Parallel

- Zero-point field

- Quantum vacuum structure
- Background field stability
- Cosmic equilibrium

Shesha = universe's substrate; Vishnu = regulator of its order.

2. Garuda — The Principle of Freedom and Velocity

The eagle-like being who carries Vishnu.

Symbolic Meaning Garuda represents the dynamic intelligence that moves through the field without resistance—speed, clarity, and awareness.

Key Interpretations

- Garuda is not a bird but the force of rapid alignment.
- He represents the mind in its highest state—free, unbound, sharp.
- His wings symbolize dual balance: action and awareness, motion and direction.

Scientific Parallel

- Electromagnetic propagation
- Field resonance
- Information transmission
- Momentum

Garuda is the carrier of equilibrium, reflecting how information flows through the cosmic field.

3. Sudarshan Chakra — The Wheel of Consequence and Alignment

The spinning disc in Vishnu's hand.

Symbolic Meaning Sudarshan Chakra is not a weapon; it is the law of consequence—the perfect, self-correcting intelligence of the universe.

Key Interpretations

- "Su-darshan" means perfect vision or clear perspective.

- The spinning motion represents constant, dynamic correction.
- The Chakra returns to Vishnu, signifying consequence returns to the source.
- It slices through ignorance, cutting misalignment instantly.

Scientific Parallel

- Feedback loops
- Corrective forces
- Natural law
- Entropy correction

Sudarshan Chakra is the algorithm of universal justice.

4. Kamadhenu — The Ecosystem of Sustenance

The divine cow that grants all nourishment.

Symbolic Meaning Kamadhenu is not a literal cow; she symbolizes nature's abundance, representing ecosystems that provide nourishment when maintained with balance.

Key Interpretations

- The cow symbolizes sustainable resources.
- "Kamadhenu" means fulfiller of essential desires—food, stability, continuity.
- She represents the circular economy of nature: what you give returns multiplied.

Scientific Parallel

- Renewable systems
- Ecological cycles
- Biodiversity
- Soil–water–life interdependence

Kamadhenu reminds us that Earth gives everything when treated with intelligence.

5. Mount Meru — The Axis of Reality

The cosmic mountain at the center of the universe.

Symbolic Meaning Mount Meru is the central axis of existence—the balancing point around which cosmic order is established.

Key Interpretations

- Represents axis mundi—the "pivot of worlds."
- Symbolizes center of gravity, stability, and alignment.
- Depicts levels of consciousness from base to peak.
- Serves as a conceptual model for inner and outer universes.

Scientific Parallel

- Galactic axis
- Rotational symmetry in physics
- Energy gradients
- Human spinal alignment & consciousness

Meru represents the stable center around which existence spirals.

6. Amrit–Vish — The Duality of Creation

The nectar of immortality and the poison of dissolution.

Symbolic Meaning Amrit and Vish are not literal substances but represent positive and negative consequences arising from the same process.

Key Interpretations

- Amrit (immortality) = order, balance, stability
- Vish (poison) = imbalance, excess, misalignment
- Both emerge from the same churning—the same action can yield opposite outcomes.
- Shiva consumes Vish, absorbing toxicity to reset the system.

Scientific Parallel

- Byproducts of chemical reactions
- Beneficial vs harmful mutations
- Positive vs negative feedback loops
- Order vs entropy

This duality embodies the two-sided nature of every creation process.

7. Devas–Asuras — Forces of Alignment and Misalignment

Beings constantly in conflict.

Symbolic Meaning Devas and Asuras are not supernatural beings. They represent:

- **Devas**: forces that align with order, harmony, intelligence
- **Asuras**: forces that move against alignment, create imbalance, amplify ego

Key Interpretations

- Both emerge from the same origin.
- Conflict is internal and external—within the mind and society.
- Evolution happens through this tension.

Scientific Parallel

- Constructive vs destructive forces
- Evolutionary competition
- Neural pathways: higher brain vs primitive impulses
- Ecosystem balance: predator vs prey

Deva–Asura conflict is the inner battle of awareness vs impulse.

8. Samudra Manthan — The Churning of Reality

The cosmic event of churning the ocean of milk.

Symbolic Meaning Samudra Manthan is a metaphor for the churning of existence—the friction required to extract knowledge, order, and growth from the ocean of potential.

Key Interpretations

- The ocean = structured vacuum, infinite potential
- The mountain = axis of stability
- The serpent = cyclical energy
- The churning = action, experience, evolution
- The emerging items = consequences, both beneficial and harmful
- Amrit emerges last—wisdom appears only after long struggle

Scientific Parallel

- Energy extraction from fields
- Phase transitions
- Evolution through friction
- Innovation through tension
- Systemic emergence from disturbances

Samudra Manthan is the process of universal evolution summarized in one metaphor.

9. Lakshmi's Lotus & Coins — Wealth as Flow and Purity

Symbolic Meaning Lakshmi is not wealth—she is flow, the movement that keeps everything alive.

Her symbols encode two essential principles:

1. The Lotus — Purity in Complexity

- Lotus grows in mud yet remains untouched.
- Symbolizes rising above disorder, balance in complexity, purity in motion, and the mind unpolluted in chaos.

2. Gold Coins — Circulation of Energy

- Lakshmi is shown distributing coins, not hoarding them.
- Signifies wealth must flow, energy must circulate, abundance arises from movement, not stagnation.

Scientific Parallel

- Flow economics
- Energy distribution
- Homeostasis
- Market dynamics
- Ecosystem balance

Lakshmi's symbols restore the forgotten truth: **wealth is not possession—it is flow.**

Closing Insight

These symbols were not created to decorate temples or entertain audiences. They were engineered to:

- encode cosmic laws
- reveal behavioral patterns
- describe energy flow
- represent psychological states
- preserve scientific insights
- transmit ethical frameworks
- map inner and outer universes

When decoded, they reveal a civilization that understood reality in layers, metaphors, and field-based intelligence.

Each symbol is a portable model of the universe—one that can be understood by a child, a philosopher, or a scientist depending on the lens they choose.

Mythology is not fiction. It is intelligence in symbolic form.

Appendix F — Intelligence as the First Principle

(Scientific Notes)

Why intelligence is not a product of the universe, but the prerequisite for it

Modern science begins with matter and energy and tries to work upward toward intelligence. Ancient knowledge begins with intelligence and works downward to matter and energy. Both meet at the same point, but from opposite directions.

This appendix provides a rigorous yet accessible exploration of why intelligence cannot be emergent—it must be the first principle from which all other principles arise.

1. Mathematical Laws Require an Underlying Intelligence

The universe behaves mathematically. This is a remarkable fact that often goes unnoticed.

Why should the universe follow laws at all?

- Equations don't arise from randomness.
- Patterns don't self-enforce.
- Geometry does not assemble itself.

The coherence of physical laws implies:

- relational structure
- internal consistency
- definable limits
- predictable transitions

- symmetry and symmetry-breaking
- conservation rules
- nested hierarchies

These features are signatures of an underlying intelligence-driven architecture.

Physics reveals intelligence through:

- Maxwell's equations: perfect symmetry of electric & magnetic fields
- Einstein's field equations: geometry responds to mass-energy
- Dirac's equation: deep symmetry between matter and antimatter
- Quantum mechanics: discrete, rule-bound probability spaces
- Thermodynamics: directional logic embedded into matter

When mathematics describes the universe so accurately, it implies that the universe is mathematically constructed, not accidentally assembled.

Mathematics is not a language we discovered—it is the operating system encoded into reality.

2. Fine-Tuning of Constants — Evidence of Intentional Calibration

The universe is alarmingly precise. Fundamental constants seem "designed" to allow complexity, consciousness, and life.

Examples:

- Gravitational constant (G): too weak → universe never forms; too strong → collapses instantly.
- Cosmological constant (Λ): tuned to 1 in 10^{120} precision.
- Electron-proton mass ratio: perfect for chemical bonding.
- Strong nuclear force: slightly weaker → no atoms; slightly stronger → no stars.
- Speed of light: sets the structure of causality.
- Planck constant: tunes quantum stability.

These constants behave like calibrated values, not lottery variables.

Three possibilities exist:

1. The universe tuned itself randomly — statistically impossible.
2. There are infinite universes — unproven and unfalsifiable.
3. The universe is encoded with intelligence — the simplest explanation.

Fine-tuning is mathematical intentionality. Ancient texts called this *Rit*—the cosmic order.

3. Quantum "Observer" Problems — Consciousness as a Requirement

Quantum mechanics forces science to acknowledge what philosophy always knew: the observer changes the observed.

The measurement problem reveals:

- A particle exists as probability until observed.
- Observation collapses the wavefunction.
- Reality takes definite form only in the presence of awareness.

Therefore:

- Matter alone cannot define reality.
- Consciousness plays a structural role.
- Intelligence interacts with quantum fields.

This is identical to the ancient insight: *"The universe arises in awareness; it is not separate from the seer."*

Quantum behavior strongly supports intelligence as a precondition, not a byproduct.

4. Self-Organizing Systems — Complexity Without a Designer?

Across nature, order appears spontaneously:

- galaxies form spiral patterns
- snowflakes create fractal geometry
- ecosystems balance themselves
- embryos self-assemble
- proteins fold into perfect shapes
- neurons self-organize into networks
- ant colonies exhibit collective intelligence

None of these require central control, yet all exhibit intentionality-like behavior.

Self-organization suggests:

- built-in rules
- embedded intelligence
- feedback-driven adaptation
- consequence sensitivity
- pattern stability

These are qualities of intelligent systems, not random matter.

Ancients encapsulated this as *Shakti*—inherent dynamic intelligence.

5. Why Intelligence Cannot Be Emergent

The modern assumption that intelligence "emerges" from matter has several logical flaws.

Flaw 1 — Emergence Cannot Create New Principles Emergence reorganizes existing parts; it cannot create fundamentally new laws. If intelligence emerges, it must already be encoded.

Flaw 2 — Consciousness Cannot Arise from Non-Conscious Matter No model explains how subjective experience arises from physical particles.

Flaw 3 — Matter Lacks Directionality Random motion cannot produce:

- purpose
- awareness
- values

- ethics
- creativity
- imagination

These require intentional architecture.

Flaw 4 — Evolution Requires Intelligence to Progress Adaptation presupposes:

- learning
- memory
- pattern recognition
- response to consequence

All of which are cognitive processes, not purely biological.

Conclusion: Intelligence cannot be the last step. It is the first input. Matter behaves intelligently because intelligence precedes matter.

6. Comparative View: Vedic Brahman vs Modern Unified Field

Ancient seers described Brahman as:

- infinite
- self-aware
- non-material
- timeless
- formless
- source of all laws
- ground of consciousness
- origin of the universe

Modern physics describes the Unified Field as:

- fundamental
- all-pervading
- non-material

- mathematically structured
- vibration-based
- symmetry-driven
- origin of particles and forces

Parallels:

Vedic Brahman	Unified Field (Physics)
Conscious substrate	Mathematical substrate
Source of all forms	Source of all particles
Non-dual	Single field with excitations
Timeless	Beyond classical time
Infinite	Omnipresent vacuum field
Intelligence	Order and laws embedded
Cosmic vibration (*Nada*)	Quantized vibrations
Manifestation → *Maya*	Excitations → Particles

Brahman is not a deity—it is the intelligent field of existence, described long before modern physics.

The ancient view and the modern view converge on one unavoidable truth: *The foundation of reality is not matter—it is intelligence.*

Closing Insight

Across mathematics, physics, biology, and cosmology, a pattern emerges:

- Laws behave intelligently
- Constants are calibrated
- Quantum fields respond to awareness
- Systems self-organize
- Information precedes energy
- Consequences guide evolution

These point to one conclusion that ancient wisdom declared clearly:

Intelligence is the first principle. Matter is its expression. Energy is its movement. The universe is its manifestation.

This appendix completes the philosophical backbone of *Vishwarup Darshan* by demonstrating that ancient cosmology was not mystical speculation—but an advanced understanding of intelligence as the core fabric of reality.

Appendix G — Modern Science Catching Up

A Cross-Disciplinary Comparison

How ancient wisdom anticipated the discoveries of modern physics, cosmology, psychology, and biology

Ancient Indian seers did not describe the universe in equations. They described it in principles, symmetries, metaphors, and living symbols. Modern science describes these same truths in mathematics, experiments, and models.

This appendix presents a clear side-by-side comparison, demonstrating that the two are not in conflict—they are two languages describing the same reality.

1. Time, Space & Relativity

Ancient Insight	Modern Discovery	Explanation
Time flows differently in different realms — Vedas, Puranas, Bhagavatam	Time dilation (Einstein's Relativity)	Higher gravity or velocity slows time; ancient texts describe realms where "one day equals thousands of years on Earth."
Lokas with different time scales	Gravitational time differences	Time varies between planets and fields; exactly described in ancient cosmology.
Brahma's day/night cycles	Mega-timescales of cosmic evolution	4.32 billion years aligns with Earth's geological timescales.

Convergence: Ancient cosmology understood time as relative, not fixed—millennia before physics.

2. Energy, Wealth & Flow (Lakshmi)

Ancient Insight	Modern Discovery	Explanation
Lakshmi = flow, circulation, movement	Energy Flow / Thermodynamics	Energy must circulate; stagnation = decay. Lakshmi's coins symbolize dynamic energy transfer.
Lotus represents purity in complexity	Self-regulation & homeostasis	Systems maintain balance despite chaotic surroundings.
Wealth is sustained by flow	Flow Economics & Systems Theory	Economies collapse when flow stops; identical to Lakshmi's symbolism.

Convergence: Lakshmi is not "goddess of money"—she is the metaphor for energy dynamics.

3. Dissolution, Entropy & Reset (Shiva)

Ancient Insight	Modern Discovery	Explanation
Shiva dissolves forms	Entropy & decay	All structures break down naturally over time.
Shiva as cosmic dancer	Oscillation & vibration	Matter exists through constant vibration; Shiva's dance = quantum motion.
Pralaya = cosmic dissolution	Heat death / Big Crunch	Universe ends in dissolution before new cycles begin.

Convergence: Shiva represents the thermodynamic and cosmological recycling engine.

4. Stability, Order & Equilibrium (Vishnu)

Ancient Insight	Modern Discovery	Explanation
Vishnu maintains cosmic balance	Equilibrium laws in physics	Systems seek stable states under internal and external forces.
Vishnu lies on Shesha (field)	Structured vacuum & zero-point field	Stability arises from quantum fields beneath matter.
Ten avatars restore balance	Evolutionary corrections	Evolution adapts to restore ecological and systemic balance.

Convergence: Vishnu symbolizes stability in a dynamic universe.

5. Shakti — Conservation, Power & Fundamental Forces

Ancient Insight	Modern Discovery	Explanation
Shakti = underlying force	Conservation of energy	Energy can neither be created nor destroyed—only transformed.
Shakti manifests through forms	Fields produce particles	Modern physics sees matter as excitations of fields —mirroring Shakti's manifestations.
Devi as dynamic potential	Potential energy fields	Existence rests on energy gradients, identical to Devi's metaphysics.

Convergence: Shakti = the foundational energy of the universe.

6. Yugas — Cyclic Universes

Ancient Insight	Modern Discovery	Explanation
Yugas repeat in cycles	Cyclic Universe Models	Cosmology increasingly favors expansion–contraction cycles.
Ages of rise and decline	Entropy & cosmic evolution	Universe moves from order to disorder to reset and renewal.
Mahayuga = 4.32 million years	Geological & astronomical cycles	Reflects long climate, extinction, and orbital cycles.

Convergence: Ancient time was cyclic, matching modern astrophysics.

7. Dashavatara — Biological Evolution

Ancient Insight	Modern Discovery	Explanation
Fish → Amphibian → Mammal → Primate → Human	Darwinian Evolution	The avatar sequence mirrors evolution perfectly.
Each avatar appears to correct imbalance	Adaptive evolution	Species evolve in response to environmental pressure.
Vamana, Parashurama, Rama, Krishna, Buddha represent mind-evolution	Cognitive evolution	Human evolution is as much mental as physical.

Convergence: Dashavatara = the world's earliest evolutionary model.

8. Creation, Sustenance & Dissolution — Trinity Framework

Ancient Insight	Modern Discovery	Explanation
Brahma creates	Big Bang / emergence	Universe arises from a singular state.
Vishnu sustains	Cosmic equilibrium	Universe maintains structure for billions of years.
Shiva dissolves	Entropy & cosmic collapse	Universe ends in entropy or collapse.

Convergence: The Trinity is a unified cosmology.

9. Maya — Perception & Cognitive Filters

Ancient Insight	Modern Discovery	Explanation
Maya = illusion of independent reality	Neuroscience: brain as model-builder	Reality is a sensory construction, not direct perception.
Mind shapes experience	Cognitive biases & predictive coding	The brain constructs reality based on expectations.
Awareness dissolves Maya	Meta-cognition	Higher awareness overrides cognitive illusions.

Convergence: Maya is the neural, perceptual, and psychological filter through which humans experience existence.

10. Samudra Manthan — Emergence Through Friction

Ancient Insight	Modern Discovery	Explanation
Churning creates both nectar & poison	Systems theory: emergent trade-offs	Complex processes yield both progress and risk.
Cooperation of opposing forces	Interplay of constructive & destructive dynamics	Evolution progresses through tension, not harmony.
Amrit emerges last	Delayed reward / emergent solutions	Highest-order solutions appear after maximum complexity.

Convergence: Samudra Manthan describes the mechanics of emergence.

11. Duality: Devas & Asuras

Ancient Insight	Modern Discovery	Explanation
Deva = alignment; Asura = misalignment	Constructive vs destructive forces	Systems evolve via both stabilizing and destabilizing inputs.
Conflict drives evolution	Evolutionary pressure	Competition and conflict accelerate development.
Both originate from same source	Duality in physics (matter–antimatter, charge ±)	Opposites emerge from single symmetry.

Convergence: Deva–Asura conflict is the dual nature of the universe.

12. Structured Vacuum — Vishnu on Shesha

Ancient Insight	Modern Discovery	Explanation
Shesha = infinite substratum	Quantum vacuum field	Space is not empty—it is structured energy.
Vishnu rests on Shesha	Equilibrium arises from vacuum structure	Stability emerges from field uniformity.
Serpent coils = potential energy loops	Vacuum fluctuations & field coherence	Energy is stored in field patterns.

Convergence: Ancient cosmology anticipated field-based physics.

Closing Insight

Across disciplines—physics, cosmology, neuroscience, systems theory, biology, psychology, and information science—modern discoveries consistently echo ancient insights.

The convergence is not coincidental. Both traditions attempt to describe:

- structure
- order
- flow
- consequence

- evolution
- perception
- intelligence

The ancients used symbols, stories, and cosmological models. Modern scientists use mathematics, equations, and empirical data.

The truth they describe is the same. The universe is one system, one field, one intelligence. The languages differ. The reality does not.

Appendix H — A Short Reader's Glossary

Clear, modern definitions of key terms to help international readers follow the terminology without confusion

Sat: The state of pure being. Truth, essence, and the underlying reality that does not change.

Rit: Cosmic order. The principle of harmony, rhythm, and alignment that governs the universe.

Dharma: Right action. The ethical principle of living in alignment with Sat (truth) and Rit (order).

Shakti: Dynamic energy. The inherent power of creation, transformation, and movement within the cosmos.

Maya: Illusion. The perception of separateness that conceals the unity of existence.

Atman: The inner self. The eternal consciousness within each being, beyond body and mind.

Brahman: The ultimate reality. Infinite, formless intelligence—the source and ground of all existence.

Pralaya: Cosmic dissolution. The phase of reset when the universe dissolves before renewal.

Yuga: An age or cycle of time. Four Yugas (Satya, Treta, Dvapara, Kali) describe phases of cosmic and human alignment.

Kalpa: A "day of Brahma." A vast cosmic cycle of creation and dissolution, spanning billions of years.

Avatar: A manifestation of Vishnu. Symbolic representation of evolutionary or corrective forces in the universe.

Purana: Ancient narrative texts. Encoded system models that describe cosmic principles, evolution, and human behavior through stories.

Veda: The foundational texts of ancient India. Poetic codes encoding universal laws of existence, energy, vibration, and consciousness.

Appendix I — The Architecture of Reality

A Unified Model (Non-Equation Format)

How reality is structured, functions, evolves, and appears dynamic—without requiring mathematics

Modern science dissects the universe into particles, forces, and equations. Ancient wisdom sees the universe as patterns, flows, and intelligence. This appendix bridges both perspectives through a single, coherent model—presented without formulas, without metaphysics, and without mythology. Only reality as it is.

1. The Structure of Existence — Three Layers of Reality

Reality is not built from matter outward. It is built from fields inward.

Every phenomenon emerges from three nested layers:

1. The Foundational Field (Substrate Layer)

- omnipresent
- continuous
- structured, not empty
- source of stability
- holds potential in suspended form

This is the "ground"—the background against which everything happens.

2. The Energy Layer (Activation Layer) When the foundational field becomes active, it manifests:

- tension
- vibration

- gradients
- ripples
- disturbances

This layer gives rise to what we call energy—not as substance, but as action within the field.

3. The Matter Layer (Condensed Layer) When energy patterns stabilize:

- they condense
- form localized clusters
- appear as particles
- assemble into atoms, molecules, stars, planets, bodies

Matter is frozen patterns of activated field.

Architecture: Field → Energy → Matter (Foundation → Action → Form)

2. Field-Based Functioning — The Universe as Interconnected Patterns

Nothing in the universe functions independently.

Every event is:

- a disturbance in a field
- interacting with other fields
- creating consequences across space
- resolving toward equilibrium

Key principles of field-based functioning:

- Every action propagates.
- Every propagation interacts.
- Every interaction generates consequence.
- Every consequence reshapes the field.
- The field, in turn, reshapes matter and events.

This is why systems—from galaxies to human bodies—behave as coherent wholes, not isolated parts.

The universe does not run on "forces" pushing objects. It runs on field-tension seeking balance. Motion is simply the field resolving itself.

3. Energy → Intelligence → Order

Most models assume: *Energy creates order.* This appendix emphasizes the deeper architecture: *Intelligence precedes both energy and matter.*

Because:

- Laws require logic.
- Patterns require consistency.
- Stability requires calibration.
- Evolution requires feedback.
- Complexity requires direction.

Nothing in reality behaves accidentally.

The correct sequence is: Intelligence → Energy → Order → Form

- Intelligence provides the rules.
- Energy enacts the rules.
- Order stabilizes the rules.
- Form expresses the rules.

This is why the universe behaves with:

- mathematical precision
- conservation principles
- symmetry and symmetry-breaking
- feedback and adaptation
- coherent organization at all scales

Intelligence is the logic of the universe.

4. Cycles of Stability and Motion — The Universe's

Operating Rhythm

Reality unfolds through two alternating states:

A. Stability (Rest State)

- fields are balanced
- gradients are minimal
- energy is potential
- systems are aligned

This is the default state of existence.

B. Motion (Active State)

- imbalance introduces tension
- tension creates action
- action propagates as waves, currents, or motion
- systems destabilize and re-stabilize

Motion is not the natural state—it is the correctional response to imbalance.

Cycle: Stability → Disturbance → Realignment → Stability

This cycle powers:

- electron transitions
- chemical reactions
- planetary orbits
- evolution
- consciousness
- thought
- birth, growth, decay, renewal
- cosmic cycles

The universe is not moving randomly. It is moving to restore balance.

5. Why the Universe Appears Dynamic Despite Underlying Equilibrium

At its core, the universe is perfectly stable. Yet what we see is constant motion.

This paradox dissolves when we understand how perception works.

A. We witness only disturbances, not equilibrium. Equilibrium is silent, invisible, unchanging. Disturbances are visible, energetic, loud, measurable. Our senses capture only the "noisy part" of reality.

B. All motion is local, not universal. The foundational field remains still. Local imbalances create currents, orbits, waves, forces, phenomena. The field itself does not move—only disturbances move through it.

C. Consciousness interprets the ripple as motion. We perceive planets "moving," light "traveling," particles "jumping," matter "vibrating." But what truly moves is: tension → resolution → tension → resolution. A continuous ripple-dynamic.

D. Dynamic appearance is the consequence of realignment. The universe is always returning to equilibrium. What we call "motion" is simply the path of correction.

6. A Unified, Non-Equation Summary of Reality

1. Existence is a structured field. Not empty space. Not void. A patterned, stable foundation.
2. Energy is the field in motion. Not substance. Not particles. A disturbance.
3. Matter is stabilized disturbance. Condensed, patterned, repeatable.
4. Intelligence is the rulebook. Embedded logic. Consequential architecture. Self-maintaining order.
5. Motion is the consequence of imbalance. Nature correcting itself. Every event is a return-to-balance cycle.
6. Perceived reality is ripple-dynamics. What we see is not the stable foundation—but the corrections happening within it.
7. The universe does not move. It reacts. And reaction looks like motion.

Closing Insight

This appendix offers a unified model of reality without equations or mysticism. It shows:

- why existence is stable
- why motion is an appearance
- why energy is structured
- why matter forms patterns
- why systems self-organize
- why intelligence cannot be emergent
- why cycles rule the cosmos
- why the universe looks dynamic but rests on equilibrium

References & Suggested Readings

The following works—spanning cosmology, physics, philosophy, systems theory, neuroscience, mythology, and ancient Indian literature—provide contextual grounding for the ideas explored in *Vishwarup Darshan*. They serve as reference points rather than direct sources, supporting a cross-disciplinary understanding of reality.

Ancient Indian Texts & Commentaries

- **Rig Veda** — Hymns on cosmic order (*Rit*), creation, and the nature of existence.
- **Yajur Veda** — Ritualized systems encoded as cosmological principles.
- **Sama Veda** — Vibration, resonance, and the auditory structure of reality.
- **Atharva Veda** — Metaphysics, healing systems, and energy dynamics.
- **Upanishads** — Non-duality, consciousness, and the architecture of reality.
- **Bhagavad Gita** — Field, action, consequence, and universal order.
- **Puranas (selected)** — Symbolic cosmology, avatars, and cyclical time.
- **Yoga Vasistha** — Observership, mind, and universality of consciousness.
- **Brahma Sutras** — Philosophical architecture of existence.
- **Sri Aurobindo — The Life Divine**
- **S. Radhakrishnan — Indian Philosophy**

These works form the philosophical backbone of India's cosmological vision.

Physics & Cosmology

- Richard Feynman — *The Feynman Lectures on Physics*
- Stephen Hawking — *A Brief History of Time*
- Roger Penrose — *The Road to Reality*
- Leonard Susskind — *The Cosmic Landscape*
- Brian Greene — *The Fabric of the Cosmos*
- Carlo Rovelli — *Reality Is Not What It Seems*
- Lee Smolin — *Time Reborn*
- Max Tegmark — *Our Mathematical Universe*
- T. Padmanabhan — *Structure in the Universe*
- Sean Carroll — *The Big Picture*

These texts support discussion on fields, time, cosmological cycles, structured vacuum, and mathematical order.

Quantum Theory, Consciousness & Perception

- Niels Bohr — Papers on complementarity
- John Archibald Wheeler — *Law Without Law*
- Wojciech Zurek — Decoherence research
- Francisco Varela, Evan Thompson, Eleanor Rosch — *The Embodied Mind*
- David Chalmers — Works on the hard problem of consciousness
- Anil Seth — *Being You*
- Donald Hoffman — *The Case Against Reality*

These materials help connect observer-based quantum phenomena and ancient insights about perception.

Systems Theory & Complexity

- Ludwig von Bertalanffy — *General Systems Theory*

- Ilya Prigogine — *Order Out of Chaos*
- Ervin Laszlo — *The Systems View of the World*
- Niklas Luhmann — Systems and structures
- James Gleick — *Chaos: Making a New Science*

These support the idea of self-organization, consequence-driven order, and cyclical equilibrium.

Evolution, Biology & Life Sciences

- Charles Darwin — *On the Origin of Species*
- Stephen Jay Gould — *The Structure of Evolutionary Theory*
- Richard Dawkins — *The Selfish Gene*
- Simon Conway Morris — *Life's Solution*
- Terrence Deacon — *Incomplete Nature*

These references align with the Dashavatara–evolution synthesis.

Mythology, Symbolism & Comparative Philosophy

- Joseph Campbell — *The Hero with a Thousand Faces*
- Heinrich Zimmer — *Myths and Symbols in Indian Art and Civilization*
- Wendy Doniger — Interpretations of Puranic symbols
- Raimundo Panikkar — *The Vedic Experience*

These works contextualize symbolic-metaphorical interpretation.

Modern Interpretative & Integrative Works

- Fritjof Capra — *The Tao of Physics*
- Ken Wilber — *A Brief History of Everything*
- Amit Goswami — *The Self-Aware Universe*
- Danah Zohar — *The Quantum Self*

These writings explore intersections of science, consciousness, and cosmology.

Independent Contemporary Thought

Research articles, papers, and philosophical writings on:

- Structured vacuum
- Field-based cosmology
- Observer-dependent physics
- Non-linear dynamics
- Unified field perspectives
- Consciousness studies

These serve as conceptual parallels rather than direct sources.

Note for Readers

This reference list is intentionally cross-disciplinary. No single field can fully explain existence; understanding emerges when physics, philosophy, cosmology, biology, and symbolic knowledge are viewed together.

The purpose of these references is not to justify the book's statements but to show how various disciplines are converging on insights known to ancient civilizations thousands of years ago.

Closing Note

Every attempt to understand the universe is, ultimately, an attempt to understand ourselves. In exploring the architecture of existence—its fields, cycles, symbols, and intelligence—we inevitably confront the quiet truth that the boundary between the observer and the observed is far thinner than it appears.

Vishwarup Darshan is not a conclusion. It is an invitation.

An invitation to look beyond the familiar equations, stories, and inherited beliefs; to see the underlying logic that holds everything together; to sense the intelligence that operates beneath movement, matter, and mind. The ancient seers expressed this through metaphors and symbols. Modern science expresses it through models and measurements. But the reality behind both is singular.

If this book has offered you clarity, it is because the universe itself is clear. If it has raised new questions, it is because the universe is alive. And if it has sparked a deeper curiosity, it is because the journey of understanding is meant to continue.

No text can fully explain the vastness of reality—not this one, not any other. But a text can serve as a lens, a reminder, a spark. What you do with that spark becomes your own exploration.

Thank you for choosing to walk through these ideas with openness and patience. May your inquiry remain fearless. May your insights remain fluid. And may your vision of the universe grow as expansive as the universe itself.

The journey ahead is yours. The universe is waiting.

Acknowledgements

A work of this nature is rarely the outcome of solitary effort. It is the result of countless conversations, reflections, and the silent influence of people, ideas, and experiences that shape one's understanding of reality.

My foremost gratitude goes to the **ancient thinkers and seers** who observed the universe with an openness and clarity that modern science is only beginning to rediscover. Their symbolic brilliance and intuitive precision form the foundation on which this book stands. Their courage to explore existence without instruments, institutions, or incentives continues to inspire me.

I am deeply grateful to the **teachers, mentors, and intellectual companions** who shaped my scientific mind and encouraged my lifelong curiosity. Every class I taught, every question raised by a student, and every discussion in the corridors of learning added a subtle thread to the fabric woven here.

A special acknowledgment is due to the **scientists, researchers, and thinkers across disciplines**—from physics and cosmology to psychology and systems theory—whose work challenges the limits of our understanding. Their discoveries, paradoxes, and questions form the bridge between the ancient and the modern.

To my **family**, whose quiet presence grounds me and gives meaning to the endless hours spent in reflection and writing—you are the reason behind every line, and the strength behind every idea. Your support, patience, and love remain the unseen but unshakeable foundations of this journey.

To my **students**, past and present—you are the constant reminder that knowledge must stay alive, clear, and fearless. Your curiosity keeps my own mind in motion.

And finally, to the **readers** who pick up this book with an open mind—thank you for your willingness to explore a worldview where science and spirituality are not opponents, but collaborators in a larger truth. Your engagement gives purpose to this exploration.

This book is a small offering in the vast continuum of human inquiry. If it brings clarity, sparks curiosity, or encourages deeper reflection on the architecture of reality, the effort has found its rightful place.

About the Author

Sandeep Chavan is an independent thinker, educator, and prolific author whose work spans physics, philosophy, psychology, cosmology, and the deeper questions of human existence. With a background in engineering and decades of experience as a respected physics teacher, he has guided thousands of students while simultaneously pursuing an unbounded intellectual journey of his own.

His writing is rooted in a rare blend of *scientific clarity and philosophical intuition*, allowing him to decode complex ideas and present them in a fluid, accessible, and deeply insightful manner. Over the years, he has developed a distinctive worldview that connects ancient Indian cosmology with modern scientific understanding—reinterpreting concepts like consciousness, energy, intelligence, and universal order through a contemporary lens.

Sandeep has authored an extensive body of work that includes explorations of human behavior, intelligence, universal dynamics, spiritual inquiry, and metaphysics. His books challenge entrenched assumptions, bridge fragmented fields of knowledge, and invite readers to observe the universe through a more integrated and consequence-driven perspective.

As a teacher, he is known for breaking down the most difficult concepts with simplicity and precision. As a researcher, he is fearless in asking foundational questions that mainstream frameworks often avoid. And as an author, he remains committed to presenting truth without mystification, ideology, or complexity—offering clarity as the highest form of knowledge.

Vishwarup Darshan reflects this lifelong pursuit: an attempt to see reality as a unified whole, where ancient insights and modern science converge into a coherent vision of existence.

Chavanian Gems

Must Reads & Paradigm Shifting Works

The journey does not end here. Each book is a ripple in a larger continuum — a field of ideas that challenge assumptions, reframe realities, and open new pathways of thought. Explore these Chavanian works to step deeper into the architecture of consequence, energy, and human possibility.

Foundational Philosophy & Consequence Dynamics

- The Law of Consequences
- Ethics & Morale: Shades of Consequence
- Universal Skill: Navigating Consequences
- Philosophy 2.0: A Structural Manifesto
- Chaos: A Gentle Guide to the Unresolvable

Groundbreaking Science & Cosmology

- $E \neq mc^2$: The Collapse of Classical Assumptions
- Chavan's Theory of Everything
- Chavan vs Einstein: The Universe Was Never Curved
- Black Hole Don't Exist
- Light: Neither a Wave, Nor a Photon
- The End of Particle Age

AI & Human Futures

- It's Not AI, It's AHI – Amplified Human Intelligence

- Doctor AI: The Diagnosis of Data
- The Human Upgrade
- The Jobless Future
- Stop Acknowledging AI
- The Real Story of AI

Society, Politics & Human Narratives

- Malicious Script of Indian Polity
- Engage Beyond Elections
- Culture, Identity & Change: The Evolution of Indian Society
- Statue vs Scaffold: MODI vs RAHUL
- Never Trust Without Doubt
- The Happiness Scam

Spiritual & Existential Explorations

- Moksha: The Liberation
- Aham Brahmasmi
- The Moon: Co-Author of Life's Script
- The Return Journey
- The Cosmos: The Still Universe
- Breath
- Restoring Bhagavad Gita

Universal Frameworks & Ripple Architecture

- Unified Energy Dynamics
- Chavan's Universal Framework for Everything
- Ripple Centrism: From Copernicus to Chavan
- The Structure of Reality (UED 2.0)

Don't miss out!

Visit the website below and you can sign up to receive emails whenever Sandeep Chavan publishes a new book. There's no charge and no obligation.

https://books2read.com/r/B-A-EPGPC-FGSLI

BOOKS 2 READ

Connecting independent readers to independent writers.

Did you love *Vishwarup Darshan*? Then you should read *Chavanian Psychology*[1] by Sandeep Chavan!

[2]

Chavanian Psychology introduces a groundbreaking field-based model of the human mind — a paradigm that transcends traditional theories rooted in behavior, cognition, or trauma. In this pioneering work, Sandeep J. Chavan redefines the mind as a **dynamic field of awareness**, shaped not by mental structures but by **ripples of emotion, thought, intention, and consequence.**

Instead of treating consciousness as a product of the brain, this book frames it as **an energetic phenomenon** governed by coherence, alignment, and field resonance. Every emotion becomes a ripple. Every decision becomes a consequence pattern. Every disturbance becomes a misalignment seeking correction. And every moment of clarity becomes a return to stillness — the field's natural state.

Across four comprehensive parts, the book explores:

1. https://books2read.com/u/mYLzvM

2. https://books2read.com/u/mYLzvM

The mechanics of ripple dynamicsEmotional amplitude, frequency, and coherenceAwareness as the stabilizing intelligence of the fieldThe Law of Consequence (LOC) as the universal regulatorThe architecture of misalignment and the pathway to healingThe psychology of relationships, empathy, and communicationThe mind's evolution from instinct to field-based intelligenceThe rising challenge of AI and the role of human coherenceThe future of humanity as conscious participants in a coherent field

Practical tools — such as the Emotional Ripple Map, the Psychological Law of Coherence (P-LOC), alignment exercises, and field-based mindfulness methods — allow readers to experience these concepts directly. Through guided reflection and awareness training, the book helps individuals navigate internal turbulence, resolve emotional patterns, and realign their field with clarity and resilience.

Chavanian Psychology is more than a theoretical contribution — it is a usable model for modern life. It answers questions that traditional psychology often leaves unresolved:

Why do emotions repeat?Why does clarity disappear under stress?Why do relationships collapse even when intentions are good?How does healing truly occur?Why does the mind feel fragmented in a hypercomplex world?

The answers emerge from the field: coherence, not complexity, defines a healthy mind. Healing is not forgetting — it is **resonating differently**. Awareness is not passive — it is **the mind's real intelligence**. And evolution is not biological — it is **the field remembering itself**.

With clarity, elegance, and depth, this book marks a definitive shift in the way we understand consciousness, emotion, behavior, and inner balance. It is an essential guide for thinkers, seekers, students, psychologists, educators, leaders, and anyone committed to living with alignment and awareness.

Read more at https://www.sandeepjchavan.com/.

www.ingramcontent.com/pod-product-compliance
Lightning Source LLC
LaVergne TN
LVHW090304210926
848480LV00001B/121
* 9 7 9 8 2 3 2 4 1 9 7 2 1 *